THE ANCIENT ETHNOSTATE

BIOPOLITICAL THOUGHT IN CLASSICAL GREECE

by

GUILLAUME DUROCHER

Kindle Direct Publishing Edition
2021

ISBN: 9798450658995
Independently published
Book version: 1.04

Cover image:
Thomas Seddon, *Penelope*, 1852.
Sotheby's

[T]he old Greeks ... stood some grades higher in intellect than any race that has ever existed ... The western nations of Europe, who now so immeasurably surpass their former savage progenitors, and stand at the summit of civilization, owe little or none of their superiority to direct inheritance from the old Greeks, though they owe much to the written works of that wonderful people.

– Charles Darwin, *The Descent of Man*

The thought of what America,

The thought of what America,

The thought of what America would be like

If the Classics had a wide circulation

      Troubles my sleep.

– Ezra Pound, *Cantico del Sole*

CONTENTS

Preface...vii

Foreword by Kevin MacDonald..ix

The Wisdom of the Ancients...1

Homer's *Iliad*: Vital Barbarism, Decadent Civilization 24

Homer's *Odyssey*: The Return of the Father...40

Hesiod's *Works & Days*: Peasants & Their Posterity............................59

Herodotus I: The Struggle of Nations & Cultures 63

Herodotus II: Hellenic Freedom & Unity in the Persian Wars 88

Aristotle: The Biopolitics of the Citizen-State....................................119

Athens & Sparta: An Analysis of Two Ethnostates 151

    "Courage Is Freedom": Ancient Athens as a Spirited & Nativist
    Democracy..153

    "Giving Birth to Men": Sparta as the First Ethnostate..................163

    Thucydides' Bitter Epilogue: State over Blood in the Peloponnesian
    War 183

Plato: The Ethno-Statal Philosopher 191

    Plato's Racial *Republic*..195

    The *Laws*: Plato's Sacred Ethnostate..207

    Platonic Confederalism: Greek Unity Against Barbarians.............235

    National Leadership & Confederalism in the Myth of Atlantis....239

    Plato's Sicilian Project...241

    Plato's Group Evolutionary Strategy 244

By Way of Conclusion 251

Bibliography 260

PREFACE

I must seem like a temple robber! You have in your hands a survey of ancient Greek literature, from Homer to Aristotle, analyzed from an evolutionary and *biopolitical* perspective. In each case, I have sought to bring out what these great poems, histories, lectures, and dialogues have to say about the governance of human life, the definition of the in-group, inter-group conflict, and reproduction. Put another way, what do these works have to say about how a people may survive and thrive?

This book then straddles the line between my two fields of predilection: history and politics. The reader will decide whether it meets the standards of either or both.

I have extensively relied on academic sources and have always striven to ensure that my interpretations are not at odds with the academic mainstream.[1] Indeed, this work makes no claim at originality except in its evolutionary angle of perspective.

I hope it may serve as a useful introduction to the Hellenic canon and to the mindset and values which underpinned our Greek forebears' extraordinary success. I wish that this humble

---

[1] See for instance: Mika Ojakangas, *On the Origins of Greek Biopolitics: A Reinterpretation of the History of Biopower* (London and New York: Routledge, 2016); Lynette Mitchell, *Panhellenism and the Barbarian in Archaic and Classical Greece* (Swansea, Wales: Classical Press of Wales, 2007); Susan Lape, *Race and Citizen Identity in Classical Athenian Democracy* (Cambridge: Cambridge University Press, 2010); Benjamin Isaac, *The Invention of Racism in Classical Antiquity* (Princeton, New Jersey: Princeton University Press, 2004); and David J. Galton, "Greek theories on eugenics," *Journal of Medical Ethics* (1998, 24: 263-267). There are similar observations in the older literature, e.g., Fustel de Coulanges, *La Cité antique* (Paris: Flammarion, 1984 [1864]), Allen G. Roper, *Ancient Eugenics: The Arnold Prize Essay for 1913* (London: Oxford University Press, 1913), Hans F. K. Günther, *Platon als Hüter des Lebens: Platons Zucht- und Erziehungsgedanken und ihre Bedeutung für die Gegenwart* (Munich: 1928).

book may help the reader to learn to *think freely* of contemporary constraints and may inspire them to discover the Classics for themselves and, ultimately, to live more nobly.

The bulk of this book was first published as essays for *The Occidental Observer/Quarterly* between 2016 and 2018. This seems particularly fitting given that the editor of these periodicals, Professor Kevin MacDonald, has largely inspired them. His evolutionary analysis of ancient and traditional Judaism represents an attempt, both rare and powerful, at consilience between the social and biological sciences.[2] Only by understanding the complex and dynamic interaction between human societies' biological and cultural characters will we be able to have some inkling of mankind's future trajectory. We await the scholars who will undertake similar evolutionary studies of the varieties of Hinduism, Buddhism, Christianity, Islam, and other ethical-civilizational systems.

In this age of deplatforming and shadowbanning, this edition, whether dead-tree or e-book, provides readers with an object which the powers that be cannot easily take away. The chapters have been ordered according to the spiritual arc of Greek history. Hence for the most part the works are presented in chronological order. I have minimally revised the original essays to strengthen the book's coherence.

I have benefited from much generous help that has enabled this brain-child to see the light of day. I thank the many friends who contributed to proofing and improving the final book, in particular Anatoly Karlin for his contributions and for our always stimulating intellectual exchanges. Last but not least, I thank my wife for her constant encouragement and support.

Bonne lecture !

---

[2] See in particular: Kevin MacDonald, *A People That Shall Dwell Alone: Judaism as a Group Evolutionary Strategy, with Diaspora Peoples* (Lincoln, Nebraska: Writers Club, 2002).

FOREWORD

BY KEVIN MACDONALD

Guillaume Durocher has produced an authoritative, beautifully written, and even inspirational account of the ancient Greeks. Although relying on mainstream academic sources, he adds an evolutionary perspective that is sorely lacking in contemporary academia at a time when ancient Greek civilization, like the Western canon *in toto*, has been subjected to intense criticism reflecting the values of the contemporary academic left. To get a flavor of the current state of classics scholarship, consider the following from the *New York Times*:

> Long revered as the foundation of "Western civilization," the field [of classics] was trying to shed its self-imposed reputation as an elitist subject overwhelmingly taught and studied by white men. Recently the effort had gained a new sense of urgency: Classics had been embraced by the far right, whose members held up the ancient Greeks and Romans as the originators of so-called white culture. Marchers in Charlottesville, Va., carried flags bearing a symbol of the Roman state; online reactionaries adopted classical pseudonyms; the white-supremacist website Stormfront displayed an image of the Parthenon alongside the tagline *"Every* month is white history month." ...
>
> For several years, [Associate Professor of Classics at Princeton University Dan-el Padilla] has been speaking openly about the harm caused by practitioners of classics in the two millenniums since antiquity: the classical justifications of slavery, race science, colonialism, Nazism and other 20th-century fascisms. Classics was a discipline around which the modern Western university grew, and Padilla believes that it has sown racism through the entirety of higher education. Last summer, after Princeton decided to remove Woodrow Wilson's name from its School of

Public and International Affairs, Padilla was a co-author of an open letter that pushed the university to do more. "We call upon the university to amplify its commitment to Black people," it read, "and to become, for the first time in its history, an anti-racist institution." Surveying the damage done by people who lay claim to the classical tradition, Padilla argues, one can only conclude that classics has been instrumental to the invention of "whiteness" and its continued domination.

In recent years, like-minded classicists have come together to dispel harmful myths about antiquity. On social media and in journal articles and blog posts, they have clarified that contrary to right-wing propaganda, the Greeks and Romans did not consider themselves "white," and their marble sculptures, whose pale flesh has been fetishized since the 18th century, would often have been painted in antiquity. They have noted that in fifth-century-B.C. Athens, which has been celebrated as the birthplace of democracy, participation in politics was restricted to male citizens; thousands of enslaved people worked and died in silver mines south of the city, and custom dictated that upper-class women could not leave the house unless they were veiled and accompanied by a male relative. They have shown that the concept of Western civilization emerged as a euphemism for "white civilization" in the writing of men like Lothrop Stoddard, a Klansman and eugenicist. Some classicists have come around to the idea that their discipline forms part of the scaffold of white supremacy — a traumatic process one described to me as "reverse red-pilling" — but they are also starting to see an opportunity in their position. Because classics played a role in constructing whiteness, they believed, perhaps the field also had a role to play in its dismantling.[3]

---

[3] Rachel Poser, "He Wants to Save Classics from Whiteness. Can the Field Survive?," *New York Times* (February 2, 2011). https://www.nytimes.com/2021/02/02/magazine/classics-greece-rome-whiteness.html; see also Donna Zuckerberg, *Not All Dead White*

Durocher's treatment is a refreshing antidote to this contemporary academic orthodoxy. Unlike so many scholars, whose main concern is to score political points useful to the anti-White left and thereby improve their standing in the profession, he has attempted to present an accurate account of these writers and the world they were trying to understand and survive in. The phrase "so-called white culture" in the above quotation from Rachel Poser's *New York Times* article is indicative of this mindset. Durocher does not shy away from discussing slavery, the relatively confined role of women, or the cruelty that Greeks could exhibit, even toward their fellow Greeks. But he also emphasizes the relative freedom of the Greeks, their intellectual brilliance, and the ability of the two principal city-states, Athens and Sparta, to pull together to defeat a common foe and thereby save their people and culture from utter destruction.

The contemporary academic left has abandoned any attempt to understand the Greeks on their own terms in favor of comparing Western cultures (and typically *only* Western cultures) to what they see as timeless moral criteria—criteria that reflect the current sacralization of diversity, equity, and inclusion. But even the most cursory reflection makes it obvious that moral ideals such as valuing diversity, equity, and inclusion are not justified because of their value in establishing a society that can survive in a hostile world. They are valued as intrinsic goods, and societies that depart from these ideals are condemned as evil. Recently there was something of a stir when a video was released by the website of *Russia Today*, a television station linked to the Russian government, comparing ads for military service in Russia and the United States.[4] Ads directed at Russians show determined, physically fit young men engaged in disciplined military units and difficult, dangerous activities under adverse conditions. On the other

---

Men: Classics and Misogyny in the Digital Age (Harvard University Press, 2018).

[4] https://www.youtube.com/watch?v=ZEnxmzqXJN8

hand, the recruitment ad for the U.S. military features a woman who, although physically fit, dwells on her pride in participating in the marriage of her two 'mothers.' The contrast couldn't be more striking. The Russian military is seeking the best way to survive in a hostile world, while the American military is virtue-signaling its commitment to the gender dogmas of the left.

Durocher emphasizes that the Greeks lived in a very cruel world, one in which war often concluded with the enslavement or extermination of the defeated. We in the contemporary West have a life of relative ease, wealth, and security that was unknown to the ancient Greeks, who were threatened not only by other Greek *poleis*, but by foreign powers, particularly the aggressive and much more populous Persian Empire. In such an environment, there is no room for virtue signaling. Survival in a hostile, threatening world was a fundamental goal and this meant citizenship entailed a communitarian ideal of solidarity and sacrifice in shared struggles.

ARISTOCRATIC INDIVIDUALISM

Ancient Greece was an Indo-European culture, and thus prized military virtues, heroism, and the quest for honor, fame, and glory. These were most memorably expressed in the great poems of Homer, the *Iliad* and the *Odyssey*. Homer's world features mistrust for strangers, sexual competition, and an ethos of bold enterprise and risk-taking for the sake of wealth, honor, and personal glory.

This sense of heroic struggle in a hostile environment is central to classical Greece and Rome; and was also evident among the Germanic peoples who inherited the West after the fall of the Roman Empire. As Ricardo Duchesne notes, the Indo-European legacy is key to understanding the restless, aggressive, questing, innovative, "Faustian" soul of Europe. Indo-Europeans were a "uniquely aristocratic people dominated by emerging chieftains for whom fighting to gain prestige was the all-pervading ethos. This culture [is] interpreted as 'the Western state of nature' and as the primordial source of Western restlessness."[5] Durocher expands on this beautifully:

> This Aryan ethos is what so appealed to Nietzsche: a people not animated by pity or guilt, nor trying to achieve impossible or fictitious equality in an endlessly vain attempt to assuage feelings. Rather, Hellenic culture, driven by that aristocratic and competitive spirit, held up the ideal of being *the best*: the best athlete, the best warrior, the best poet, the best philosopher, or the most beautiful. This culture also held up the collective ideal of being the best as a whole society, for they understood that man as a species only flourishes as a community.

This competitive ethic so central to the West is fundamentally individualistic, not based on extended kinship. It is in strong contrast to the contemporary West where the main goal of far too many of its traditional peoples is to uphold moral principles and to feel guilt for differences in wealth and accomplishment. In individualist Western culture, reputation is paramount, and in the modern West, reputation revolves mainly around being an honest, morally upstanding, trustworthy person, with moral rectitude defined by media and academic elites hostile to the Western tradition. In my *Individualism and the Western Liberal Tradition*, I ascribe this fundamental shift in Western culture to the rise of the values of an egalitarian individualist ethic that originated among the northwestern European hunter-gatherers—an ethic that is in many ways the diametrical opposite of the Indo-European aristocratic tradition.[6] This new ethic began its rise to predominance with the English Civil War of the seventeenth century and remains most prominent in northwest Europe, particularly Scandinavian cultures.

The aristocratic individualism of the ancient Western world implies a hierarchy in which aristocrats have power over

---

[5] Ricardo Duchesne, *The Uniqueness of Western Civilization* (Leiden: Brill, 2011), p. 51.

[6] Kevin MacDonald, *Individualism and the Western Liberal Tradition: Evolutionary Origins, History, and Prospects for the Future* (Seattle: CreateSpace, 2019).

underlings (although there was the expectation of reciprocity). There is however an egalitarianism among aristocratic peers. In the *Iliad*, the Achaean army is made of several kings and is therefore fractious, with no one having absolute power over the rest. The leading king is a first among equals who may be criticized by his peers. Decisions require consensus and consultation. Aristocratic individualism is always threatened by what one might term a degenerate aristocracy — such as those dominated by the ancient tyrants and the early modern European monarchs who aspired to complete control. For example, King Louis XIV of France (reigned 1643-1715) had power over the nobility undreamed of in the Middle Ages while his legacy of absolute rule led ultimately to the French Revolution.

The historian Herodotus notes that a common strategy for ruling elites was to form a distinct and solidary extended family by only marrying among themselves, for example the ruling Bacchiadae clan of Corinth (Herodotus, 5.92). This also occurred in the European Middle Ages and later as elites severed ties with their wider kinship groups and married among themselves — likely a tendency for any aristocratic society.

But even apart from peers, there was an ideal of reciprocity within the hierarchy — a fundamental feature of Indo-European culture. As I noted in *Individualism and the Western Liberal Tradition*:

> Oath-bound contracts of reciprocal relationships were characteristic of [Proto-Indo-Europeans] and [Indo-Europeans] and this practice continued with the various I-E groups that invaded Europe. These contracts formed the basis of patron-client relationships based on reputation — leaders could expect loyal service from their followers, and followers could expect equitable rewards for their service to the leader. This is critical because these relationships are based on talent and accomplishment, not ethnicity (i.e., rewarding people on the basis of closeness of kinship) or despotic subservience (where followers are essentially unfree). (p. 34)

Such reciprocity is apparent in Homer's world, the relationship between a king and his people being ideally one of asymmetric mutual responsibilities, ultimately to the benefit of both.

GREEK COLLECTIVISM: THE NECESSITY OF SOCIAL COHESION

Given the exigencies of survival in a hostile world, Greek conceptions of the ideal society were firmly based on realistic assessments of what was necessary to survive and flourish. In *Individualism and the Western Liberal Tradition*, I noted that the Puritan-descended intellectuals of the nineteenth century, like today's academic and media left, were moral idealists, constructing ideal societies on the basis of universalist moral principles, such as abolitionist ideology opposing the evil of enslaving Africans. The Greeks also had ideas on the ideal society, but they were not based on moral abstractions independent of survival value. And among those values, social cohesion was paramount. Because of its inherent individualism and the practical necessity of social cohesion, Western culture has always been a balance between its individualism and some form of social glue that binds people together to achieve common interests, including forms of social control that impinge on the self-interest of at least some individuals, while also providing citizens with a stake in the system.

There is thus a major contrast between the Greeks and an autocratic society such as the Persian Empire—a contrast the Greeks were well aware of. Western social cohesion has typically resulted from all citizens having a stake in the system. Homeric kings understood that they would benefit if their peer and subordinates are willing to fight and die for their homeland. Herodotus noted that Athens became a superior military power after getting rid of tyrants and developing a citizenry with a stake in the system.

My interest in understanding the West has always revolved around kinship, marriage, and the family as bedrock institutions amenable to an evolutionary analysis. An important aspect of social cohesion in the West has been institutions that result in relative sexual egalitarianism among males, in contrast to the common practice (e.g., in classical China and the Middle East, including Greece's main foreign enemy, the Persian Empire) where wealthy, powerful males maintained large harems, while many men were unable to procreate. In ancient Greece, the importance of social cohesion can be seen in Solon's laws on marriage (early sixth century BC). Solon's laws had a strongly egalitarian thrust, and indeed, the purpose of his laws was to "resolve problems of deep-seated social unrest involving the aristocratic monopoly on political power and landholding practices under which the 'many were becoming enslaved to the few.'"[7] His reforms abolished existing private debts and banned usurious loans, which had on default led to the enslavement many Athenians and harmed social cohesion.

The concern therefore was that such practices were leading to a lack of social cohesion — with people not believing they had a stake in the system. As in the case of the medieval Catholic Church, the focus of Solon's laws on marriage was to rein in the power of the aristocracy by limiting the benefits to be gained by extra-marital sexual relationships. In Solon's laws, legitimate children with the possibility of inheritance were the product of two Athenian citizens, a policy approved by popular vote in 451 B.C. Bastards were to be "excluded from both the responsibilities and privileges of membership in the public household."[8] Given that wealthy males are in the best position to father extramarital children and provide for multiple sexual partners, it is critical that Solon's legislation (like the Church's policies in the Middle Ages) was explicitly aimed at creating sexual egalitarianism among men — giving all male citizens a stake in the system.

Greek thinkers and lawgivers thus had no compunctions about reining in individual self-interest in the interest of the

---

[7] Susan Lape, "Solon and the institution of 'democratic' family form," *Classical Journal* 98.2 (2002–2003), pp. 117-139, p. 117.

[8] C.B. Patterson, *The Family in Greek History* (Cambridge, MA: 2001, Harvard University Press), p. 110.

common good, notably in the area of population policy. The Greeks took for granted that the reproduction of the citizenry was a fundamental matter of public interest: the new generation should be bred and educated in the right numbers and to the highest quality possible. The public interest in achieving a society able to withstand the hostile forces arrayed against it was paramount, not the interests of any particular person or segment of the society, including the wealthy.

Greek cultures therefore often had strong social controls aimed at creating cohesive, powerful groups where cohesion was maintained by regulating individual behavior, effectively making them group evolutionary strategies. These cultures certainly did not eradicate individual self-interest, but they regulated and channeled it in such a manner that the group as a whole benefited. For example, in constructing an ideal society, Aristotle rejected a mindless libertarianism in favor of a system that had concern for the good of the society as a whole. Anything that interfered with social cohesion or any other feature that contributed to an adaptive culture had to be dealt with — by whatever means necessary.

Solon's laws on marriage and inheritance would therefore have been analyzed by Aristotle for their effect on social cohesion. Egalitarianism, like everything else, had to be subjected to the criterion of what was best for the community as a whole and that meant that societies should be ethnically homogeneous and led by the best people. Aristotle's arguments for moderate democracy are not founded on abstract 'rights' or a moral vision, ideas that have dominated Western thinking since the Enlightenment, but on whatever benefits the community as a whole and enables its flourishing. On these grounds, he notably argued for regulated private property and concord between social classes. The social cohesion needed in a hostile world was a fundamental value that trumped any concern for individual rights. Durocher:

> Aristotle's *unabashed* ethics are typically Hellenic: there is no egalitarian consolation for the ugly and the misbegotten, there is no pretense that *all* human beings can be happy and actualized. Rather, Aristotle, like the Greeks in general,

celebrates excellence. ... This vision is in fact unabashedly communitarian and aristocratic: Firstly, the human species cannot flourish and fulfill its natural role unless it survives and reproduces itself in the right conditions; secondly, the society must be organized so as to grant the intellectually-gifted and culturally-educated minority the leisure to exercise their reason.

Sparta was even more egalitarian among the Spartiates, giving the citizens a stake in the system, but with an ethic that rejected effeminacy and weakness and in which individuals strived to achieve excellence in military skills. Also likely promoting social cohesion was that the Helot slave class was an outgroup that Spartans understood needed to be rigorously controlled, setting up a very robust ingroup-outgroup psychology that promoted social cohesion and high positive regard for the ingroup along with disparagement and even abuse of the outgroup. Spartan social cohesion is legendary and was instrumental to defeating, in alliance with Athens, the far more numerous Persians, thus preserving Greek freedom. The results have resounded down the ages.

This emphasis on giving individuals a stake in the system as a mechanism for social cohesion thus has strong roots in Western culture. The political system of the Roman Republic was far from democratic, but it was also far from being a narrow oligarchy, and the representation and power of the lower classes gradually increased throughout the Republic (e.g., with the office of tribune of the plebs). The highest offices, consuls and praetors with military and judicial functions, were elected by the *comitia centuriata*, a convocation of the military, divided into centuries, where people with property had the majority of the vote (people were assigned to a century depending on five classes of property ownership, with the lower classes voting after the wealthy; the election was typically decided before the poorer centuries could vote).

A deep concern with social cohesion enabled by having a stake in the system was also apparent in the Germanic world after the fall of the Roman Empire. Although unquestionably hierarchical, early medieval European societies had a strong sense that cultures ought to build social cohesion on the basis of reciprocity, so that, with the exception of slaves, even humble members near the bottom of the social hierarchy had a stake in the system. The ideal (and the considerable reality) is what Spanish historian Américo Castro labeled "hierarchic harmony."[9]

For example, the seventh-century Visigothic Code promulgated by King Chindasuinth of Spain illustrates the desire for a non-despotic government and the social cohesion that results from taking account of the interests of all but slaves. Regarding despotism:

> It should be required that [the king] make diligent inquiry as to the soundness of his opinions. Then, it should be evident that he has acted not for private gain but for the benefit of the people; so that it may conclusively appear that the law has not been made for any private or personal advantage, but for the protection and profit of the whole body of citizens.[10]

Thus the concern with social cohesion is a strong current in Western history.

ETHNIC DIVERSITY & LACK OF SOCIAL COHESION

Aristotle was well aware that extreme individualism may benefit some individuals who gain when a culture discourages common identities. I recall being puzzled when doing research on the Frankfurt School that intellectuals who had been steeped in classical Marxism had developed an ideology that prized individualism — jettisoning ethnic and religious

[9] Américo Castro (trans. Edmund L. King), *The Structure of Spanish History*, (Princeton, NJ: Princeton University Press, 1954), p. 497; see also Américo Castro (trans. Willard F. King and Selma Margaretten), *The Spaniards: An Introduction to Their History*, (Berkeley: University of California Press, 1971).

[10] The Visigothic Code (Forum judicum), trans. S. P. Scott (Boston, MA: Boston Book Company, 1910; online version: The Library of Iberian Resources Online, unpaginated), Titles I, II.
http://libro.uca.edu/vcode/visigoths.htm

identities in favor of self-actualization and acceptance of differences.

> In the end the ideology of the Frankfurt School may be described as a form of radical individualism that nevertheless despised capitalism — an individualism in which all forms of gentile collectivism are condemned as an indication of social or individual pathology. ... The prescription for gentile society is radical individualism and the acceptance of pluralism. People have an inherent right to be different from others and to be accepted by others as different. Indeed, to become differentiated from others is to achieve the highest level of humanity. The result is that "no party and no movement, neither the Old Left nor the New, indeed no collectivity of any sort was on the side of truth ... [T]he residue of the forces of true change was located in the critical individual alone."[11]

The Greeks would have seen such thinking as fatally detrimental to social cohesion and ancestral identity. In particular, they were well aware that ethnic diversity leads a dangerous absence of common identity and ultimately to conflict. As Aristotle noted, many cities fell into civil strife because of failure to assimilate immigrants, often culminating in the elimination of either the natives or the newcomers (*Politics*, 1303a13). He also observes that both extreme democrats and tyrants encouraged the mixing of peoples and loss of old identities and loyalties so as to consolidate their own power (*Politics*, 1319b19). Thus, there is a long history of power-hungry statesmen taking advantage of evolutionary realities to undermine the solidarity of the people they ruled over.

---

[11] Kevin MacDonald, *The Culture of Critique: An Evolutionary Analysis of Jewish Involvement in Twentieth-Century Intellectual and Political movements* (Bloomington, IN: Authorhouse, 2002; originally published: Westport, CT: Praeger, 1998), p. 165, quoting J. B. Maier, "Contribution to a critique of Critical Theory," in *Foundations of the Frankfurt School of Social Research*, ed. J. Marcus & Z. Tar (New Brunswick, NJ: 1984, Transaction Books).

It is interesting in this regard that such efforts to undermine the homogeneity of populations continue in the contemporary West. In the wake of World War II, the activist Jewish community, in part inspired by the writings of the Frankfurt School,[12] made a major push to open up immigration of Western countries to all the peoples of the world, their motive being a fear of ethnically homogeneous White populations of the type that had turned against Jews in Germany after 1933.[13] Corroborating this assessment, the historian Otis Graham notes that the Jewish lobby on immigration "was aimed not just at open doors for Jews, but also for a diversification of the immigration stream sufficient to eliminate the majority status of western Europeans so that a fascist regime in America would be more unlikely."[14] The motivating role of fear and insecurity on the part of the activist Jewish community thus differed from other groups and individuals promoting an end to the national origins provisions of the 1924 and 1952 laws which dramatically lowered immigration and restricted immigration to people largely from northwestern Europe. These same intellectuals and activists have also pathologized any sense of White identity or sense of White interests to the point that it is common for White liberals to have negative attitudes towards White people. More recently, the media has played a leading role in stoking left-wing racial discontent and 'woke' ideology.[15]

GREEK RACE REALISM

The ancient Greeks were vitally concerned with leaving descendants and they understood that heredity was important in shaping individuals—a view that is obviously adaptive in an evolutionary sense. Having indigenous, ancient, and

---

[12] *Ibid.*, Ch. 5.

[13] *Ibid.*, Ch. 7.

[14] Otis Graham, *Unguarded Gates: A History of American's Immigration Crisis* (Rowman & Littlefield, 2004), p. 80.

[15] Zach Goldberg, "How the Media Led the Great Racial Awakening," *Tablet*, 5 August 2020.

distinguished ancestors were all signs of "good birth" (Aristotle, *Rhetoric*, 1.5). Congruent with contemporary behavior genetic research, there was an expectation that children would inherit the traits of parents (apparent as early as Homer, e.g. *Odyssey* 4.61-64, 4.611).

The Greeks also had a sense that they shared a common ethnicity and culture with other Greeks. There were frequent expressions of pan-Hellenic identity and kinship in culture, political discourse, religion, and sporting events. And, as Durocher notes, pan-Hellenic rhetoric and calls of solidarity were pervasive throughout the Persian Wars.

The Greeks were thus proud of their lineage and had a sense of shared kinship. However, it was not the sort of extensive kinship that is typical of so much of the rest of the world. There was an individualist core to Greek culture stemming from its Indo-European roots, resulting in the famously fractious Greek culture, with wars between Greek city-states. Even during the Persian wars, most Greek city-states failed to join the coalition against Persia and many prominent Greek leaders collaborated with the enemy.

As in individualist cultures generally, lineage is confined to close relatives, and there are no corporate kinship-based groups that own property or where brothers live together in common households: "Despite typically vague modern notions of a primitive clan-based society as the predecessor to the historical society of the *polis*, early Greek society seems securely rooted in individual households—and in the relationships focused on and extending from those households."[16]

Reflecting the common Greek view that it was necessary to regulate society to achieve the adaptive goals of the city as a whole, the Greeks accepted the idea that individual behavior needed to be regulated in the common interest, resulting in eugenic proposals by philosophers and, in the case of Sparta at least, practices such as killing weak infants. Both Plato and Aristotle accepted eugenics as an aspect of public policy. Plato

---

[16] C.B. Patterson, *The Family in Greek History* (Cambridge, MA: 2001, Harvard University Press), pp. 46–47.

was particularly enthusiastic about eugenics—Durocher labels it "an obsession." Like many evolutionists, such as Sir Francis Galton, Plato was much impressed by animal breeding as a paradigm for eugenic policies for humans. For Plato, eugenics was part of a broader group evolutionary strategy he proposed for the Greeks. As Durocher notes, Plato advocated

> a great reform of convention grounded in reason and expertise, to transform Greece into a patchwork of enlightened, non-grasping city-states, cultivating themselves intellectually and culturally, reproducing themselves in perpetuity through systematic and eugenic population policies, avoiding fratricidal war and imperialism among themselves, and working together against the barbarians, under the leadership of the best city-states. Taken together, I dare say we can speak of a Platonic Group Evolutionary Strategy for Greece.

It is worth noting in this context that the basic premises of eugenics are well-grounded in evolutionary and genetic science and were broadly accepted in Western culture, even among progressives, from the late nineteenth century until after World War II when the entire field became tarred by association with National Socialism. It is thus part of the broad transformation among Western intellectuals away from thinking in terms of racial differences and the genetic basis of individual differences—to the point that it is currently fashionable to deny the reality of race and any suggestion that race differences in socially important traits such as intelligence could possibly be influenced genetically. This denial of human biodiversity is now being paired with a suppression of Western ethnic pride and identity; tendencies which if, maintained, are likely to prove fatal for the nations concerned

SCIENTIFIC THINKING AS CHARACTERISTIC OF THE WEST

The ancient Greeks were pioneers of scientific thinking. This included, among much else, naturalistic theories on the origins and character of the universe, the emergence of certain geographical formations, and the effect of the natural environment on human biology and culture.

Analogical thinking is fundamental to science. Later examples include Christiaan Huygens' use of light and sound to support his wave theory of light and Darwin's analogy between artificial selection and natural selection, and the conception of the mind as a blank slate or computer. Scientific thinking is thus apparent in Greek philosophers' eugenic recommendations based on analogies with animal breeding.

Such scientific thinking is a unique characteristic of Western individualist culture. In his book *The WEIRDest People in the World*, Joseph Henrich describes "WEIRD psychology" — i.e., the psychology of Western, educated, industrialized, rich, and democratic people. A major point is that the psychology of Western peoples is unique in the context of the rest of the world: "highly individualistic, self-obsessed, control-oriented, nonconformist, and analytical ... When reasoning WEIRD people tend to look for universal categories and rules with which to organize the world."[17]

Henrich notes that people from cultures with intensive kinship are more prone to holistic thinking that takes into account contexts and relationships, whereas Westerners are more prone to analytic thinking in which background information and context are ignored, leading ultimately to universal laws of nature and formal logic. I agree with this,[18] but, while Henrich argues that analytical thinking began as a result of the policies on marriage enforced by the medieval Church, this style of thinking can clearly be found among the ancient Greeks. Consider Aristotle's logic, a masterpiece of field independence and ignoring context, in which logical relationships can be deduced from the purely formal properties of sentences (e.g., All x's are y; this is an x; therefore, this is a y); indeed, in *Prior Analytics* Aristotle used the first three letters

---

[17] Joseph Henrich, *The WEIRDest People in the World: How the West Became Psychologically Peculiar and Particularly Prosperous* (New York: Farrar, Straus, & Giroux, 2020), Ch. 1.

[18] MacDonald, *Individualism and the Western Liberal Tradition*, pp. 112-113.

of the Greek alphabet as placeholders instead of concrete examples. Or consider Euclidean geometry, in which theorems could be deduced from a small set of self-evident axioms and in which the axioms themselves were based on decontextualized figures, such as perfect circles and triangles, and infinite straight lines. Despite its decontextualized nature, the Euclidean system has had huge applications in the real world and dominated thinking in geometry in the West until the twentieth century.

Ancient Greece was an Indo-European-derived culture (*Individualism*, Ch. 2) and, beginning in the Greco-Roman world of antiquity, logical argument and competitive disputation have been far more characteristic of Western cultures than any other culture area. As Duchesne notes:

> the ultimate basis of Greek civic and cultural life was the aristocratic ethos of individualism and competitive conflict which pervaded [Indo-European] culture ... There were no Possessors of the Way in aristocratic Greece; no Chinese Sages decorously deferential to their superiors and expecting appropriate deference from their inferiors. The search for the truth was a free-for-all with each philosopher competing for intellectual prestige in a polemical tone that sought to discredit the theories of others while promoting one's own.[19]

In such a context, rational, decontextualized arguments that appeal to disinterested observers and are subject to refutation win out. They do not depend on group discipline or group interests for their effectiveness because in Western cultures, the groups are permeable and defections based on individual beliefs are far more the norm than in other cultures. As Duchesne notes, although the Chinese made many practical discoveries, they never developed the idea of a rational, orderly universe guided by universal laws comprehensible to humans. Nor did they ever develop a "deductive method of rigorous demonstration according to which a conclusion, a

---

[19] Duchesne, *The Uniqueness of Western Civilization*, p. 452.

theorem, was proven by reasoning from a series of self-evident axioms,"[20] as seen in Aristotle's *Prior Analytics*. Indeed, I can't resist noting the intelligence and creativity that went into creating the incredibly intricate Antikythera Mechanism designed by an unknown Greek (or Greeks). Dated to around 150-100 BC and "technically more complex than any known device for at least a millennium afterwards," it was able to predict eclipses and planetary motions decades in advance.[21]

Schematic of the Antikythera Mechanism

Western scientific and technological creativity did not begin after the influence of Christianity, the Renaissance, or the Industrial Revolution. As Durocher notes, "The fruits of Hellenic civilization are all around us, down to our very vocabulary."

CONCLUSION

The Ancient Ethnostate should be at the top of everyone's reading for those interested in understanding Western origins and the uniqueness of the West. It is also an inspiring work for

---

[20] *Ibid.*

[21] S. Freeth *et al.*, "Decoding the ancient Greek astronomical calculator known as the Antikythera Mechanism," *Nature* 444 (November 2006), pp. 587-591, p. 587.

Foreword

those of us who seek to reinvigorate the West as a unique biocultural entity. The contemporary West, burdened by loss of confidence and moral and spiritual decay, cannot be redeemed by a fresh influx of ethnically Western barbarians as happened with the collapse of the Roman Empire and the rise of Germanic Europe. There are no more such peoples waiting in the wings to revive our ancient civilization.

Reinvigoration must come from within, but now it must do so in the context of massive immigration of non-Western peoples who are addicted to identity politics and are proving to be unwilling and likely unable to continue the Western traditions of individualism and all that that implies in terms of representative, non-despotic government, freedom of speech and association, and scientific inquiry. Indeed, we are seeing increasing hatred toward the people and culture of the West that is now well entrenched among Western elites and eagerly accepted by many of the non-Western peoples who have been imported into Western nations, many with historical grudges against the West. It will be a long, arduous road back. *The Ancient Ethnostate* contains roadmaps for the type of society that we should seek to establish.

Kevin MacDonald, Professor Emeritus of Psychology at
California State University–Long Beach
August 2021

The Wisdom of the Ancients

Like too many of our generation, I was raised and 'educated' without acquiring any real knowledge of European identity or our Western tradition. The Classics lay unopened. Though I may have tried once or twice to read them, they always left me baffled. I was too ignorant to even attempt to lessen my ignorance through them. I then did not know where we, our great civilization and family of nations, came from, and I took them for granted. 'The West' meant little more to me than a set of very recent and highly questionable values largely imposed in the last century or so.

Having become conscious of my ignorance, I sought to rectify this, and I began reading some of the Classics — especially those of the ancient Greeks — and, to my joy, I found that this time I could read them and that they often had very relevant insights for our times. I believe the difference is that I am a bit older, a bit wiser, and that I have been able to emancipate myself from the very impoverished view that postwar consumer democracy represents the highest possible form of human life. Having shed my liberal and egalitarian assumptions, I could finally appreciate these works.

In highlighting a few major insights and themes from the Classics, I hope to provide a useful introduction and whet the appetite of my readers to (re)discover our peerless Western tradition. This should not be done in an antiquarian spirit. The Greeks, a brilliant people living in the harsh world of the ancient Mediterranean, discovered truths and techniques of timeless value, things not to memorize, but *to live by*. If one has understood anything, one begins to see life in a different way, and one begins, however modestly, to change one's life, day by day.

Love & War

In our world, at least so far as living creatures are concerned, all revolves around a ceaseless struggle for survival and reproduction. All creatures exist as the culmination of a magnificent chain of generations, each of which triumphed in vicious competition both nutritional and sexual — eat, or be eaten, mate or see your lineage die with you. We all exist because each of our ancestors was ultimately successful in this ceaseless struggle of love and war. The very lessons of that struggle are inscribed as the hardest-won wisdom upon our genes: in our propensity for pleasure and pain, hunger and lust, boldness and timidity, intuition and rationality, and indeed in every aspect of our physique and personality.

Whether by intuition or reason, the oldest Greek literature which comes down to us ascribes foundational and even cosmic significance to these two basic forces, love and war. The poet Hesiod, in his genealogy of the gods, puts the god of love, Eros, at the beginning of creation, enabling every other divine and animal generation:

> Eros, the most handsome among the immortal gods, dissolver of flesh, who overcomes the reason and purpose in the breasts of all gods and men. (*Theogony*, 96-129)

The philosopher Heraclitus, known as "the obscure," produced cryptic sayings which form some of the most ancient fragments of Western thought. His famous saying on war has virtually become a proverb: "War is the father of all things." More exactly, he said:

> War is father of all and king of all. Some he reveals as gods, others as men; some he makes slaves, others free.[22]

This is as true in the animal world as in the human. The Greeks knew this intimately: any city-state deficient in martial valor and organization was enslaved or destroyed, whether by fellow Greeks, the expanding Persian Empire, or some other barbarians. The fate of the vanquished was often supremely grim: the men could be exterminated, the women and children enslaved as so much war booty. Our generation too often

---

[22] Robin Waterfield (ed. and trans.), *The First Philosophers: The Presocratics and Sophists* (Oxford: Oxford World's Classics, 2000), p. 40.

forgets that our political order exists by virtue of a succession of wars — from the revolutionary wars of the Enlightenment to the World Wars of the Twentieth Century — and it cannot be otherwise.

Homer too tells a significant story about the gods of love and war: Aphrodite and Ares. The two wished to make love, but the lame smith-god Hephaestus had been promised Aphrodite as his wife. The smith forged a metallic net to put above his conjugal bed and, finding Aphrodite and Ares making love there, trapped them inside, to their humiliation. A metaphor for the unconquerable sex drive's crude taming by the constraints of civilization?[23]

---

[23] The Greek myths ascribe cosmic, world-generating power to sex and violence. The titan Cronus castrated his own father, the sky-god Uranus, from whose blood sprouted Aphrodite, the goddess of love. Cronus himself, embodying many a father's fear of being overshadowed by his progeny, devoured his own children before being toppled by his son Zeus. Zeus himself is no less a slave to erotic desire and it is said in the fragmentary poem *Aegimius* that because of the thunder-god's adultery "oaths touching the matter of love do not draw down anger from the gods." All's fair in love and war!

The *Hymn to Aphrodite* recalls the power that goddess holds over the entire Animal Kingdom:

Muse, tell me the deeds of golden Aphrodite the Cyprian, who stirs up sweet passion in the gods and subdues the tribes of mortal men and birds that fly in the air and all the many creatures that dry land rears, and all that the sea: all these love the deeds of rich-crowned Cytherea.

As virgins, Athena, Artemis, and Hestia are immune. As for Zeus, Aphrodite "beguiles even his wise heart whenever she pleases."

The *Cypria*, a general mythological history, sees war as a necessary means of reducing the number of men burdening the Earth:

There was a time when the countless tribes of men, though wide-dispersed, oppressed the surface of the deep-bosomed earth, and Zeus saw it and had pity and in his wise heart resolved to relieve the all-nurturing earth of men by causing the great struggle of the Ilian [Trojan] war, that the load of death might empty the world. And so the heroes were slain in Troy, and the plan of Zeus came to pass.

Homer's *Iliad*, the oldest Western epic poem to come down to us, is a great tale of love and war. The poet tells of a terrible war sparked by sexual competition, to win the heart of beautiful Helen, and its inevitable tragedies. But the maudlin self-pity and effeminacy of our time is unknown to Homer: if tragedy is inevitable in the human experience, the poet's role is to give meaning and beauty to the ordeal, and to inspire men to struggle for a glorious destiny.

Homer's *Odyssey*, which tells the tale of Odysseus' return from the Trojan War to his homeland of Ithaca, is also a story substantially driven by love and war, or rather, kinship and violence. Odysseus is doomed to wander the Mediterranean amidst hostile strangers who would "bring havoc on men of another stock."[24] The hero faces savages and monsters; and is often tempted to settle away from home with divine beings. But Odysseus cannot help longing for his wife Penelope and family, his "kith and kin,"[25] and his "own country,"[26] that of his forefathers.

Odysseus perseveres by clinging to his identity and triumphs through courage and cunning. His household had "no man left with the mettle of Odysseus to ward off ruin."[27] He returns to find his home overrun by parasitic suitors who wish to usurp his wife and birthright. Odysseus joins with his son Telemachus to plot revenge. Telemachus himself had a duty to find his father and redeem his household, for he is said to belong to "the race of heaven-protected and sceptered kings."[28] Odysseus' revenge upon the suitors and their collaborators is ruthless and brutal, a dark deed necessary to restore his honor and authority.

Love would also have a central importance in later Greek philosophy. Plato's *Symposium* sublimates sexual desire into a powerful ethical force enabling one to unite with kindred spirits and gravitate towards the truth.

[24] Homer, *Odyssey*, 3.36-121.

[25] *Ibid.*, 2.158-241.

[26] *Ibid.*, 7.329-47.

[27] *Ibid.*, 2.1-75.

[28] *Ibid.*, 4.61-64.

THE GREEK CITY-STATES, THE FIRST ETHNOSTATES

For the Greeks, citizenship meant belonging to a city-state, the polis, grounded in very different principles than the ones we have come to know. Many of these principles however are very relevant for any people struggling for self-determination and survival in a world of hostile tribes competing for limited resources.

Before anything else, a good city-state was one with the qualities necessary to survive in the face of aggressive foreign powers. This was ensured by solidarity among the citizens, each being willing to fight and die beside the other. Hence the citizen was also a soldier-citizen. The completion of military training and the ability to purchase the hoplite soldier's armor for oneself were typical criteria for full citizenship. The city-state was small, most numbering less than 50,000 people, and a minority of the population were citizens. This made politics a face-to-face affair between leaders and fellow citizens who knew each other personally.

For the ancient Greeks, political freedom was a holistic enterprise involving the entire community. They had no notion of individual liberty outside of the *polis*. The citizen in his capacity as a private individual was known as an *idiōtēs*, the semantic ancestor of our "idiot." All would be free or slaves together, depending on the well-being and survival of the community and its state. Hence, Aristotle argued that "justice consists in what tends to promote the common interest" (*Politics*, 1282b14), rather than in the pursuit of some individualist or egalitarian ideal. Aristotle's political ethics takes a holistic, communitarian approach typical of the Greeks, for: "A whole is never intended by nature to be inferior to a part" (*Politics*, 1288a15). To those tempted by the illusions of individualism, Xenophon writes eloquently on the self-destructive foolishness of those who believe that there can be freedom without self-discipline (one is then beholden to one's belly) or by being a stateless rootless cosmopolitan (one's freedom is then beholden to the good-will of the foreign state one is residing in).[29]

The *polis* was then unabashedly authoritarian and collectivist, the good lawmaker being he who could inspire good habits and morals in the citizenry. The citizens themselves accepted the city's disciplines by having a role in their making and by identifying with the community. There was no sense that an individual had "rights" to live an unregulated or capricious private life according purely to his own whims. The society and state as a whole, which were one in the city-state, then regulated the lives of citizens, often harshly, in order to promote the public good. One indeed can say of the ancient Greek ideal of citizenship: *Gemeinnutz vor Eigennutz*.[30] As Paul Cartledge observes: "Whatever the ancient Greek *polis* and politics were, they were emphatically *not* 'liberals' as that term is today understood in mainstream political theory. Any attempt to detect even a quasi-metaphorical 'liberal temper' in Greek politics is deeply misguided."[31]

Solidarity and group cohesion were ensured not only by the civic participation and familiarity enabled by the small size of the city, but also by ties of blood. Both Athens and Sparta, the leading Greek city-states, limited citizenship to descendants of the original founding population, allowing for few exceptions. Non-Greeks especially were typically excluded from citizenship. More generally, kinship lay at the very core of the Greek *polis*, being the fundamental foundation for identity and solidarity. The Greek city-states were *Herrenvolk* republics, quite diverse in their internal organization and degree of enfranchisement, the exclusion of non-citizens and enslavement of foreigners being paired with a level of civic participation and popular self-government unmatched in ancient history.

---

[29] See in particular, Socrates' debate with the hedonistic philosopher Aristippus and Heracles' myth of Vice and Virtue: Xenophon, *Memorabilia*, 2.1.

[30] The public good before the private interest.

[31] Paul Cartledge, *Ancient Greek Political Thought in Practice: Key Themes in Ancient History* (Cambridge/New York: Cambridge University Press, 2009), p. 131.

The ancient Greek's concentric circles of kinship defined his identity and bonds of solidarity, from the family up through to the nation. The family under a powerful father was the basic building block of society. The city-state was an organic entity as a real and imagined extended family. In thinking of the *polis*, we must avoid the bureaucratic and impersonal connotations of our word "state." As Melissa Lane observes, the Hellenic state or *polis* was defined above all not by its administration, but by *its people*:

> While land was important to a *polis*'s identity, both practically and symbolically, it was ultimately secondary to the identity of its inhabitants. A *polis* was defined most fundamentally in terms of its people. The Greeks never spoke of "Athens" or "Sparta" as political actors ... they spoke of "the Athenians" or "the Spartans." And, in desperate moments the survival of the *polis* meant the survival of the people holding *ta politika* [political things] in common, even at the cost of sacrificing some of their land ... *Polis* is often translated as "citizen-state," since it was the people, more than the place, who made the *polis*. [32]

Indeed, on one occasion "the Athenians" fled their city *en masse* when it was invaded and torched by the Persians, but they fully retained their identity as a people.

The city-state itself was contained within other circles of kinship and solidarity. If a mother-city were to create new settlements, these cities recognized their kinship and would seek good relations with one another. The *ethnos*, meaning a regional-linguistic intra-Greek tribe, was another tier of identity, which was often the basis for villages or cities to coalesce into confederations and leagues (notably in Achaea, Arcadia, and western Crete). Finally, the Greeks as a whole, whatever their internal divisions and dispersion across the Mediterranean, had a powerful and enduring sense of common identity, separateness, and superiority in the face of foreigners.

---

[32] Melissa Lane, *Greek and Roman Political Ideas* (London: Penguin, 2014), pp. 13-14.

In resisting the Persian invasions, the 31 out of the approximately 700 mainland Greek cities which fought under Spartan and Athenian leadership proudly called themselves "the Greeks," thus claiming to fight for the survival of the Greek nation as a whole (even though, in fact, more Greeks served on the stronger and wealthier Persian side). The Greeks themselves recognized that, whatever loyalty each had to their *polis*, there was also a wider spiritual, cultural, and ethnic kinship among all Greeks. In light of their shared blood and culture, the Greeks believed that they should be gentler with one another and unite against barbarian aggressors, but political divisions meant they rarely attained this ideal.

The Greeks ardently held what should be a common-sense view: that the rearing of prosperous descendants is central to human life, both as individuals and as communities. The Greeks generally held a very adaptive conception of happiness: a man is only happy if his descendants are prosperous. As Aristotle wrote: "That the fortunes of descendants and of all a man's friends should not affect his happiness at all seems a very unfriendly doctrine, and one opposed to the opinions men hold" (*Nicomachean Ethics*, 1.11). The gods were said to punish the impious by making their lineage barren. Conversely, having children was held as a great social honor. Homer is supposed to have said in one of his *Epigrams*: "Children are a man's crown." Children owed honor and economic support to their parents. The Greeks took for granted that they would wish to have the best children possible, praying to the gods for good offspring and practicing primitive eugenics.

In line with these values, the Greeks believed that state and society had a duty to encourage and regulate the citizenry beget and raise children. And in the right numbers at that: neither too many for Greece was poor in land, nor too few for this meant a declining state. This was achieved through social pressure, legal penalties and encouragements, and marriage. The latter was not conceived as a private pact meant for the convenience and pleasure of two consenting individuals, but as a sacred institution aiming to produce the best children possible, in the service of the well-being and perpetuity one's lineage and of the society as a whole.

In ancient Greece, religion worked *with* the tribal instinct in wondrous harmony in order to magnify and sacralize every circle of kinship and identity — namely the family, the city-state, and the Hellenic nation as a whole. The nineteenth-century French historian Numa Denis Fustel de Coulanges documented in his classic study *La Cité antique* the degree to which religion, society, and polity were inseparable in ancient Greece. The ancestral Pagan Indo-European religion prescribed no moral universalism, but rather that men perpetuate their family line so as to forever honor their ancestors:

> As religious chief [the father] is responsible for the cult's perpetuity and, therefore, for the family.[33]

> If [this religion] ignores the duties of charity [towards outsiders], it at least traces for man with an admirable clarity his familial duties. It makes marriage mandatory; celibacy is a crime in the eyes of a religion which makes the continuity of the family the first and the holiest of duties.[34]

When the first Greek cities were founded, essentially by groups of armed men capable of defending them, this eminently adaptive piety was then projected onto society as a whole:

> The comparison of [Indo-European] beliefs and laws shows that the primitive religion created the Greek and Roman family, established marriage and paternal authority, fixed the hierarchy of kinship, consecrated the right of property and the right of inheritance. This same religion, after having enlarged and extended the family, shaped a wider

---

[33] Fustel de Coulanges, *La Cité antique* (Paris: Flammarion, 1984 [1864]), p. 135. Available online in English translation: Fustel de Coulanges, *The Ancient City: A Study on the Religion, Laws, and Institutions of Greece and Rome* (Kitchener, Ontario: Batoche Books, 2001; originally published in 1862). https://socialsciences.mcmaster.ca/econ/ugcm/3ll3/fustel/Ancient City.pdf

[34] *Ibid.*, p. 143.

association, the city, and reigned in it as in the family.[35]

[T]his explains the patriotism of the ancients, a vigorous sentiment which was for them the supreme virtue and that which all the others culminated in ... Love of country is piety to the ancients.[36]

Such religious beliefs, urging people to have children and defend their community, were obviously highly adaptive. Greek religion with its sacrifices and festivals was eminently public, political, and indeed omnipresent. As Coulanges observes: "There was not a single act of public life in which one did not have the gods intervene."[37] Through these obligatory communal rituals, citizens symbolically worked together to please the gods, themselves embodying the incomprehensible superior forces that make and destroy human things, and thus protect the community. The Greeks as a whole celebrated their common identity in joint religious festivals and sporting events, most famously the Olympic Games.

The ancestral Greek religion thus inspired values that prized both the perpetuation of one's family lineage and the collective survival and prosperity of one's people. The Athenian lawgiver and sage Solon was said to have described a certain Tellus as the happiest man in the world because:

Tellus had sons who were fine, upstanding men and he lived to see them all have children, all of whom survived. ... [And he had] a glorious death. You see, in battle at Eleusis between Athens and her neighbors he stepped into the breach and made the enemy turn tail and flee; he died, but his death was splendid, and the Athenians awarded him a public funeral on the spot where he fell, and greatly honored him. (Herodotus, 1.30)

The politics of democratic Athens were typically particularistic. The Athenian statesman Pericles, noted for his

---

[35] *Ibid.*, p. 36.

[36] *Ibid.*, pp. 278-79.

[37] *Ibid.*, p. 230.

democratic reforms assisting poorer citizens and giving them more say in government, paired his efforts with tightening citizenship requirements by limiting it to those descending from two Athenian parents. Modern liberals may be surprised to see such extreme 'chauvinism' from the world's first democracy. In fact, Pericles' generosity and exclusion go hand in hand: the more discriminating one is between a well-defined in-group and out-groups, the more generous one can afford to be with the in-group. The ancients in general rejected any undiscerning and unreciprocated universal altruism.

Furthermore, Montesquieu reports that foreigners found to be illegally voting in the Athenian assembly paid the supreme penalty: death. Such was the price Athenian democrats extracted from those who would dilute the sovereignty of the people and the state. Restriction of citizenship is one of the most striking aspects in the development of the West's first and most famous democracy (another is Solon's institution of debt forgiveness).

In contrast with Athenian democracy, the Spartans had an admired "mixed constitution" with monarchical, oligarchic, and democratic elements, leaning towards aristocracy. Full citizens, known as Spartiates, ruled as a unique class of professional soldiers over a conquered population of Helots ("probably just about the most difficult and contentious institution in the entire Greek world," notes Plato [*Laws*, 776c]). The Spartan lawgiver Lycurgus had given that state its peculiar institutions, demanding systematic military training of the youth, eating in common mess halls to bond citizens, and measures to improve their biological quality (including the killing of deformed newborns). Sparta also had laws to improve fertility: fathers with three sons were relieved from military service and those with four sons paid no taxes (Aristotle, *Politics*, 1270b6).

Lycurgus instituted a harsh system. And yet, it was through such laws, and the unity and discipline that resulted, that Sparta, numbering perhaps 50,000, had the power to defeat a far richer and more populous Athens of 250,000 in the Peloponnesian War. And prior to this, Athenian and Spartan power together had been necessary to save Greece from total destruction in the Persian Wars. Indeed, the sacrifice of the Spartan King Leonidas and his 300 men at Thermopylae resonates to this day even in popular culture, most recently with the *300* films. In his *Laws*, Plato recounts what would have happened to Greece had the city-states been too weak and the Persians triumphed:

> If it hadn't been for the joint determination of the Athenians and the Spartans to resist the slavery that threatened them, we should have by now virtually a complete mixture of the races — Greek with Greek, Greek with barbarian, and barbarian with Greek. We can see a parallel in the nations whom the Persians lord it over today: they have been split up and then horribly jumbled together again into the scattered communities in which they now live. (*Laws*, 693a)

And that would have been the end of the Greek people and their unparalleled cultural achievements, and Western civilization as we know it would not exist. Fortunately, "the Persian attack on the Greeks — on virtually everyone living in Europe," failed (*Laws*, 698b).

Insofar as citizenship was genetically-defined through descent and the authorities took an active role in promoting reproduction, we can say that the ancient Greek city-states were indeed the first ethnostates, each with their own primitive group evolutionary strategies. These city-states constantly struggled with each other and against barbarians. What we would call today pure and simple ethnic cleansing was not an uncommon fate for the losing side of a war in the ancient world—the winner physically often replacing his adversary with settlers. The struggle for life was central to Greek politics.

NATURE & THE GODS: SACRED LAWS

Greek thinkers often debated the nature of the gods and of the universe itself — or nature — and their relationship with the city's laws. Many Greeks denounced their traditional stories about passionate and violent gods as impious. Some denounced their city's laws as contrary to nature. The Greeks were typically Western in their willingness to question convention.

The Greeks almost universally believed that anyone who violated the will of the gods or nature, whether out of ignorance or contempt, would inevitably be ruined and destroyed as a result. In a quite literal sense then, to be impious or to do the unnatural meant for the Greeks to be engaging in *maladaptive* behavior. Homer's capricious gods and the suffering of his heroes, who may have unknowingly offended a god, reflect the anxiousness of men, facing death and danger at every turn, to respect the inscrutable higher powers that hold sway over their lives.

This point is perhaps made most explicitly in one of Xenophon's dialogues on the subject of incest:

Socrates: Those who transgress the laws laid down by the gods pay a penalty which no man can escape in the way that some transgressors of man-made laws escape paying the penalty, either by escaping detection or by the use of force.

Hippias: What penalty, Socrates, cannot be escaped by parents who copulate with their children or children who copulate with their parents?

Socrates: The greatest of all, I can tell you, what greater misfortune could happen to human beings in the procreation of their children than to procreate badly? (*Memorabilia*, 4.4.17-25)

The prohibition on incest is therefore a divine or natural law. This interdiction is a perfectly adaptive principle, even though the Ancients could know nothing about the genetic reasons for consanguineous diseases or inbreeding depression. In Xenophon's dialogue, Hippias and Socrates observe two further customs besides incest which, being shared by (virtually) all human societies, likely reflect natural law: "among all peoples the first established custom is to worship gods" and "to honor parents." I would argue both are fundamental adaptive principles. To honor one's parents means to know one's preceding kin, to be in solidarity with them, and, to a certain extent, to inscribe ourselves in their wider plan. Elsewhere, Xenophon observes that a mother's love for her own children is also a "natural law," which again is self-evidently adaptive (*Oeconomicus*, 9.16-10.8).

Piety, I would argue, represents an in-born drive for obedience and enforcement of group norms, defined by the reigning religion. A religion's principles can of course be maladaptive (I think especially of universalist religions, often promoted and manipulated by rulers of multiethnic empires). However, traditional tribal religions seem to virtually always have adaptive values on the whole. Judaism, Hinduism, or Shinto clearly have adaptive ethnocentric principles. Greek polytheism, besides promoting the family and values of personal heroism and sacrifice, emphasized loyalty to the city-state, which as we have seen was a kinship group. The universal abhorrence for impiety in traditional societies represents, in my view, an instinctive aversion to normlessness, a society with no direction or ordering is felt to be a revolting sacrilege. Religion can be likened to a kind of social software: it enables both group unity and potentially radical changes in social behavior through various mechanisms (guilt, enforcement), without waiting for invariably slow genetic change—what evolutionists refer to as cultural group selection.

This by no means exhausts the discussion of natural law. I observe however that the usual Greek conception, that what is unnatural and impious is self-destructive/maladaptive, tends to imply duties rather than rights.[38] The Greek conception of natural law means individuals and communities have a duty to not engage in behavior which will ruin them. Conversely, as we Westerners are transforming our societies in utter contempt for the laws of tribalism in human beings and of heredity in all

---

[38] A "natural right" would then, I suppose, only be a right which if violated would tend to destroy the community. There might then be a "natural right" to a degree of private property, insofar as wholly communist economies, in disregarding individual rationality and the slowness of the state, are invariably failures. Modern "human rights" can be considered an egalitarian and individualist outgrowth of ancient "natural law."

living creatures, so we become steadily weaker with every generation.

It follows that for the Greeks, ethics — personal or political — could only be known through knowledge of the natural and divine laws of the universe. The good state would hence seek to harmonize its laws with those of the universe. As Heraclitus says: "all human laws are in the keeping of the one divine law; for the one divine law has as much power as it wishes, is an unfailing defense for all laws, and prevails over all laws."[39] A possible implication is that if the state's laws are unnatural and maladaptive for one's people, one has the right and duty to violate and replace those laws.

The philosophers then had a quest to discover nature's laws and to inspire their society to live in harmony with them. This however had obvious antidemocratic implications. Democritus, a philosopher famous for his positing the existence of indivisible atoms, believed that it was "wrong to assess the truth by majorities and minorities."[40] Indeed, by definition, those with the best knowledge of truth are a tiny minority — just as the best sprinters, the best ship-builders, the best doctors, etc., form tiny minorities in their respective fields.

Much later, the philosopher-emperor Julian, the last Roman ruler to seek to revive the old pagan religion and Greek philosophy, summarized things thus: "the end and aim of ... every philosophy is happiness, but happiness that consists in living according to nature and not according to the opinions of the multitude" (*To the Uneducated Cynics*). Cultural and political leadership was then meant to belong to those who had both the in-born intellect and goodness, and the best training and education, to know the truth.

THE RECOGNITION OF INEQUALITY: FOUNDATIONAL TO ETHICS

For the ancient philosophers, the recognition of inequality was foundational to ethics. An egalitarian was effectively

---

[39] Waterfield, *First Philosophers*, p. 39.
[40] *Ibid.*, p. 177.

morally blind. Inequality extended to all spheres. In the Socratic tradition's evaluation of the individual soul, reason was considered superior to emotions, and emotions superior to mere pleasure. In the best human beings, those who fulfill our true potential as distinct from irrational beasts, reason rules over pleasure and pain, with the assistance of emotions. Since reason was not distributed equally among all people, human inequality was a fact of nature — a truth that has since been scientifically shown repeatedly in the literature on the behavioral genetics of intelligence and self-control.

At the level of the universe, species and things were unequal in the same regard: gods were superior to men, men to animals, and animals to inanimate objects. In this schema, humans should worship and serve the gods, while rightly ruling over animals, and finally animals over mere matter. Between individual man and the universe, there is the city. And here again one finds inequality and diversity everywhere in any human society, much of it in-born. Again, the better — those who are more enlightened, by whatever happy combination of natural ability and good upbringing — should lead those with lesser abilities.

The inequality of all things in the universe is axiomatic for the Greeks. And equally axiomatic is the rule that the better should rule the worse, and not otherwise. As the gentle Marcus Aurelius, another Roman philosopher-emperor, would write in his famous *Meditations*: "Is it not clear that inferior beings were made for the sake of the superior, and superior beings for the sake of one another?" (5.16). And again, with his trademark magnanimity towards the less enlightened, he said: "Try to persuade them, but act even against their will if the principles of justice demand it" (6.50).

One does not find much of an individualist strain in ancient Greek politics. But one does find an egalitarian one. Sometimes this was justified, as over time land and wealth tended to accumulate into few hands and the people became indebted through usury. There were periodic revolutions to spread the land more equally among citizens. However, as so often in Western history, the egalitarian tendency frequently lapsed into self-destructive excess. As Heraclitus observed with damning eloquence:

> For banishing Hermodorus, who was the best man among them, the Ephesians deserve to be hanged, every last one of them, and to leave the city to boys. They said, "Let no single one of us be best, or else let him be so elsewhere, among others."[41]

The aristocratic and antidemocratic strain throughout the entire ancient philosophical tradition cannot be overemphasized. This goes far beyond the understandable frustration of Athenian philosophers at the defeat of their incompetent democratic regime during the Peloponnesian War and their revulsion at the democracy's execution of Socrates, a man in all respects superior to the mob. Rather, it is a point of principle, as Plato is at pains to emphasize in his *Laws*: *the unequal should be treated unequally*, and justice "consists of granting the 'equality' that unequals deserve to get" (756e-758a). On this point, Aristotle agreed with his teacher Plato, writing:

> [J]ustice is considered to mean equality. It does mean equality — but equality for those who are equal, and not for all. Again, inequality is considered to be just; and indeed it is — but only for those who are unequal, and not for all. (*Politics*, 1280a7)

Modern philosophers such as Rousseau and Nietzsche also affirmed this 'geometrical' or 'proportionate' notion of equality, as opposed to the 'arithmetical' one which sees all human beings as interchangeably equal. Greek philosophers more generally understood that gifted men with the opportunity to dedicate their lives to the pursuit of the truth would be far closer to that truth than the common man, let alone a fickle mob, whose opinions were at best the product of folk-wisdom and popular culture.

---

[41] *Ibid.*, p. 45.

SELF-IMPROVEMENT: NATURE & NURTURE

Today, egalitarian blank-slatism pervades much of academia and official discourse. The Greek had a far more realistic view, believing that an individual's qualities were the fruits of nature *and* nurture. Even the sophist Protagoras, a thinker of democratic leanings and an educator of the people, argued: "Teaching requires natural endowments and training; one should begin to learn when one is young."[42] The recognition of in-born human inequality in no way implied that the well-endowed should rest on their laurels. On the contrary, *all* humans should constantly work to maximize their potential through training and education.

There was widespread recognition that human inequality was not only substantially in-born but also hereditary. One of the earliest and most vigorous proponents of this view was the poet Theognis of Megara, who lamented that humans did not care for their own reproduction as much as did animal breeders, men often marrying for money rather than the quality of their wives:

> In rams and asses and horses ... we seek the thoroughbred, and a man is concerned therein to get him offspring of good stock; yet in marriage a good man thinketh not twice of wedding the bad daughter of a bad sire if the father give him many possessions, nor doth a woman disdain the bed of a bad man if he be wealthy, but is fain rather to be rich than to be good. For 'tis possessions they prize; and a good man weddeth of bad stock and a bad man of good; race is confounded of riches. In like manner, son of Polypaus, marvel thou not that the race of thy townsmen is made obscure; 'tis because bad things are mingled with good. (Theognis, 183-92)[43]

---

[42] *Ibid.*, p. 219.

[43] Theognis furthermore asserts that even the best education cannot correct someone of bad in-born character:

> To beget and breed a man is easier than to put into him good wits; none hath ever devised means whereby he hath made a fool wise and a bad man good. If God had given the Children of Asclepius

Charles Darwin himself, the founder of modern evolutionary thinking, said of these poems:

> [I]t was a well recognised principle with the Greek, that men ought to select their wives with a view to the health and vigour of their children. The Grecian poet, Theognis, who lived 550 BC, saw how important selection, if carefully applied, would be for the improvement of mankind. He saw likewise that wealth often checks the proper action of sexual selection.[44]

Based on this belief in heredity, intuitively believed among those who claimed good birth and following logically from the successful practice of animal breeding, the Greeks practiced eugenics, albeit generally in an unsystematic way. The Greek more generally developed techniques to maximize their human potential. They were remarkably cognizant of the means available: good education, constant training, healthy habits, and socialization with good individuals. Through self-discipline and piety, reason could rule over emotions, pleasures and pains. The Greeks considered a life of belly-chasing, death-fearing, and comfort-clinging to be an evil, subhuman one, no better than that of the lower beasts. Politically, moral education of the citizens was considered practically the first duty of the state, to be achieved through training, culture, public religion, and laws.

None went further than the divine Plato in imagining how humanity might tend towards superhuman perfection. His ideal republic is a state effectively led by an enlightened and pious order of warrior-monks as a cognitive and moral elite drawn from the best of the whole people. This elite then

---

the art of healing a man's evil nature and infatuate wit, they would receive wages much and great; and if thought could be made and put into us, the son of a good father would never become bad, because he would be persuaded by good counsel. But by teaching never shalt thou make the bad man good. (429-38)

[44] Charles Darwin, *The Descent of Man* (London: Penguin, 2004 [1879]), p. 47.

systematically educates and trains itself, and to the extent possible the people, towards the good. But Plato goes further than most philosophers and follows the Spartan lawgiver Lycurgus in making *biological improvement* of the population through good breeding a sacred moral imperative. This principle, while it follows quite naturally from humanity's many successes in plant and animal breeding, is nonetheless remarkable given that Plato wrote long before the scientific facts about Darwinian evolution, heredity, and genetics were known.

For too long, Western civilization has operated in contempt of the blood. Western man does seem to have a tendency to love contemplation of the divine. Yet higher consciousness, which may reasonably be deemed a supreme goal of intelligent life, is only a flicker in the dark if it ends with one's bloodline. As even the blue-eyed Buddha in India, perhaps a contemporary of Socrates, observed: "this body ... produced from a mother and father ... is what [the ascetic's] consciousness depends on, what it is bound up with."[45] And the body assuredly derives from the blood.

Universalist religions have often forgotten this, urging the most pious to become childless monks or priests. There is a case for our best minds to not be distracted by family life so that they may fully pursue philosophical truth and political activism. But I would limit that to a minuscule minority. The best of our people must know they have a duty to perpetuate their line. Humans are by nature genetic, social, and cultural creatures, our political goals naturally flow from this: the genetic, social, and cultural improvement of our people.

TRUTH-TELLING & CULTURAL STRUGGLE

European Identitarians and other violators of political correctness must bear the burden of being considered heretics. This is not only painful and unglamorous, but indeed can

---

[45] Rupert Gethin (trans.), *Sayings of the Buddha: A selection of suttas from the Pali Nikayas* (Oxford: Oxford World's Classics, 2008), "The Fruits of the Ascetic Life," p. 30.

prove financially and socially ruinous. Yet, here too, there is inspiration in the Hellenic tradition and we find that not all is new under the sun.

Greek philosophy itself, as it comes down to us, really flourished following the eternal example of Socrates. In no other man is the contradiction between social acceptability and the pursuit of truth so apparent. Socrates was a good soldier when Athens called upon him to fight for his country. He was also a father and family man, though perhaps a somewhat neglectful one. He preferred to live in relative poverty, questioning those who claimed to be wise, and refusing to take corrupting fees for his teachings. Socrates' self-discipline was legendary, being immune to cold, drunkenness, or sleepiness, spending hours or whole days and nights meditating.

The detail of Socrates' views will remain forever unknown to us. But we know some things by his way life. Describing himself as the "gadfly" of Athens, Socrates was what we would call today an ethical 'troll': urging his fellow citizens to become aware of their ignorance and showing established authorities to not be as wise as they claimed. He praised the value of political expertise as against the assumptions of Athenian direct democracy. He said that the only genuine good, for an intelligent being, was in the good of the soul, rather than external goods or even health. For if you give a foolish man wealth and power, he would only use these foolishly, at best wasting them and perhaps even harming himself further. And indeed, is not power and wealth without purpose the very story of America and of Western civilization itself over the past century? We are victims of our foolishness and apparent successes.

Socrates fell afoul of the democratic authorities of his day. He was accused, like all unpopular truth-tellers, of "impiety" and of "corrupting the youth." Do not we heretics today know these charges well? The women too lamented. But Socrates would not back down. In the face of the mob, he put his words into practice, preferring death to a life in which he could not live by philosophy. The story, as magnificently told by Plato, is all the more poignant in that Socrates refused to flee his execution. Socrates was no liberal: while boldly questioning convention, he honored the right of the Athenian state to do as it saw fit in the name of public morals, and he submitted, for without respect for the laws there is only anarchy. By his willingness to sacrifice himself, the philosopher shows his superior piety, his adherence to his own internal moral law, itself acquired through training and reflection. This is piety a mob cannot even conceive of, let alone have. The egalitarian executioner is shamed forever, the philosopher by his exemplary death becomes immortal in the minds of men.

Socrates' sacrifice inspired all the Greco-Roman philosophical schools that endured until the end of antiquity. In terms of individual ethics and lifestyle, all merely elaborated upon his principles. His example lives with us still. Remember that you have only one life and death is inevitable, that we are all subjects of the laws of the universe whether we like it or not, that you have nothing but your soul, and that your blood begot your spirit.

The Emperor Julian, that final flowering of the Hellenic spirit, showed the way in recalling the two fundamental principles of his philosophy: "Know thyself" and "restamp the common currency." In other words, discover your own nature and then, based on this truth, *change the culture*, change what people value, for what they value today is utterly worthless. And there will even be joy and that rarest of things in our nihilistic age: a life full of meaning. For as Julian also said, those who have had a taste of the truth, however small, are seized by that "sacred frenzy," that ecstatic feeling which inspires us to order our life accordingly and to zealously fight to enlighten our kinsmen.

The threats faced by the European race today are unprecedented. Many individual European tribes have been exterminated in the past. But never before as in this century has our entire race faced such collective decline and utter dispossession in our ancestral homelands. Yet, on a personal level, the struggle for truth remains in many ways similar to that faced by our Greek forefathers. If we dare to learn and live by our ancestral wisdom, if words are every day met with

22

deeds great and small, we need fear nothing.

The challenges are enormous, but certainly no greater than the travails our ancestors triumphed over century after century. In that struggle for survival, amidst the primordial force which has shaped all life, our ancestors have left timeless wisdom imprinted not just in our culture but in our very genes. And hence the Western youth of today can take heart and inspiration, just as Telemachus did upon hearing the words of Athena: "If the gods let Penelope bear such a son as you, they did not mean for your lineage to be inglorious in times to come."[46]

---

[46] Homer, *Odyssey*, 1.197-278.

HOMER'S *ILIAD*
VITAL BARBARISM, DECADENT CIVILIZATION

Every organism and every species is engaged in a ceaseless struggle for survival and reproduction. This is equally true of peoples: throughout history, those with the values and genes necessary to reproduce and triumph in war prospered, while the rest have already perished. Human behavior being determined not only by genes, but also by culture, we would expect the cultural artifacts and practices of successful peoples to reflect values which enabled them to survive and conquer. Such values, reflecting the harsh laws of life and struggle, are clearly embodied in the most ancient sacred text to have come down to us in the Western tradition: Homer's *Iliad*.

The hundreds of thousands of years of humanity's prehistory appears to us in mere glimpses, like the occasional memories of our earliest childhood. We know so very little about the lives of our ancestors, their travails and triumphs. What is the *Iliad*, this enigmatic epic which the Greeks considered worth singing generation after generation? The *Iliad* is the earliest recordings of Hellenic and indeed of Western consciousness: following the long-forgotten night of our prehistory, this great, feverish poem reads like the reminiscences of a long, blood-soaked dream.

In his poems, Homer encapsulates the familial, aristocratic, competitive, manly, and warrior values which enabled the ancient Greeks to impose themselves in the world. These values formed the underlying morality of the *polis*, what Nietzsche called "the naïve barbarism of the Greek state."[47] Homer expresses an ethos inspired by Nature herself, truly "red in tooth and claw."

If Hesiod's genealogy of the gods portrays the primordial

---

[47] Friedrich Nietzsche (trans. Carol Diethe), "The Greek State" (1871/2), in Keith Ansell-Pearson (ed.), *On the Genealogy of Morals* (Cambridge: Cambridge University Press, 2006).

sex and violence at the origin of the creation, the *Iliad* recounts the violence of love and war at the dawn of civilization. The poet tells of a terrible war between the Greeks, whom the poet calls Achaeans, and the Asiatic Trojans. Homer's portrayal of "the great leveler, war" is by no means sugar-coated. The killings of over two hundred men are individually described, dying by having their brains splattered, bladders pierced, or innards slopping out … By these and so many other ways, "the swirling dark" falls before the eyes of countless men. The *Iliad* immortalizes the Greek variant of a wider warrior ethos: that of the Aryans who burst forth into Europe some four thousand years ago and conquered the indigenous hunter-gatherers and farmers. The Europeans have, ever since, been profoundly influenced by the genes, languages, and martial way of life of these peoples.

The heroic values of Homer are by our standards extremely harsh, even barbaric.[48] I will show however that these values are supremely adaptive: values of conquest, community, competition, and kinship. These reflect the spirit of the Bronze Age with its countless forgotten wars between peoples. From an evolutionary point of view, these men embraced a high-risk, high-reward strategy: victors in battle won wealth, women, and honor. Their boldness and prowess indeed remain imprinted on our very genes: scientists have found that around 90 percent of Britain's gene pool was replaced over a few centuries in this period and indeed that half of European men descend from a single Bronze Age king.[49]

The *Iliad* is also worth reading to understand the ancient Greeks and the values which they lived by to survive in the brutal world of the ancient Mediterranean. Indeed, Homer's

---

[48] There is irony here in that "barbarian" is the Greek word initially meaning foreigner. The semantic slippage towards "uncivilized savage" is significant and likely reflects the Greeks' own historical trajectory from civilization to decadence.

[49] Iñigo Olalde *et al*, "The Beaker Phenomenon and the Genomic Transformation of Northwest Europe," *bioRxiv*, May 9, 2017. Sarah Knapton, "Half of Western European men descended from one Bronze Age 'king,'" *The Daily Telegraph*, April 25, 2016.

influence over Greek culture was enormous, akin to the Bible in medieval Europe. As Bernard Knox notes, the Greeks believed the Trojan War actually occurred and, as their Year Zero, was central to their national identity:

> But though we may have our doubts, the Greeks of historic times who knew and loved Homer's poem had none. For them history began with a splendid Panhellenic expedition against an Eastern foe, led by kings and including contingents from all the more than one hundred and fifty places listed in the catalogue in Book 2. History began with a war.[50]

THE IRRESISTIBLE POWER OF LOVE

The Trojan War itself took place because of love—and the inevitable competition this entails. Paris the Trojan was asked to choose which of the three goddesses Aphrodite, Hera, or Athena was the fairest. He chose Aphrodite, goddess of love, who had promised him the most beautiful woman in the world, Helen. Thus, Paris incurred the wrath of the other two goddesses as well as Helen's husband, "red-haired" Menelaus, a Greek king. The fact that Paris did this while being a guest of Menelaus in Sparta was the ultimate violation of *xenia*, or guest-friendship, a serious impiety.

"Fair-haired" Helen herself laments being overpowered by love, dragging her against her will away from "the life-giving earth of Lacedaemon, the dear land of her fathers" (3.243-44). Upon seeing the massing Achaeans, her former husband, "her kinsmen and people," she says: "if only death had pleased me then, grim death that day I followed your son to Troy, forsaking my marriage bed, my kinsmen, and my child" (3.173-75). Upon meeting Aphrodite again, Helen says: "Maddening one, my Goddess, oh what now? Lusting to lure me to my ruin yet again?" (3.399-401).

Even wise and all-powerful Zeus, king of the gods, is not immune to the power of love. Hera manages to enable her

---

[50] Bernard Knox, "Introduction," in Homer (Robert Fagles trans.), *The Iliad* (New York: Penguin Books, 1990), p. 24.

favored Achaeans to win the upper hand in battle by distracting Zeus for a time, seducing and making love with him, and sending him into a deep slumber. Hera had called out to Aphrodite for help: "Give me Love, give me Longing now, the powers you use to overwhelm all gods and mortal men!" and thus gained "the heat of Love, the pulsing rush of Longing, the lover's whisper, irresistible — magic to make the sanest man go mad" (14.198-217).

But while impetuous love and retaliatory honor, brought the war about, Homer makes clear that love has no place on the battlefield. This is strikingly portrayed in Book 5 by Aphrodite's appearance and severe wounding by a mortal, the Achaean fighter Diomedes. The goddess of love is then forced to flee from the carnage of men. There is a whiff of that typically Western Promethean excess in Diomedes: even before the gods he refuses to give up the fight and even dares to injure one. He suffers no revenge however, for he knows to back down eventually when facing Apollo, a god more capable in battle.

A SOCIAL WORLD OF LINEAGE & KINSHIP

The society which Homer portrays revolves around lineage and kinship. In a dangerous world of often hostile strangers, family and fatherland are what one can most count on. Exile is a dreaded fate, especially for women, who if on the losing side of a war risk being taken away "far from their fatherland." Kinship entails reciprocal rights and responsibilities. Children have a duty to respect their parents and bring honor to their family. One father sends off his son to fight at Troy saying: "Always be the best, my boy, the bravest. Never disgrace the generation of your fathers" (6.207-10). If a relative is killed, kin similarly have a duty to avenge him: "That's why a fighter prays for kin in his halls, blood kin to survive and avenge his death in battle!" (14.484-85). That is, unless the relative is satisfied with blood money as compensation, in which case "the injured kinsman curbs his pride, his smoldering, vengeful spirit" (9.632-36). Moreover, if one should die in general "distant kin would carve apart their birthright" (5.158).

The heroes love to recount their ancestors, often numbering gods among them. Heredity is a common theme. The great warrior Ajax remarks on one of the Trojans: "No coward, to judge by his looks, no coward's stock, no doubt some brother of stallion-breaking Antenor [a Trojan elder], that or his own son—the blood-likeness is striking!" (14.472-74). Virtue is said to run in aristocratic families, as when Diomedes in council debate recounts his ancestors' achievements and concludes: "You cannot challenge my birth as low, cowardly, or spurn the advice I give" (14.126-27). Those with recent divine ancestry are naturally uniquely gifted and honored as a result.

THE WARLIKE ACHAEANS

Homer's Achaeans are not a civilized bunch. Their way of life is one of "vital barbarism," having the values of ruthless conquerors, prizing loot, honor, and glory above all. The Achaean warriors are soldiers by profession, living by piracy, cattle-wrangling, and plunder. Several of the Achaean heroes are named by Homer as murderers exiled from their native lands. Wise Odysseus says the Achaeans are "the men whom Zeus decrees, from youth to old age, must wind down our brutal wars to the bitter end until we drop and die, down to the last man" (14.85-87).

Homer is frank on the horrors and hatreds of war. Fearing defeat, the Achaeans openly contemplate atrocities against their hated foes. Nestor, a venerable old king, urges the men to not flee, promising them the rape of Trojan women: "let no man hurry to sail for home, not yet … not till he beds down with a faithful Trojan wife, payment in full for the groans and shocks of war we have all borne for Helen" (2.354-56). King Agamemnon, Menelaus' brother and as the most powerful monarch the commander-in-chief of the Achaean forces, even fantasizes of killing the unborn: "Ah would to god not one of them [Trojans] could escape his sudden plunging death beneath our hands! No baby boy still in his mother's belly, not even he escape—all Ilium [Troy] blotted out, no tears for their lives, no markers for their graves!" (6.57-60).

Reputation is paramount in this society of bandits and

warriors. As Odysseus notes on the possibility of retreat: "what a humiliation it would be to hold out so long, then sail home empty-handed" (2.298). Achilles, the poem's hero with "gold-red" hair, prefers a brief but glorious life to one of lengthy obscurity. When attacked by the Trojans, the powerful Ajax urges boldness: "Quick, better to live or die, once and for all, than die by inches, slowly crushed to death—helpless against the hulls in the bloody press, by far inferior men!" (15.511-13). Again, this is an ethos embracing high risks and high rewards. As Odysseus makes clear, this entails both fortitude and a cavalier attitude towards loss of life:

> We must steel our hearts. Bury our dead, with tears for the day they [our friends] die, not one day more. And all those left alive, after the hateful carnage, remember food and drink—so all the more fiercely we can fight our enemies, nonstop, no mercy, durable as the bronze that wraps our bodies. (19.228-33)

The Achaeans are not alone in adhering to this warrior ethos. Sarpedon, a Lycian ally of the Trojans, eloquently expresses the values of these fighters, who claim to rule by their willingness to boldly risk their lives:

> [T]he duty's ours—*we* are the ones to head our Lycian front, brace and fling ourselves in the blaze of war, so a comrade strapped in combat gear may say, "Not without fame, the men who rule in Lycia, these kings of ours who eat fat cuts of lamb and drink sweet wine, the finest stock we have. But they owe it all to their own fighting strength—our great men of war, they lead our way in battle!" Ah my friend, if you and I could escape this fray and live forever, never a trace of age, immortal, I would never fight on the front lines again or command you to the field where men win fame. But now, as it is, the fates of death await us, thousands poised to strike, and not a man alive can flee them or escape—so in we go for attack! Give our enemy glory or win it for ourselves! (12.315-29)

The Achaeans are drawn from one warrior people. They do

not have one name however—being also called Danaans, Argives, and Panhellenes—and are politically divided. The Achaean forces have been formed by a coalition of kings, assembled by Menelaus and Agamemnon. This is a fractious alliance governed by rules of honor between proud kings rather than the united government of a single lawful state. The kings are almost equal between each other, indeed Achilles could freely withdraw support for the war, while each has absolute sway over his own men and can even beat inferiors with a staff.

Given their lack of common government, the Achaeans' warrior pride is both a strength in pushing them to conquer others and a weakness in causing conflict among them. The enterprise falls apart if any sovereign should come into a dispute with any of the others. This problem is at the heart of the poem: Agamemnon, being forced by Apollo to give up the captured daughter of one of his priests, decides to take Achilles' beautiful war-bride Briseis instead. Thus disrespected, Achilles is then possessed by his infamous Wrath and refuses to fight the Trojans, undermining the Achaeans at a critical moment in the war and almost causing their defeat.

DECADENT TROY

Troy is a very different state from those of the Achaeans. The Trojans are older, more well-established, and have built for themselves something like a 'super-polis,' with great walls, an enormous royal palace, temple, agora, and untold riches. The Trojans, however, are not fighters by profession, with the exception of "dark-haired" prince Hector, their general and Paris' brother. The Trojan soldiers and even aristocrats engage in various trades: they are shepherds, cowherds, shipbuilders, carpenters, masons, and merchants.

The Trojans often act as though money can solve their problems. They frequently retrieve their prisoners from the Achaeans by paying a ransom. The Trojans are not ruled by an absolute monarch, but by a divided Council of Elders, some of whose members Paris has bribed to not force him to return Helen to the Achaeans (11.122-25). In fact, Trojans from the city proper only make up about a tenth of the Trojan forces, the rest are made up of mercenary allies on the pay. This has taken a toll on the city, as Hector complains twice:

> Hear me—numberless tribes of allies living round our borders—I neither sought nor needed enormous hordes of men that day I called you here, each from your own city. What I needed was men to shield our helpless children, fighting men to defend our Trojan women—all-out—against these savage Argives. That goal in mind, I bleed my own people for gifts and food so I can build your courage, each and every man. (17.220-26)

> Time was when the world would talk of Priam's Troy as the city rich gold and rich in bronze—but now our houses are stripped of all their sumptuous treasures, troves sold off and shipped to Phrygia, lovely Maenia. (18.288-92)

The Trojans and their allies do not, like the Achaeans, form a single people. Rather, "they speak a thousand different tongues" (2.803-04).

The difference between the Achaean professional soldiers and the Trojan amateurs is sometimes striking. While the Achaeans march in disciplined silence, twice Homer compares the disorderly Trojans to noisy animals: "the Trojans came with cries and the din of war like wildfowl ... But Achaea's armies come on strong in silence, breathing combat-fury" (3.1-9). And:

> You'd never think so many troops [the Achaeans] could march holding their voices in their chests, silence, fearing their chiefs who called out clear command, and the burnished blazoned armor round their bodies flared, the formations trampling on.

> But not the Trojans, no ... like flocks of sheep in a wealthy rancher's steadings, thousands crowding to have their white milk drained, bleating nonstop when they hear their crying lambs—so the shouts rose up from the long Trojan lines and not one cry, no common voice to bind them all together, their tongues mixed and clashed, their men hailed from so many far-flung countries. (4.429-38)

31

If the Achaeans are threatened by the discord between their proud kings, the Trojans are doomed by their failure to discipline Paris, who is shamed by his brother Hector for effeminacy, but whom the corrupt and divided Council Elders ultimately allow to keep Helen.

PATRIOTISM: FOR FAMILY & FATHERLAND

An attractive feature of the Trojans, however, is their patriotism. The Achaeans fight for loot, honor, and the glory of their names and families. The Trojans' allies fight for gold. But the soldiers of the city of Troy itself are fighting to save their families and fatherland from a grim fate. When exhorting his troops to abandon their doubts and drive the Achaeans into the sea and burn their ships, Hector cries: "Fight for your country — that is the best, the only omen!" (12.243). This famous line was often cited by Greeks in later ages as a splendid sentiment, inspiring them to defend their cities even against overwhelming odds.

The Trojans, though not having the vigor of the Achaeans, also socialize and shame their members to promote manliness and sacrifice in defense of the community. The effeminate Paris tells his brother: "Mother bore me — even me — not to be a coward through and through" (13.777). Hector later urges his comrades to fight and die for family and fatherland:

> So fight by the ships, all together. And that comrade who meets his death and destiny, speared or stabbed, let him die! He dies fighting for fatherland — no dishonor there! He'll leave behind him wife and sons unscathed, his honor and estate unharmed — once these Argives sail for home, the fatherland they love. (15.494-99)

As the last line suggests, while the Achaeans are fighting for glory and plunder rather than patriotism, they too are moved by a deep love and longing for their country and kinsmen far away.

Elsewhere, the soldier Glaucus shames his Trojan allies for giving ground instead of taking the corpse of Patroclus, Achilles' dearest friend, with them: "If the Trojans had that courage, that unswerving courage that fires men who fight for their own country, beating their enemies down in war and struggle, then we could drag Patroclus back to Troy at once" (17.156-59). A Trojan later goads Achilles: "We have fighting men by the hundreds still inside her, forming a wall before our loving parents, wives, and sons to defend Troy—where you rush to meet your doom" (21.585-89).

Among the Trojans, the fates of family and country are one. There is a famous and touching scene of Hector with his wife and infant son, before battle, knowing full well their fate hangs in the balance. Homer shows us the intertwined fates of King Priam's city and family by showing us, in graphic detail, the painful deaths of many of his sons in battle. The stoic Hector in particular is cognizant of the tragedy of war. About to undertake his doomed duel with Achilles, he says: "The god of war is impartial: he hands out death to the man who hands out death" (18.309).

Familial and patriotic sentiment are not unknown to the Achaeans either, although this is less apparent in this expedition. Nestor, in council, faults those who foment civil conflict as failing both family and nation: "Lost to the clan, lost to the hearth, lost to the old ways, that one who lusts for all the horrors of war with his own people" (9.63-64). Later, Nestor, "Achaea's watch and ward," sought to inspire the troops to fight by appealing to thoughts of their families:

> Be men, my friends! Discipline fill your hearts, maintain your pride in the eyes of other men! Remember, each of you, sons, wives, wealth, parents—are mother and father dead or alive? No matter, I beg you for *their* sakes, loved ones far away—now stand and fight, no turning back, no panic. (15.661-66)

THE WAR COMMUNITY

The *Iliad* has immortalized a primordial vision of the community at war. The men must act as one or perish. In war especially, the individual's fate is bound up with the community, no matter his personal inclination. As Homer says of good Axylus:

> Diomedes killed off Axylus, Teuthras' son who had lived in
> rock-built Arisbe, a man of means and a friend to all
> mankind, at his roadside house he'd warm all comers in.
> But who of his guests would greet his enemy now, meet him
> face-to-face and ward off grisly death? (6.12-17)

Both Troy and Achaea are shame cultures. The warriors are
often gripped by fear and, when overpowered, pathetically beg
for mercy from their enemies. Against this natural sentiment,
the commanders frequently shame their comrades to fight, or
threaten them with force. The Achaeans also require "a heavy
fine" from those who refuse to serve (13.669-70).

The ideal is unity in combat, something the Achaeans excel
at. Homer portrays the order and discipline of the archaic
phalanx: "all his comrades came in a pack with one will,
massing round him, bracing shields to shoulders" (13.487-88).
Later Homer compares the soldiers to a stone wall, in a famous
passage:

> Hearing the king's command the ranks pulled closer, tight
> as a mason packs a good stone wall, blocks on granite blocks
> for a storied house that fights the ripping winds — crammed
> so close the crested helmets, the war-shields bulging, jutting,
> buckler-to-buckler, helm-to-helm, man-to-man massed tight
> and the horsehair crests on glittering helmet horns brushed
> as they tossed their heads, as the battalions bulked so dense.
> (16.210-17)

The Achaeans' is a society in which hierarchy enables a
salutary unity. And yet, these soldiers share in a certain
equality in the face of death. The two Ajaxes make this clear in
cheering and bullying the men to fight: "Friends — you in the
highest ranks of Argives, you in the midst, and you in the rank
and file, we cannot all be equal in battle, ever, but the battle lies
before us all — come see for yourselves, look straight down …
keep pressing forward, shouting each other on!" (12.269-74).

ILIADIC POLITICS: KINGSHIP & THE GOOD CITY

One may draw political insights from Homer's ideal of kingship and his portrayal of the failures of the Achaean alliance and the city of Troy. Each monarch being sovereign, the Achaeans are divided whenever any king's virtue fails. Agamemnon takes Briseis, failing to respect Achilles' status as the best warrior, while Achilles' pride and wrath drive him to let the Achaeans fall to the brink of oblivion. The Trojans, for their part, are paralyzed by a corrupt Council of Elders, which has failed to order Paris to return Helen. In both cases, there has been a failure to enforce what would be a fundamental principle of the Greek *polis*: the subordination of individual interests to those of the community.

There is no good kingship without a right hierarchy. Among the Achaeans, there is relative equality among the kings and each is meant to be treated according to his respective qualities. If anyone feels dishonored, there is strife. Subjects must respect their kings, under penalty of violence. When lowly and ugly Thersites mocks Agamemnon and the Achaeans, Odysseus beats him into silence with his scepter, prompting general laughter. Odysseus, who Homer calls "a mastermind like Zeus" (2.169), again describes best the Achaean aristocratic ideal of kingship:

> Whenever Odysseus met some man of rank, a king, he'd halt and hold him back with winning words: "My *friend* — it's wrong to threaten you like a coward, but you stand fast, you keep your men in check! ... The rage of kings is strong, they're nursed by the gods, their honor comes from Zeus — they're dear to Zeus the god who rules the world."

> When he caught some common soldier shouting out, he'd beat him with the scepter, dress him down: "You *fool* — sit still! Obey the commands of others, your superiors — you, you deserter, rank coward, you count for nothing, neither in war nor council. How can all the Achaeans be masters here in Troy? Too many kings can ruin an army — mob rule! Let there be one commander, one master only, endowed by the son of crooked-minded Cronus with kingly scepter and

35

royal rights of custom: whatever one man needs to lead his people well." (2.188-206)[51]

The kings however are not tyrants: they are expected to welcome legitimate criticism from their peers and even tolerate a good deal of backtalk. Diomedes counters Agamemnon's proposal to flee Troy, saying: "I will be first to oppose you in your folly, here in assembly, King, where it's the custom" (9.32-33). Nestor tells Agamemnon:

> Great marshal Atrides [i.e., son of Atreus], lord of men Agamemnon ... you hold sway over many warriors, vast armies, and Zeus has placed in your hands the royal scepter and time-honored laws, so you will advise them well. So you above all must speak your mind, and listen and carry out the next man's counsel too, when his spirit leads him on to speak for the public good. Credit will go to you for whatever he proposes. (9.96-102)

Troy is evidently governed by similar values in this respect. Polydamas, a Trojan warrior, often contradicts Hector, saying on one occasion:

> Hector, you always seem to attack me in assembly, despite my good advice. Never right, is it, for a common man to speak against you, King, never in open council, god forbid in war. Our part is always to magnify your power. Well, once again I am bound to say what I think best. (12.211-15)

There is in Homer an equation of piety with civility, and a sense of reciprocity between the king and his people. Achilles, Agamemnon, and Hector are all described as "shepherd of the people." The place by the ships where the Achaeans "hand down their laws" is the same where they have "built their altars to the gods" (11.805-07). The impious, be they kings or not, are harshly punished by the gods. Homer speaks of terrible storms in which

---

[51] Socrates reportedly loved to quote this passage. Xenophon, *Memorabilia*, 1.2.

Zeus flings down his pelting, punishing rains — up in arms, furious, storming against those men who brawl in the courts and render crooked judgments, men who throw all rights to the winds with no regard to the vengeful gods. (16.385-88)

Amidst Achaean barbarism and Trojan decadence, there is the famous Shield of Achilles described at the end of Book 18, which the smith-god Hephaestus has forged for the hero. On this, Hephaestus has made the image of "two noble cities filled with mortal men" which seem to portray a political and social ideal beyond the war. The great elements of life and death are there. There are weddings and wedding feasts, and young boys and girls court each other with elaborate dancing and gifts, ensuring the renewal of generations. The king watches over from his palace, while people hunt or work in the fields, vineyards, and herds.

In the City at Peace, there is a quarrel in the marketplace between two men "over the blood-price of a kinsman just murdered … The crowd cheer on both, they took both sides, but heralds held them back as the city elders sat on polished stone benches, forming the sacred circle" (18.497-504). Hence, the enmity of blood feuds and the passions of the mob are constrained by law. The City at War, however, is besieged by enemies, but "the people were not surrendering, not at all." The citizens even organize a counter-raid, killing enemy shepherds. Thus the city is prepared to fight ruthlessly for its own survival, even if innocents must die.

After Achilles defeats Hector in battle, Priam enters the Achaean camp to recover his son's corpse. The hero and the king meet and weep together, sharing in compassion in their common tragedy. Achilles' empathy makes him rejoin the world of men, pride and wrath are met with empathy, and the Greek city may be born … a city no doubt destined one day to decay like Troy. The flawed heroes Achilles and Agamemnon, with their overweening pride, seem to give way to wiser and more moderate kings, Nestor and Odysseus, who find the words for social harmony.

CONCLUSION

The *Iliad* is then a poem about the tragedy of vital barbarism and decadent civilization, ascending from one, falling from the other. This is a common enough interpretation. William Merritt Sale writes: "the poem is about the tragic growth of Achilles and the tragic death of Troy."[52] Bernard Knox argues that Homer's epic long resonated with the Greeks as a great warning:

> The Trojan War was stamped indelibly on the consciousnesses of the Greeks throughout their history, immortalized in lyric poetry, in tragedy, on temple pediments and painted vases, to reinforce the stern lesson of Homer's presentation of war: that no civilization, no matter how rich, no matter how refined, can long survive once it loses the power to meet force with equal or superior force.[53]

The *Iliad* embodies the primal values which enabled our Bronze Age ancestors, thousands of years ago, to conquer the European continent, replacing the native egalitarian hunter-gatherer cultures with ultimately stronger militaristic and aristocratic cultures. These cultures gave us not only the lights of the ancient Greeks, but also the power of the Romans and the refounding of Europe by the Germans in the Middle Ages.

The values of the *Iliad*, as I hope to have shown, are highly adaptive, being focused on pride in one's lineage, kinship as central to identity and entailing reciprocity and solidarity, subordination of individual interests to those of the community, the intertwined loves of family and fatherland, and finally the glorification of conquest and honor. These values, though often brutal, enable one's people to triumph, and surely that is also part of the tragedy Homer was trying to tell. Certainly, the *Iliad* does not present a genuine group evolutionary strategy, as exists for instance in the racial purity laws of the Jewish Tanakh or the eugenic dreams of Plato.

---

[52] William Merritt Sale, *The Government of Troy* (Washington University, 1994), p. 74.

[53] Bernard Knox, "Introduction," in *Iliad*, p. 37.

Homer's epic reflects a more instinctive and atavistic psychology and way of life enabling the triumph of oneself and one's kin.

The European patriot Dominique Venner considered the Homeric poems to be "the European Bible." The lessons of the *Iliad* indeed are as relevant today as ever. Unfortunately, one can share Ricardo Duchesne's pessimistic assessment that loss of manliness and ancestral values are part of a natural cycle of civilization, decadence, and collapse.[54] Indeed, given our unprecedented degree of comfort and miseducation, Western men today are of an unbearable and unheard-of effeminacy. As a natural result, our people are steadily declining and being physically replaced by other peoples, less gifted and accomplished by the yardstick of civilization, but who have kept that instinctive barbarian vigor. A fatal encounter, for as Achilles tells Hector in rejecting a pact: "There are no binding oaths between men and lions—wolves and lambs can enjoy no meeting of the minds" (22.262-63). There may, inevitably, be hard times for the European peoples ahead, but, as the saying goes, hard times breed hard men.

---

[54] Ricardo Duchesne, "There is Nothing the Alt Right Can Do about the Effeminacy of White Men," *Council of European Canadians*, March 28, 2017.

HOMER'S *ODYSSEY*
THE RETURN OF THE FATHER

"Who are you, and from where? Where are your city and your parents?" Thus does a stranger ask Odysseus to identify himself in Homer's poem dedicated to that hero, the *Odyssey* (10.325). Taking place after the travails of the Trojan War, the tale is fundamentally about Odysseus' struggle to find and reestablish his place in a chaotic world. During his twenty-year absence, the hero's native land of Ithaca has fallen victim to usurpers, and he must overcome innumerable obstacles to find his way home and restore his political authority as king through subterfuge and violence. Odysseus never gives up on his quest, nor does he settle down in one of the many places he visits, because he never forgets his dear family and fatherland, those two defining aspects of his social identity.

The *Odyssey* has inspired Europeans of every generation since the ancient Greeks and Romans up to the present day. Besides the picaresque quality of Odysseus' fantastic adventures, one finds an enduring story that can only resonate with all those who long for home. Odysseus, rather unlike Achilles, is close to an ideal hero: enduring, cunning, resourceful, diplomatic, and ruthless when necessary. If the *Iliad* is the memory in poetry of the archaic Greeks' countless forgotten wars of conquest and plunder, the *Odyssey* is that of their exploration and colonization of the ancient Mediterranean and Black Sea, endeavors which were often no less violent. If the *Iliad* is about the tensions between individual and community in the savagery of wartime, the *Odyssey* suggests a more constructive personal and political project: the journey home and the restoration of a good country.

Odysseus' visiting various, often dystopian, societies and his quest to restore his Ithacan kingdom indeed suggest an implicit Homeric politics. The world of Odysseus is an often brutal and lawless one in which travelers are at the mercy of the goodwill of their hosts. Without reciprocity or strength, one is liable to fall victim to depredation. In this trustless world, Homer identifies two things which can serve to create more civil societies: piety and kinship. While the ideal of the *polis*, of individual sacrifice for the common good, is indeed hinted at in the *Odyssey*, Odyssean politics however are firmly monarchic, with reciprocal duties between king and people.

Among the aristocratic ruling class Homer is dealing with, kinship is the basic foundation for identity and solidarity, and therefore of both personal and political action. Strangers are synonymous with uncertainty and potential violence. Kinship in contrast entails inherited resemblance and shared pride in and duties towards one's lineage. Among kin, there is the possibility of security. That security, however, only exists by the strength of the family father, his domestic authority, and his willingness to use violence against hostile aliens. The *Odyssey* is then also a tale of what befalls a family and country when the patriarch, by his absence, no longer meets his responsibilities.

For Homer, identity and purpose is found in one's lineage. One acts for the sake of one's ancestors and one's descendants. Odysseus and his son Telemachus resemble one another by virtue of their shared blood and must work together to save their common family house. The restoration of paternal and kingly authority in Ithaca is impossible without brutal revenge against the usurpers. And it is only within the circle of such violence that one's kin can enjoy a secure and gentle life. According to Homer, a happy man has prosperous descendants and the people thrive under a righteous king, for he rules them like a good father.

FATHERLESS ITHACA: VICTIM TO PARASITES & USURPERS

Without Odysseus the family father, Ithaca is a dystopia, vulnerable to the depredations of selfish men. The suitors, noblemen from around Ithaca, feast on his wealth and wish to marry his wife Penelope, thus usurping his legacy. Telemachus condemns the suitors: "with their greed they waste my inheritance away, and before long they will bring destruction on myself" (1.250-51). Telemachus is also deeply disappointed with Odysseus' subjects, telling them in assembly:

> I have lost my noble father, who once was king among all
> you here and ruled you as gently as a father; then something
> far worse has befallen me, which before long will ruin my
> house altogether and bring to nothing my means of living.
> My mother, greatly to her distress, has been beset by suitors,
> sons of the greatest nobles here ... they haunt my palace day
> in, day out; they slaughter my sheep and oxen and fatted
> goats; they make merry here, they selfishly drink the
> glowing wine, and thus an abundance of things is wasted.
> All this because there is no man left with the mettle of
> Odysseus to ward off ruin from the house. I myself am not
> able to ward it off; I fear I shall always be a weakling, with
> no skill to resist at all. (2.46-61)

> It is the rest of you [the people] I am indignant with, to see
> how you all sit dumbly there instead of rebuking them and
> restraining them; you are many; the suitors are few. (2.239-
> 41)

There is again supposed to be reciprocity between ruler and
people, the latter owing the former loyalty if he governs them
as though they were kin. No one can substitute for Odysseus as
patriarch. There is "no man left with [his] mettle." Telemachus
is too young, fearful of being a "weakling." Grandfather
Laertes is too old and feeble; and is left wallowing in misery on
the country farm. Penelope herself is wise and virtuous, but as
a woman she cannot challenge the suitors head-on. Twice she
is told by her menfolk to tender to the loom and her private
chambers rather than get involved. Penelope has her feminine
charms however and is able to able to stall and deceive the
suitors on occasion.

As royal heir, Telemachus has an unabashed claim to
wealth, honor, and power by birthright: "Surely kingship is no
bad thing; wealth flows into the palace readily, and the name
of king brings a man more honor ... I shall reign over my own
house and over the slaves that Odysseus once made his prize
and left to me" (1.392-98). That is what Odysseus' entire line
risks losing if he does not return, so long as Odysseus is "away

42

from his kith and kin" and the suitors can hope that he will "perish far from his people" (2.180-85). Fatherless Ithaca cannot ward off unscrupulous enemies: the patriarch must return to restore order and justice.

KIN & STRANGERS: "BRINGING HAVOC ON MEN OF ANOTHER STOCK"

As in the *Iliad*, in the *Odyssey* strangers and foreign lands are synonymous with uncertainty and violence. This is a world without mutual confidence. Even the gods do not trust in one another, as when the smith-god Hephaestus tells Poseidon: "Pledges for trustless folk are trustless pledges" (8.351). In this world of strangers, men however are bitterly driven on by "the accursed belly" to find sustenance. The only guarantee for civilized conduct is tenuous moral obligations of hospitality and reciprocity. Useless and parasitic beggar-migrants are scorned:

> No man of his own accord goes out to bring in a stranger from elsewhere, unless that stranger be master of some craft, a prophet, or one who cures diseases, a worker in wood, or again an inspired bard, delighting men with his song. The wide world over, men such as these are welcome guests. But a beggar to eat up what one has — who would invite such a guest as that? (17.382-88)

Like Odysseus, Telemachus is driven by his identity. He must assert himself and learn to be a man, not only to find his father, but also to show himself to be worthy of his royal lineage. The glorification of lineage serves a double purpose: those of good stock are reassured they have the traits necessary to triumph, but it is also an exhortation to live up to the previous achievements of their line.

Traveling to the Greek mainland in search of news of his father, Telemachus encounters Odysseus' fellow veteran of the Trojan War, the elderly King Nestor of Pylos. Nestor greets Telemachus asking: "Are you bound on some trading errand, or are you random adventurers, roving the seas as pirates do, hazarding life and limb and bringing havoc on men of another stock?" (3.72-74). The last part is a striking phrase which recurs several times in the *Odyssey*:[55] in the ancient Mediterranean, encountering strangers with no ties of kinship meant the risk of being attacked, robbed, and enslaved by them.

The Achaeans are as prone to this as anyone. In Egypt, we are told, "Menelaus with his vessels went to and fro among men who spoke an alien tongue, and he gathered much substance and much gold" (3.301-02). Odysseus' swineherd, who turns out to be the most loyal of his subjects, observes that fear of the gods' revenge is one of the few things which can motivate "men of violence and ill-will who land on a foreign coast" to not do evil (14.85-88). The same swineherd feared that Odysseus had been left "wandering foodless about some town or region of foreign speech" (14.42-43). In this mysterious and hostile world in which Odysseus must survive, kin and country are his lodestar.

LIKE FATHER, LIKE SON

Heredity is an even more pronounced theme in the *Odyssey* than in the *Iliad*. The characters frequently comment on the striking similarities between Telemachus and his father. Athena, the deity who most loves Odysseus, tells Telemachus: "are you the son of Odysseus himself? Your likeness to him sets me wondering — the head might be his, and the fine eyes" (1.207-09). She also reassures him: "If the gods let Penelope bear such a son as you, they did not mean your lineage to be inglorious in times to come" (1.222-23).

Nestor is clearly for Homer a model of the wise king and is described as a "shepherd of his people," comparable to Odysseus. He makes several hereditarian observations. Telemachus greets Nestor by hailing him as the "son of Neleus, glory of the Achaean race" (3.79). Nestor is struck by the uncanny similarities between father and son. Between remarks

---

[55] Notably by the Cyclops, who represents primitive barbarism in contrast with the wise Nestor (9.215-282), suggesting both the savage and the civilized are concerned with the issue of violence by strangers.

on Odysseus' legendary cunning and eloquence, Nestor tells Telemachus: "as I look at you I am filled with wonder. All you say has a perfect rightness; who would have thought a man so young could display such rightness in speech?" (3.123-25). He says that Athena has punished many Achaeans on their way home from Troy due to their injustice and lack of wisdom, for "is she not the child of a mighty father?" (3.135).

Nestor decides to give substantial assistance and gifts to Telemachus, also on account of his obvious kinship with his old war comrade Odysseus. Telemachus later said Nestor gave him the care "a father might give a son just home after a long absence in foreign lands" (17.109-12). For Nestor furthermore, individual happiness is synonymous with the prosperity of one's family and descendants. He remarks: "How good it is that when a man dies, a son should be left after him!" (3.196). Nestor is pious. In sacrificing a heifer to Athena, he prays for his family: "O goddess, be gracious to us now; give good renown to myself, my children, the queen my wife" (3.380-81). His wife for her part is "revered."

Now assisted by Nestor's son Peisistratus, Telemachus goes to Sparta, where he meets another comrade of Odysseus, King Menelaus, who has returned from Troy with his wife Helen. Telemachus finds Menelaus "celebrating with many clansmen a wedding feast for his daughter and his son" (4.3-4). The former is promised to a son of Achilles, the latter to a Spartan noblewoman, suggesting marriage strategies among archaic aristocracy.

Menelaus is impressed by Telemachus' bearing and is also very interested in his lineage: "Surely you two have not shamed your parentage; you belong to the race of heaven-protected and sceptered kings; no lesser parents could have such sons" (4.61-64). Menelaus later adds: "What you say, dear child, is proof of the good stock you come from" (4.611).

Both Menelaus and Helen notice the similarities between Odysseus and Telemachus:

> "This boy is far too much like Odysseus to be any other than his son [said Helen]; surely he is Telemachus ..."

Yellow-haired Menelaus answered her: "Wife, your thought
has become my thought as well. Odysseus had just such feet
and hands; his head and his hair were like this boy's; his
eyes had the same glance." (4.140-50)

Menelaus too equates blessings from heaven with
prosperous children:

There is no mistaking the child of a man whom the son of
Cronus marked out for happiness both at birth and bridal;
witness the favors bestowed on Nestor through all his
days—for himself an old age of comfort in his own palace,
for his children wisdom, and prowess with the spear. (4.207-
11)

THE JOURNEY HOME: CLINGING TO IDENTITY AMID DYSTOPIAS

Homer begins the *Odyssey* thus:

Goddess of song, teach me the story of a hero. This was the
man of wide-ranging spirit who had sacked the sacred town
of Troy and who wandered afterwards long and far. Many
were those cities he viewed and whose minds he came to
know, many the troubles that vexed his heart as he sailed
the seas, laboring to save himself and to bring his comrades
home. (1.1-5)

Despite these many troubles, "not even then was he with his
own people," this "so subtle a man and so ill-starred" (1.16-50).
The poem is an ode to the determination necessary to returning
home, clinging to one's identity, namely one's family and
fatherland, through the travails. By showing us all the societies
Odysseus visits, most of them evil, Homer also gives a kind of
implicit political theory and idea of what the good society
would not contain.[56]

Homer begins his story in the midst of the action, in his

---

[56] On this I follow Annette Giesecke, notably in "Mapping Utopia:
Homer's Politics and the Birth of the Polis," *College Literature*, 34.2,
Spring 2007, pp. 194-214.

customary manner, with Odysseus having lost his crew. He is trapped with the goddess Calypso, who promises him a strange eternal life with her. He cannot bear the thought of living forever far from his people, as Athena says: "but he—he would be well content to see even the smoke rising from his own land, and he longs to die" (1.57-59). For Odysseus, immortality is not worth losing his identity, kin, and fatherland. Calypso must let the hero go after a visit from Hermes, who says: "it is not appointed for him to find his end here, far away from his own people; he is destined to see his own kith and kin again and return to his high-roofed house and his own country" (5.113-15).

The narrative then shifts to mysterious Phaecia, on the edge of the world, where Odysseus has miraculously landed. Odysseus greets the natives with a question implying the traditional Greek equation of piety with lawfulness and sociality: "whose land have I come to now? Are the people barbarous, arrogant, and lawless? Are they hospitable and god-fearing?" (6.119-21). Fortunately for Odysseus, of all the places he visits Phaecia is evidently the most civilized and peaceful, the Phaecians being "a people whose lineage is divine" (5.35). The city has walls, a port, ships, games, dancing, and poetry. The Phaecians are perhaps even unnaturally peaceful, for they have "no regard for bow and quiver, only for masts and the oars of ships and the balanced ships themselves in which so proudly they traverse the whitening sea" (6.270-72).

Most relevant to Odysseus, Phaecia is one of the few places he visits which is welcoming to strangers and treats guests properly. For the most part, those who harm guests and violate the rules of hospitality are harshly punished in Homer's world. But the Phaecians, if anything, are a bit too welcoming. On one occasion the Phaecians were punished because, as their king Alcinous explains, "Poseidon was angry with us because we took home all manner of men without coming to any harm" (13.173-74).

The happy Phaecians live, among other things, in the hope of honoring their parents and bearing prosperous children. When Odysseus is welcomed by the lovely princess Nausicaa, he tells her: "thrice happy over is your father, happy your lady mother, happy your brothers. How often their hearts must glow with gladness because of you, as they see entering the ranks of dances this matchless flowering of their race!" (6.154-57). Nausicaa is told by Athena to dress beautifully for the sake of her parents: "Such things as these make a bride well spoken of with the people and bring her father and mother joy" (6.29-30). Odysseus is treated well by the Phaecians and the queen in particular:

> I pray that the gods may grant them [her husband and guests] happiness all their lives and that each of them may bequeath his children the wealth that he has in his own halls and whatever rights his people have granted him. As for myself—give me means to return quickly to my own land, because for this long time past I have suffered misery far from my kith and kin. (7.146-52)

Upon hearing a Phaecian bard sing about the Trojan War, Odysseus is reduced to tears. Alcinous asks him:

> Did some kinsman of yours die before Ilium, some man of courage, your daughter's husband, your wife's father? Such ties as these come nearest to men after their own flesh and blood. Or was it a friend, perhaps, one who was brave and whose thoughts were one with yours? Not less than we cherish our own brother do we cherish a wise-hearted man. (8.581-86)

Odysseus then recounts his most fantastical and famous adventures to the Phaecians. The tale begins with Odysseus' leaving Troy with twelve vessels, taking time to engage in piracy by attacking the Trojans' allies the Cicones. The loot is shared fairly, but the men indulge in wine for too long, and so the Cicones have time to counter-attack and Odysseus' men are pushed back.

Next Odysseus goes to the land of the Lotus-Eaters. Like modern-day sports-ball fans or marijuana smokers, these forget any sense of duty or fatherland by embracing a life reduced to a dull haze. They must be forced to be free by being coercively pulled away from the drug:

> Those of my men who tasted the honey-sweet lotus fruit
> had not desire to retrace their steps and come back with
> news; their only wish was to linger there with the Lotus-
> Eaters, to feed on the fruit and put aside all thought of a
> voyage home. These men I forced back to the ships; they
> were shedding tears but I made them go. I dragged them
> down under the thwarts and left them bound there. (9.94-99)

Odysseus then comes upon the country of the one-eyed
Cyclopes. These primitive and vicious beings have been taken
by later commentators—including Plato, Aristotle, and the
emperor Julian—as a metaphor for humanity's prepolitical
past, when there was no ruler beyond the father and no society
beyond the immediate family. Odysseus says:

> We came to the land of the Cyclops race, arrogant lawless
> beings who leave their livelihood to the deathless gods and
> never use their own hands to sow or plow ... They have no
> assemblies to debate in, they have no ancestral ordinances;
> they live in arching caves on the tops of high hills, and the
> head of each family heeds no other, but makes his own
> ordinances for wife and children. (9.105-15)

Shepherding is the most complex Cyclopean activity. A
lovely island nearby has much the Cyclopes could use, with
fine goats and woods, but they have not even the social
organization or ships to go there, let alone to travel or visit
foreigners in general.

Odysseus ends up in the cave of Polyphemus, a particularly
anti-social specimen:

> it was not his way to visit the others of his tribe; he kept
> aloof, and his mind was set on unrighteousness. A
> monstrous ogre, unlike any man who had ever tasted bread,
> he resembled rather some shaggy peak in a mountain-range,
> standing out clear, away from the rest. (9.188-92)

Odysseus expresses a no doubt wider fear that "the stranger
who might face us now would wear brute strength like a

garment round him, a savage whose heart had little knowledge of just laws and ordinances" (9.213-15). Polyphemus is unabashed in declaring the arrogant godlessness of his people:

> We of the Cyclops race care nothing for Zeus and for his aegis; we care for none of the gods in heaven, being much stronger ourselves than they are. Dread of the enmity of Zeus would never move me to spare either you or the comrades with you, if I had no mind to it myself. (9.275-78)

The beast is outwitted by Odysseus however, who gets him drunk with wine and stabs his single eye during his sleep, declaring himself "Noman." So when a fellow Cyclops, a rarity, comes to help Polyphemus, he is confused as to how "Noman" wounded him … Having fled to safety on his ship, Odysseus is too proud to not reveal his identity and name to Polyphemus. This comes at a cost however: the Cyclops being the sea-god Poseidon's son, the deity would make him pay the price with a difficult journey home.

Odysseus comes across another strange land in the form of the island of Aeolus, the lord of winds. This king is hospitable enough: he has a town, a palace, and … six sons married to his six daughters. Obviously such an incestuous little arrangement does not yet qualify as a society. Odysseus then meets the Laestrygonians, a race of impious and lawless giants. Unlike the Cyclopes, the Laestrygonians have a palace, an assembly-place, and a king. The encounter proves disastrous: Odysseus' men are speared like fish and eaten, and all but one of his ships are destroyed.

Odysseus then lands upon the island of Circe. His men first encounter the sorceress, who "blended for them a dish of cheese and barley-meal, of yellow honey, and Pramnian wine, all together; but with these good things she mingled pernicious drugs as well, to make them forget their own country utterly" (10.234-36). The men were then turned into pigs. Xenophon reports that Socrates considered the story a metaphor for enslavement to gluttony (*Memorabilia*, 1.3). Odysseus, with Athena's aid, is able to overcome Circe and eventually leaves the island. As with Calypso, Odysseus abandons this matriarchal society by remembering and cherishing his family and fatherland:

> My land is rugged, but knows how to breed brave sons. A man can see no country more lovable than his own, and so it is with myself and Ithaca ... neither of them [Calypso and Circe] could win the heart within me; so true it is that nothing is sweeter to a man than his own country and his own parents, even though he were given a sumptuous dwelling-place elsewhere, in a strange land and far from his parents. (9.27-36)

Odysseus goes to Hades, where he encounters ghosts. The prophet Tiresias tells him: "death will come to you far from sea. A gentle death that will end your days when the years of ease have left you frail and your people round you enjoy all happiness. This is my prophecy; it is true" (11.134-37). Odysseus says the female ghosts "each in turn told me her lineage" (11.233-34). One had been taken as a lover by Poseidon, telling her: "Girl, be happy in this our love. When the year comes round you will be the mother of glorious children, for an immortal's embrace is not in vain" (11.248-50).

Visiting an island with the cattle of the sun-god Helios, Odysseus' men decide to eat them instead of going hungry. They all perish, except Odysseus, who had wisely abstained through pious self-discipline. At the end of his tale, Odysseus is given untold treasures by the Phaecians, thus he will not return from Troy empty-handed and dishonored in that way. More important than the treasures however is no doubt the wisdom that Odysseus has acquired in overcoming his trials: in knowing "many cities and minds," in conquering himself through self-discipline, the hero is transformed and uniquely equipped to refound political order in Ithaca. Indeed, by his sufferings, there is the promise that the new order can be more perfect than the one that had been lost.

ODYSSEUS IN ITHACA: THE FATHER'S REVENGE

Finally, Odysseus makes his way home and "he rejoiced to be in his own country" (13.250-52). "King Odysseus was filled with happiness, filled with joy that this land was his. He kissed the grain-giving soil of it, then prayed to the nymphs with uplifted hands" (13.353-55). Athena transforms Odysseus' appearance to that of an old man, to better gather allies, observe the suitors' misdeeds, and prepare his revenge.

Odysseus enters the palace as an elderly beggar and is mistreated by the suitors, who have been scheming to murder Telemachus. The task will not be easy, but Odysseus affirms: "I would rather perish, rather meet death in my own palace, than look on perpetually at things as detestable as these" (16.105-07). Finally meeting Telemachus, the two emotionally embrace, but Odysseus quickly turns to business: "at Athena's bidding, I have come to this place to consult with you on the slaughtering of our enemies" (16.233-34).

When Odysseus reveals himself to the suitors, he will not be turned away from vengeance against those who "devoured my substance, forced my serving-women to sleep with you, and in cowardly fashion wooed my wife while I still was living" (22.36-38). One of the suitors offers tribute, but Odysseus will have none of it, dishonor cannot be redeemed with gold:

> [N]ot if you all gave me all your patrimony, whatever you have and whatever more you might come to have, not even then would I hold back my hands from slaughter till every suitor had paid for the whole transgression. (22.61-64)

Through subterfuge and prowess, Odysseus and his few allies are able to overcome and kill the suitors. They are not the only ones who must pay. While the few in Odysseus' household who helped the suitors unwillingly are spared, the willing collaborators must pay, notably the servant-women, who are hanged. As Telemachus says: "Never let it be said that sluts like these had a clean death from me. They have heaped up outrage on me and on my mother; they have been the suitors' concubines" (22.462-64). The punishments are monstrous, but the guilty perpetrated evil deeds, and the gods willed retribution.

The suitors overthrown and his authority restored, Odysseus can then finally unite with Penelope, who recognizes him in their own bed. Penelope has remained faithful to Odysseus and, with her handmaidens, maintained "the hearth's unflagging fire" (20.123). Thus, the family has been saved. There is something touching in the couple's complicity. As Odysseus had previously said: "There is nothing nobler, nothing lovelier than when man and wife keep house together with like heart and with like will. Their foes repine, their friends rejoice, but the truth of it all is with her and him" (6.182-85). The family members' faithfulness to one another has allowed their collective survival.[57]

This is only a brief respite, for in a social world defined by kin, Odysseus knows that the suitors' families will not be long in retaliating for what has happened. But the three generations, Laertes, Odysseus, and Telemachus, find confidence and joy in the honor and prosperity of their line:

> King Odysseus … said forthwith to his son Telemachus: "My son, when you enter the battlefield where warriors prove their mettle, you need not be told not to shame the lineage of your fathers. In courage and manliness we have long been foremost, the whole world over."
>
> Thoughtful Telemachus replied: "Father, if you are minded so, you shall watch me in my present spirit by no means shaming the lineage that you speak of."
>
> So he spoke, and Laertes, in his joy cried out: "Dear gods, what a day is this for me! What happiness, when my son and my grandson are vying for the prize of valor!" (24.505-15).

ODYSSEAN POLITICS: KING ODYSSEUS & THE GOOD CITY

One can read an implicit political philosophy into Homer's tale. No doubt the "many cities and minds" Odysseus comes to know present so many (counter-)models to the state he will be refounding in Ithaca. Fatherless Ithaca under Penelope is

---

[57] In stark contrast, Agamemnon is murdered upon his return home from the Trojan War with the complicity of his unfaithful wife, Clytemnestra.

powerless to prevent depredations. The strange matriarchies of Calypso and Circe are rejected. The dazed Lotus-Eaters and pre-social Cyclopes live subhuman existences. Nor do the monstrous Laestrygonians or incestuous Aeolus have true cities. Only the Phaecians—with their city walls, assembly, port, marketplace, and good king—can be seen as a model, and even they are perhaps a bit too civilized.

The Phaecians honor their parents and hope for the prosperity of their children. Kings Menelaus and Nestor on the mainland, visited by Telemachus, also provide positive models. Both are welcoming to guests and honor Telemachus as obviously of the same blood and spirit as their old comrade-in-arms Odysseus. Nestor in particular is presented as a paragon of wisdom, piously honoring both the gods and his family in the same breath.

The Homeric ideal of kingship is one of familial solidarity, moderation, trust, piety, strength, and reciprocal duties between king and people, to the benefit of one another. Hierarchy and community are fundamentally necessary in Homer's world. Followers require leadership, especially once a period of servitude has made them torpid and foolish. Odysseus' dog Argos, upon seeing his master return for the first time, is seized by joy and promptly dies. The swineherd says: "When masters are not there to command, serfs lack zeal to do as they should, for Zeus the Thunderer takes half the virtue away from a man when once the day of bondage has come on him" (17.320-23). Loyalty is supremely valued, as when Telemachus tells a wavering follower: "It will do you no good to serve many masters" (21.369).

The *Odyssey*'s political ideal is a firm and fatherly kingship. Odysseus' men are destroyed by their greed, lack of trust, and impiety. The good king in contrast is, like Odysseus, pious, ruthless, cunning, and self-disciplined. As King Alcinous says: "the heart within me is never tempted to groundless anger; right measure in everything is best" (7.309-10). Sociality and piety are equated. Just rule is inspired by the divine, as evidenced when Odysseus encounters the mythical Cretan king Minos in Hades:

Then I saw Minos the son of Zeus holding a golden scepter and delivering judgments among the dead. There he sat, and around him the others sat or stood in the ample-gated house of Hades, seeking from this master of justice the firm sentences of law. (11.568-71)

Odysseus' moderation and piety do not exclude the most blood-curdling ruthlessness, however, whenever necessary. When his second-in-command Eurylochus proves unreliable and challenges his authority, Odysseus recalls: "I was half minded to draw the long keen sword from my sturdy thigh, strike off his head and send it to meet the ground, although he was close kin of me" (10.438-41). Odysseus' revenge upon the suitors and their collaborators is brutal, a dark deed necessary to restore his honor and authority.

Reflecting on the basic insecurity of men, Odysseus wishes that men be god-fearing, hospitable, and lawful. While disguised as a beggar, he says:

Of all things that breathe and move on earth, earth mothers nothing more frail than man. As long as the gods grant him prosperity, as long as his limbs are lithe, he thinks he will suffer no misfortune in times to come; but when instead the Blessed Ones send him sorrow, he bears these also with endurance, because he must. The father of the gods and men makes one day unlike another day, and earthlings change their thoughts on life in accord with this. Even I myself seemed once marked out as a prosperous man, and I did many reckless deeds to sate my desire for power and mastery, putting great faith in my father and my brothers. And so I would have no man be lawless, rather let each accept unquestioningly whatsoever gifts the gods may grant him. (18.130-42).

Under a pious and just king, the people flourish. Odysseus says that Penelope's fame is

like that of a virtuous king who fears the gods and who rules a strong well-peopled kingdom. He upholds justice, and under him the dark soil yields wheat and barley; trees are weighed down with fruit, sheep never fail to bear young and the sea abounds with fish—all this because of his righteous rule, so that thanks to him his people prosper. (19.109-14)

This order of law and generosity, ultimately benefiting the people, however can only be built by the hero's embrace of kinship and violence. The *Odyssey* reaffirms the *Iliad*'s tragic message: that good order and the community can only be guaranteed by the willingness to fight and die for family and fatherland. Upon hearing about the Trojan War, Odysseus wept:

It was as when a woman weeps with her arms around her darling husband, one who has been defending his country and countrymen, striving to keep the day of mercilessness far from his city and his children, but now has fallen and is dying and gasping out his life. (8.523-26)

CONCLUSION

Homer's *Odyssey* does not present a fully-fledged ethno-political ideal, perhaps the latter is even less present than in the *Iliad*. The contrasts are between civilization and savagery, kin and strangers, rather than an ethnocentric idea as such. Furthermore, the work is more personal than political. The ideal and practice of the Greek *polis*, while hinted at, remains to be developed, as later recounted in the works of Herodotus and Aristotle.

The *Odyssey* is however a tale fundamentally about kinship and identity, with politics and personal behavior reflecting a familial, aristocratic, and patriarchal ethos. Telemachus goes forth into the world and attempts to become a man to live up to his lineage. Many remark upon the resemblance between father and son. Happiness is equated with prosperous descendants. And Odysseus faces frequent dangers and temptations to abandon his quest, but never surrenders, on the grounds that his homeland and family are worth more than anything else. Identity is destiny.

Odysseus embodies the ethos and qualities of the

unpretentious, competitive, and enterprising Greeks of the age of exploration and colonization. This contested king of a modest realm is also a pirate, an explorer, a carpenter, an archer, and even a farmer. Odysseus provides a model of personal behavior and kingship, characterized by determination, pragmatism, cunning, and ruthlessness. G. S. Kirk writes that Odysseus is not only a good fighter and "a man of many wiles":

> But he is also long-suffering, patient, wise, humane, resigned, philosophical, hard-headed, practical, brutal when circumstances demand it, boastful at times ... He is a survivor who fights his way home to take up life again where it should be taken up after war: among one's own people, surrounded by the possessions one has fought for, and solaced by the wife who is one's partner and whom one has struggled to win. That at least is what the Greeks of the heroic tradition believed in.
>
> To achieve all that, Odysseus has to hold firmly to the past, to what happened at Troy, to what he knows himself to be. With Calypso, that means above all remembering that he is mortal, a social being, not destined for solitary love with a creature of another kind.[58]

The world of Odysseus is riven by conflicts between families and strangers, from the Cyclopes and Aeolians, who have no society beyond the family, to the warring clans of Ithaca. Fatherless Ithaca's decline shows that a righteous social order can only be restored through the father's ruthlessness in alliance with his family. The good society is held together by powerful familial and religious sentiments, including fierce pride in one's lineage and reverence for the gods. One can interpret the turmoil of the Trojan War and Odysseus' journey as metaphors for the Greeks' violent primordial past and rise to civilization. The Wrath of Achilles gives way to an ideal of kingship: that of a god-fearing, powerful, and moderate king,

---

[58] G. S. Kirk, "Introduction," in Homer (trans. Walter Shewring), *The Odyssey* (Oxford: Oxford University Press, 1980), p. xix.

who rules his flourishing people as a father would.

The *Odyssey* has resonated with Europeans throughout the ages. The sophist Alcidamas called Homer's second poem "a beautiful mirror of human life" (quoted in Aristotle, *Rhetoric*, 3.3). Anyone who has felt themselves exiled, physically or psychologically, from their kin and homeland cannot help but identifying with Homer's wandering hero. Children as much as adults can still cheerfully learn from this ancient tale.

One of the most famous and evocative scenes in the poem occurs when Odysseus must sail past the Sirens, whose seductive song promises knowledge of the entire world:

> Never has any man passed this way in his dark vessel and left unheard the honey-sweet music from our lips; first he has taken his delight, then gone on his way a wiser man … we know of all things that come to pass on this fruitful earth. (12.186-91)

Are not Western men—so bold, so restless, so curious, so wishing to overcome their own limited nature and embrace the whole—most tempted by such a promise? The Sirens of course lie: any man who listens will only be bewitched, forget himself, and drown as his ship is dashed upon the rocks. Yet Odysseus cannot resist listening: while he has his men block their own ears with wax, he orders them to tie him to the mast, so he might still hear the Sirens' song. Is all this perhaps a metaphor for Western man's recurring temptation to forget himself, including the necessary limitations and foundations of his nature, in pursuit of forbidden knowledge and superhuman ambitions? While recognizing the value of such drive, the lesson of the *Odyssey* is clear: the most valuable thing you have in this world are your honor and your own people.

HESIOD'S *WORKS & DAYS*
PEASANTS & THEIR POSTERITY

If Homer gives us the grand tales of proud warlords and princely pirates, Hesiod's *Works and Days*, is a compendium of practical advice and traditional ethics for humble Greek farmers. Through the second-oldest surviving Greek poet, we hear of the aspirations and hardships of the common people who are the foundation of every traditional society. As much as Homer, Hesiod sees kinship as central to finding solidarity and happiness in a harsh and uncertain world: children owe their parents reverence, siblings owe each other a special respect, good men and happy kings preside over a prosperous posterity, and evil men will suffer a barren lineage.

We find the peasant's traditional common sense: work brings prosperity (an attitude radically different from the typical aristocratic Greek hostility to labor), laziness brings hunger and beggary, and one should get to know one's neighbors. There is an early Greek expression of the Silver Rule: "A man fashions ills for himself who fashions ill for another, and the ill design is most ill for the designer" (264-65). Furthermore, those who do evil hurt not only themselves but also their descendants: "whoever deliberately lies in his sworn testimony, therein, by injuring Right, he is blighted past healing; his family remains more obscure thereafter, while the true-sworn man's line gains in worth" (281-84).

Some later Greeks found much to appreciate in Hesiod as a constructive and pacific poet. The *Contest of Homer and Hesiod* provides a fictional account of a poetic competition between the two men. It was said that:

> [T]he Hellenes applauded Homer admiringly, so far did the verses exceed the ordinary level; and demanded that he should be adjudged the winner. But the king gave the crown to Hesiod, declaring that it was right that he who called upon men to follow peace and husbandry should have the

prize rather than one who dwelt on war and slaughter.

Later still, it was said that Homer was the poet of the Spartiates and Hesiod that of the enslaved Helots, "because the former encouraged men to make war, and the latter to farm."[59]

The *Works and Days* contains much advice suggesting distrust of others. One should give only to those who will reciprocate, not to others (353-54). One should be kind with visitors, the traditional pacifying Greek view; however, Hesiod affirms that kinship especially demands responsibility and solidarity. The goddess Hecate blesses the winner of athletic contests, "conferring glory on his parents" (*Theogony*, 435-38). One should not sleep with a brother's wife "in breach of all propriety" (327-28). One should not "make a friend on a par with a brother" (706).

The *Works and Days* is a melancholy song, evidently reflecting a world of hard labor, uncertainty, and poverty. Women are portrayed as a terrible burden which men must provide for. Seafaring professions are discouraged, the sea being a place of danger. Hesiod argues for having only one son, who can then happily inherit the whole family household, rather than have multiple brothers doomed to poverty.

Rightly or wrongly, men throughout the ages have believed that our best days were behind us, and Hesiod was among them. He recounts the famous myth of the degeneration of mankind through five epochs since the Golden Age, culminating in the current unhappy generation. The prophesied fall of this "race of iron" will include the supreme disasters of ill-birth and collapse of family bonds:

Would that I were not then among the fifth men, but either dead earlier or born later! For now it is a race of iron; and they will never cease from toil and misery by day or night, in constant distress, and the gods will give them harsh troubles. Nevertheless, even they shall have good mixed with ill. Yet Zeus will destroy this race of men also, when at

---

[59] Plutarch, *Sayings of the Spartans*, "Cleomenes Son of Anaxandridas," 1.

birth they come out gray at the temples. Nor will father be like children, nor children to father, nor guest to host nor comrade to comrade, nor will a brother be friendly as in former times. Soon they will cease to respect their aging parents, and will rail at them with harsh words, the ruffians, in ignorance of the gods' punishment; nor are they likely to repay their aging parents for their nature. (173-87)[60]

Hesiod, like Homer, prefigures the principle of the *polis* in asserting that an entire community can be ruined by a single bad individual. The community's misfortune is equated with childlessness and the decline of households:

> But those who occupy themselves with violence and wickedness and brutal deeds, Cronus' son, wide-seeing Zeus, marks out for retribution. Often a whole community together suffers in consequence of a bad man who does wrong and contrives evil. From heaven Cronus' son brings disaster upon them, famine and with it plague, and the people waste away. The womenfolk do not give birth, and households decline, by Olympian Zeus' design. (237-44)

Hesiod condemns the corrupt government of "bribe-swallowers," praising instead the goddesses "Lawfulness, Justice, and Flourishing Peace, who watch over the works of mortal men" (*Theogony*, 901-3).

Hesiod broadly shares the same ideal of kingship as Homer. In the *Theogony*, his genealogy of the gods, the heaven-blessed kings have a divinely-inspired charisma and ability to create concord:

> Whomsoever great Zeus' daughters favor among the kings that Zeus fosters, and turn their eyes upon him at his birth,

---

[60] The collapse of familial responsibilities and ties is a common theme in traditional mythology. In Norse myth, it is said that at Ragnarök, the Doom of the Gods: "Brothers will kill brothers for the sake of greed, and neither father nor son will be spared in the killings and the collapse of kinship" (Snorri Sturluson [trans. Jesse L. Byock], *The Prose Edda* (London: Penguin, 2005), p. 71). The term used for "collapse of kinship," *sifjaslit*, has connotations of incest.

upon his tongue they shed sweet dew, and out of his mouth the words flow honeyed; and the peoples all look to him as he decides what is to prevail with his straight judgments. His word is sure, and expertly he makes a quick end of even a great dispute. This is why there are prudent kings: when the peoples are wronged in their dealings, they make amends for them with ease, persuading them with gentle words. When he goes among a gathering, they seek his favor with conciliatory reverence, as if he were a god, and he stands out among the crowd. (*Theogony*, 81-92)

In the *Works and Days*, Hesiod says that good kings witnesses the flourishing of his community and the bearing of children who resemble their parents:

As for those who give straight judgments to visitors and to their own people and do not deviate from what is just, their community flourishes, and the people blooms in it. Peace is about the land, fostering the young, and wide-seeing Zeus never marks out grievous war as their portion. Neither does Famine attend straight-judging men, nor Blight, and they feast on the crops they tend. For them Earth bears plentiful food, and on the mountains the oak carries acorns at its surface and bees at its center. The fleecy sheep are laden down with wool; the womenfolk bear children that resemble their parents; they enjoy a continual sufficiency of good things. (224-35)

Under the good king, according to Hesiod, the people reproduce themselves and retain their identity across the generations. Homer is not much different. Both poets have the same inspired intuition, no doubt drawn from the healthy instincts and hard-won experience of a primeval culture: the good man enjoys a prosperous posterity and the good king secures the same for his people.

HERODOTUS I
THE STRUGGLE OF NATIONS & CULTURES

In defense of history, the Roman orator Cicero said: "To be ignorant of what occurred before you were born is to remain forever a child."[61] In history, we find the past trajectory of human events and insights into the nature of human existence in other circumstances, two powerful guides for the future. The first historian was Herodotus, a Greek who lived some 2,500 years ago. His massive *Histories* are in fact more than a mere recounting of past events: they are an encyclopedic snapshot of that epoch, an enormous collection of stories on the many nations of the known world which he had gathered during his travels.

Herodotus is a perceptive observer of human nature. His humans are indeed riven with contradictions and subject to extreme pressures, torn between often-conflicting personal, familial, and political loyalties. Herodotus' is a world of sex and violence, tribes and cultures, barbarism and civilization, republics and empires. Reading Herodotus remains a rewarding experience, for our human nature has not changed much over the past two-and-a-half millennia. I propose an evolutionary analysis of the *Histories*, highlighting in particular the complex and dynamic relationship between environment, culture, and ethnicity. As we shall see, national identity, ethnocentrism, and the condemnation of decadence—what we would call maladaptive culture—are major themes in Herodotus' work.

The known world of Herodotus stretched across three continents from the mouth of the Mediterranean in the west to India in the east and from the Black Sea in the north to the edge of the Sahara in the south. While Herodotus consciously writes as a Hellene with a Greek cultural frame, his political history is very much centered on the Persian Empire, by far the largest

---

[61] Cicero, *De Oratore*, 34.120.

and most powerful state of that time. In this vast world, the Greeks were a young people, though already a "well-travelled race" (1.56), scattered across the Mediterranean "like frogs around a pond" (Plato, *Phaedo*, 109b). The Greeks were well-aware of the other great and often ancient peoples around them: the Semitic trading-nation of Phoenicia in the Levant, the wild nomadic Scythians in the north, the mysterious Ethiopians in the south and Indians in the east, the massive city of Babylon in Mesopotamia, and the venerable Egyptians, among others.

Herodotus' world certainly featured peaceful commerce, cultural exchange, and ethnic intermarriage among these peoples — the historian is quite broad-minded and free of chauvinism in this respect.[62] At the same time, Herodotus is clearly writing from a patriotic Greek perspective with a particular interest in issues insofar as they pertain to Greeks. He also makes clear that this was a world of extreme ethnocentrism and brutal wars. The highly diverse material of the *Histories*, which features myths, stories, and ethnographic portraits of the many peoples of the known world, is united around the rise and decline of the Persian Empire: each people is described when they encounter the Persians, the latter being invariably bent on conquest. The work climaxes with the great struggle of an unlikely coalition of Greek city-states led by Athens and Sparta and their ultimate triumph over the Persian invaders. Meditation on war and commemoration of Greek unity and freedom are then at the center of Herodotus' narrative. One may be pleasantly surprised to learn that many of the most iconic lines and scenes in the otherwise unrealistic film *300* are actually directly drawn from Herodotus.

With the *Histories*, we can discover the ancient world as seen through the eyes of a well-traveled and endlessly curious Greek. Herodotus' world is one of hearsay, myth, and superstition. In the absence of written documents, knowledge of events in far-away places or even of a few generations earlier

---

[62] Herodotus says for instance on religion: "Because I believe that everyone is equal in terms of religious knowledge, I do not see any point in relating anything I was told about the gods" (2.3).

was dependent on often highly-unreliable and romanticized oral transmission. In these largely oral cultures, information overwhelmingly spread through Chinese whispers. Thus, the stories Herodotus dutifully reports from his various sources are often inaccurate and fantastical—yet if anything this gives us an even better sense of the mental universe of the Ancients, inhabiting a world which was at once mysterious and full of meaning.

For all that, we can also clearly see in the *Histories* the beginnings of scientific thought concerning both nature and society, for instance with his plausible speculations about the formation of the Nile Delta, micro-climates, and the effect of the natural environment on human biology and culture. Herodotus is a particularly perceptive observer of the role of culture and ethnicity in human societies. In a famous passage, the historian says that "King Custom" (or *nomos*) rules all human societies, that all these societies tend to think their own customs are superior, and hence paradoxically that cultural chauvinism is a human universal.

Furthermore, Herodotus' stories frequently revolve around the theme of kin-solidarity, within both families and ethnic groups. In another famous passage of the *Histories*, the Athenians justify their resistance to the Persians on the grounds of their Greek national identity, defined by shared blood, language, religion, and custom. This is a powerful working definition of nationhood that is still useful today. Herodotus then shows that compelling ethnocentric sentiment was present at the dawn of recorded human history, cultural chauvinism and ethnic kin-solidarity working in tandem.

One can also infer clear cases of gene-culture interaction in the *Histories*. The cultures Herodotus describes often promote, as an overwhelming imperative, what are in effect evolutionarily adaptive values at both the individual and social levels. Family formation, solidarity with immediate kin, and filial piety frequently appear as supreme ethical and even religious duties. Some customs, such as limiting intermarriage to within certain classes or ethnic groups, lead to the creation of new, genetically-unique populations.[63] There is extreme concern about suppressing many behaviors we would consider maladaptive, such as contempt for kin and effeminacy.

Selection, it would seem, could also occur at the level of the group. War is a common tragedy between the nations described by Herodotus, frequently concluding in ethnic cleansing in the form of mass enslavement, expulsion, or simple extermination. Entire societies are frequently annihilated culturally and sometimes genetically as well. Herodotus is keenly aware that a people's culture can either help or hinder their struggle for survival, with cultural practices often being aimed at increasing toughness, group solidarity, and martial valor. He is deeply concerned with luxury, effeminacy, and decadence causing the fall of great empires and nations. From Herodotus' account, one can surmise that King Nomos, culture's influence on human behavior, is clearly powerful enough to affect the composition of the gene pool across generations, and thus the course of human evolution.

I dare say one can even see in Herodotus the glimmer of a general theory of cultural and ethno-national change, with complex and dynamic interaction between populations and cultures, both being furthermore influenced by their natural environment. Populations and cultures rise and fall across this world—interacting peacefully or violently according to character and circumstance. Cultural practices and knowledge, especially if useful, may spread among the nations. At times, however, cultures are simply incompatible, such as the Persian

---

[63] A common example of this was limiting marriage to members of the in-group and limiting citizenship to those born of such unions. Herodotus claims that at one time Egypt was divided in twelve allied kingdoms whose royal families married exclusively with one another. He also says that Egyptian swineherds were only allowed to marry within the families of other swineherds. Over time, such populations would then become genetically distinct populations with different phenotypical characteristics. The most extreme examples of such limits on intermarriage in ancient times appear to have been those practiced by the Jews and the Hindus, the genetic and therefore phenotypic consequences of this are evident to this day.

custom of imperial expansion conflicting with the Greek custom of civic self-government. Here we witness a clash of *nomoi*. War is a recurring fact of life, brought about by competition for limited resources, the arrogance of conquerors, or, most often according to Herodotus, the vicious circle of tit-for-tat retaliatory escalation, nations starting new wars by citing old crimes (Herodotus for instance tells a story claiming that the Persians' hostility to the Greeks dates from the mythical destruction of the Eastern city of Troy). Whatever the causes of conflict, the nations with cultures promoting strength defeat those with cultures promoting weakness. Thus, a strong national-cultural pair spreads together: the weak conquered nations are either exterminated, meaning biological extinction, or subjugated, meaning the end of their cultural sovereignty.[64]

Over time, one would expect to see a selection for cultures and genes promoting group solidarity and manliness. Indeed, this is what Charles Darwin describes in his *Descent of Man*:

> A tribe including many members who, from possessing in high degree the spirit of patriotism, fidelity, obedience, courage and sympathy, were always ready to aid one another, and to sacrifice themselves for the common good, would be victorious over most other tribes; and this would be natural selection.[65]

Tribes which are able to sustain such adaptive culture could be expected to survive longer, while those who fail to do so, can be said to be decadent.

Interestingly, Herodotus sees both nations and cultures as being powerfully influenced by their natural environment.

---

[64] Few peoples, it would seem, have the natural ability to maintain their identity and way of life across the centuries as a non-ruling minority in other nations. Diaspora ethnic groups, most notably the Jews and the Gypsies, have proven capable of maintaining their identity, culture, and in-group loyalty as minorities in other societies. Most human populations, however, evidently require sovereignty and/or a majority presence in their own territory to maintain their way of life and identity.

[65] Darwin, *Descent of Man*, pp. 157-8.

Nature (*physis*) can both change a people physically and, depending on its harshness, determine the toughness of its culture. This a major cause of the self-correcting nature of Herodotus' world: as a strong nation/culture conquers and expands, it tends to become wealthy and arrogant, leading to softness and excess, and thus to defeat at the hands of still-virile peoples. This is the recurring fate of the Persian armies, defeated by the Scythians, the Ethiopians, and finally the Greeks.

Herodotus' discussion of the Ethiopians is a good case study of all these influences between environments, populations, and cultures. South of the Nile, Herodotus says "it is so hot there that the people are black" (2.22). The Ethiopians' culture was also changed by the settlement of Egyptian soldiers in the area: "As a result of their living there, the Ethiopians have learned Egyptian customs and become less wild" (2.30). According to Herodotus, a Persian army invading Ethiopia met its doom starving in the barren desert, the hardy Ethiopians remaining free.[66] By this example, we can see the world of Herodotus as

---

[66] Herodotus' discussion of Black people in general is worthy of comment. Herodotus uses the term "Ethiopian" to refer to people of color, both African and Indian: "The eastern [Indian] Ethiopians have straight hair, while the Libyan [African] ones have curlier hair than any other people in the world" (7.70). Herodotus describes the Egyptians as dark-skinned and curly-haired (2.104), but distinguishes between them and Ethiopians, saying 18 of 330 historical pharaohs were of Ethiopian origin (2.100).

Herodotus' discussion of Ethiopians is sometimes realistic, clearly referring to actual peoples, and sometimes fantastical, following the mythical descriptions of "Ethiopians" described in Homer, as a semi-divine people on the edge of the world, as unreal as the Hyperboreans (*Iliad* 1.423, 23.206; *Odyssey* 1.22, 5.282). On the mythical side, Herodotus speaks of certain Ethiopians as the "tallest, best-looking, and longest-lived men in the world" (3.114). Elsewhere, Herodotus speaks of fleet-footed cave-dwelling Ethiopians that eat reptiles and squeak like bats (4.183). In between myth and reality, there are reports that possibly refer to Pygmies. Libyans are said to have crossed the desert and encountered "small men of less than normal human stature [who] had black skin" (2.32). Carthaginians

one of evolving peoples and cultures, interacting and conflicting with one another, all under the influence of nature.

"KING NOMOS": THE POWER OF CULTURE & THE UNIVERSALITY OF CULTURAL CHAUVINISM

Herodotus had traveled far and wide across the Mediterranean, thus coming across nations with often radically different cultural assumptions and ways of life. Accounting for this astonishing diversity, Herodotus is extremely impressed by the social power of culture and ethnocentrism:

> If one were to order all mankind to choose the best set of rules in the world, each group regards its own as being by far the best ... There is plenty of other evidence to support the idea that this opinion of one's own customs is universal. ... Pindar was right to have said in his poem that custom is king of all. (3.38)

Herodotus says this in the context of the Persian king Cambyses killing a sacred bull during his stay in Egypt, a bull which the Egyptians had considered to be their god Apis. The historian considers Cambyses' sacrilegious contempt for local Egyptian custom as proof of his madness, an infamy on a par with his murder of his own brother and sister. (Cambyses dies shortly thereafter as a result of his actions.) Herodotus also takes the example of how Greeks and Indians treat corpses differently: Greeks burn their corpses, while Indians (allegedly) ate them, the practice of each being equally repulsive to the other. Hence, by giving societies radically different norms, taboos, and assumptions, cultural drift tends to polarize humanity into different, mutually-uncomprehending groups.

The supremacy of "King Nomos," or custom, in every society reflects the power of culture to shape that society's behavior. If genes and physique are the hardware of humanity, culture and ideas are our software. The world-view,

---

who claim to have circumnavigated Africa say that during their travels they discovered "a country inhabited by small people who wore clothes made out of palm leaves" (4.43).

assumptions, values, and taboos of a society have a powerful effect on human behavior, even if this can never eliminate our in-born proclivities. Herodotus makes clear that the power of a society's culture is necessarily paired with a sense of superiority over foreign customs. Indeed, how could it be otherwise? If the members a society thought foreign customs superior, would they not seek to make them their own? A corollary however is that if peoples with starkly different cultures and values must live in close proximity, they are liable to come into conflict. Among foreign cultures, the wise man will tread carefully.

All this does not mean that national cultures are completely closed-off and autarkic memetic units. On the contrary, Herodotus is quite cognizant of the cultural porosity and mutual influence between nations. He freely admits barbarians' superior achievements, such as the Egyptians' calendar and their monumental pyramids, and their influence over Greek culture. The Greeks, he says, owe their alphabet to the Phoenicians and much of their religion and basic geometry to the Egyptians. It is furthermore striking that the first great philosophical flourishing of the Greek world, the so-called Ionian Renaissance, occurred in the Persian-occupied Greek cities of Asia Minor (today's western Turkey). The Persians themselves were apparently the most culturally open-minded people in the world, for they "adopt more foreign customs than anyone else" (1.135).

Despite this, Herodotus records innumerable examples of cultural chauvinism and of reverence for ancestral tradition, two characteristics which would obviously help a culture to perpetuate itself. He makes clear that ancient societies were often highly chauvinist, deprecating other cultures, and putting a supreme value on the perpetuation of their own traditions. This is perhaps not surprising: the longest-lasting customs would precisely be those which were most impervious to spontaneous innovation and foreign influence.

The ancient Greeks were notoriously xenophobic. Among their greatest thinkers, Plato thought Greeks should avoid conflict with one another on grounds of their ties of kinship;

while Aristotle believed barbarians were incapable of freedom, and were rightly enslaved by Greeks. The Greeks were not alone in their chauvinism however. The Persians may have been open to foreign customs, but they deprecated foreign peoples on the most literal ethnocentric grounds: "they regard themselves as by far the best people in the world in all respects, and others as gradually decreasing in goodness, so that those who live the furthest away from them are the worst people in the world" (1.134).

The peoples of Herodotus' world are often hostile to the adoption of foreign customs. He says that the Scythians, a warlike nomadic Aryan nation who lived on the northern edge of the known world, in today's Ukraine, southern Russia and central Asia, "are another people who are absolutely set against adopting customs imported from anyone else, especially Greeks" (4.76). Herodotus says that at least one Scythian leader was killed for adopting Greek customs. The Egyptians were perhaps the most chauvinist of nations, having the most ancient culture and limited contact with foreigners. Herodotus says: "They perpetuate their traditional customs rather than acquire new ones" (2.79). Furthermore: "The Egyptians refer to anyone who does not speak the same language as them as a barbarian" (2.158).[67] Interestingly, Herodotus tied the uniqueness of Egyptian customs to their being "exceedingly religious," thus recognizing a strong role for religion in the maintenance of social norms. Surely the most effective way to make a custom enduring is to make it a religious obligation.

Perhaps we would say that an adaptive national culture would distinguish between those foreign cultural practices which can be beneficial to one's people and those which undermine one's own identity and adaptive values. In any event, culture had an overwhelming role in Herodotus' world, both in determining behavior within a society and magnifying

---

[67] The historian Carolyn Dewald says that in this context the term is clearly xenophobic. She elsewhere says that many of the tales Egyptian priests told Herodotus were "nationalist propaganda" (in Herodotus, *Histories*, p. 624).

the differences between societies. Despite cultural porosity and mutual influence, cultural chauvinism and reverence for ancestral tradition were common, two factors which allowed customs to sustain themselves in the face of both time and foreign influence.

FAMILIAL KIN-SOLIDARITY

In addition to culture, kinship, both familial and ethnic, is a pervasive theme throughout the *Histories*. Again and again, Herodotus tells stories in which kinship is sufficient grounds for solidarity and mutual duties, especially among immediate family members.[68] A closely related theme is filial piety,[69] of which the Persians in particular had an extremely elevated notion:

They say that no one has ever killed his own father or mother. They insist that all such incidents would inevitably

---

[68] A Persian, when asked to kill an infant, responds: "There are plenty of reasons why I won't kill the child, not the least of which is that he's a relative of mine" (1.109). When two Scythians come into conflict, one asks: "You are my sister's son. Why should we fight each other?" (4.80). Herodotus thinks it noteworthy that two Spartan brothers and their descendants quarreled constantly, despite their kinship (6.52). The Agarthysians, a Scythian tribe, in a prefiguring of the radical suggestions in Plato's *Republic*, were said to not have distinct families, so that familial solidarity would extend to the entire community: "Any woman is available to any man for sex, to ensure that the men are all brothers and that they are on amicable and good terms with one another, since they are all relatives" (4.104).

Other tribes, such as the Nasamones (4.172) and the Auseës of Libya are also said to practice such sexual sharing of women. Herodotus says of the Auseës: "They have intercourse with women promiscuously; rather than living in couples, their sex life is like that of herd animals. When a woman's baby is grown, in the course of the third month the men all convene and the child is taken to be the son or daughter of whichever of the men it resembles" (4.180).

[69] A Greek father whose son had run away and rejected his authority lamented: "I am the last person in the world you ought to treat this way ... You now know ... what it is like for people to be angry with their parents and their betters" (3.52).

be found on examination to have been the work of a child substituted for a genuine child, or of a bastard; they simply deny the plausibility of a full parent being killed by his own child. (1.138)

A Persian nobleman, prior to sending his daughter on a dangerous mission to determine whether the throne has been usurped by non-kin, says: "Daughter, your noble birth means that you have to accept any risk I, your father, tell you to run" (3.69).

Familial kinship and solidarity were overwhelming factors in ancient politics, many monarchic and oligarchic regimes being nothing more than family mafias. The power of kinship could be exploited for political strategies in both domestic politics and international relations. A common strategy for ruling elites was to form a distinct and solidary extended family by only marrying among themselves. This was practiced by the ruling Bacchiadae clan of Corinth (5.92). The half-dozen conspirators who seized power and restored the Persian monarchy under Darius decided that "the king was not to marry outside the families of his fellow revolutionaries" (3.84). Such strategies could also extend to international relations, in attempts to moderate the unstable and often violent relationships between states. Upon making a peace treaty, the Lydians and Medes decided to organize a marriage among the ruling families "on the grounds that strong treaties tend not to last in the absence of strong ties" (1.74).

It is said in the *Histories*: "the most valuable possession in the world is an intelligent, loyal friend" (5.24).[70] Both within and between societies, much of history has arguably been determined by whichever *loci* of kinship-solidarity were strongest: family, clique, clan, city, or nation? The level at

---

[70] Pericles would similarly later say: "Intelligence without clear communication is no better than an empty mind; a man with both these abilities but no loyalty to his country is less likely to speak for the interests of the community, let him have loyalty also, but if the man is venal this one fault puts all his other qualities up for sale" (Thucydides, 2.60).

which identity and solidarity were strongest was also the level at which there was the most collective agency, a conscious and solidary group always overcoming a disorganized mass.

Reproduction is a common imperative in the world of Herodotus. Among the Greeks, one's duty towards one's kin was above all that towards one's parents, and that included a religious duty to perpetuate the family line. Among the Persians, Herodotus claims that Cambyses once asked whether he was a greater man than his father, Cyrus the Great, who had founded the Persian Empire. One adviser said Cambyses was greater, for his empire was bigger, another disagreed, saying: "In my opinion, my lord, you do not bear comparison with your father, because you do not yet have a son of the caliber of the one he left behind" (3.34). Cambyses was reputedly "delighted" with this answer. Having prosperous descendants was a fundamental marker of success in life. Conversely, the gods would strike the impious and immoral with a lack of descendants as a supreme punishment. The oracle of Apollo at Delphi warned on one occasion that dishonesty and theft would mean "All a man's offspring, all his house" are destroyed, "But an honest man's offspring will gain in the long run" (6.86).[71]

HERODOTUS' DEFINITION OF NATIONAL IDENTITY

Solidarity on grounds of kinship extended not only to a

---

[71] Many of Herodotus' stories have to do with individuals being forced to choose between various extreme imperatives: duties to self, to family, and to the state often clash with one another. On one occasion, a Persian woman is told she may save one member of her immediate family. She chooses to save her brother rather than her husband or children, saying: "God willing, I may get another husband and more children, if I lose the ones I have at the moment. But my parents are dead, so there's no way I can get another brother" (3.119). Thus, in this instance, the woman put her duty towards her own ancestral line ahead of that towards her husband and children. On another occasion, Persian overlords abuse their Macedonian hosts by molesting their wives and daughters at the dinner table. The Macedonians then conspire to slaughter the Persians (5.18-20).

family or a clan, but indeed to entire ethnic groups. Expressions of solidarity were common among Greeks as well as among kindred cities (mother cities and the new settlements they created continued to consider each other relatives, even if they came into conflict). Herodotus famously quotes a speech in which the Athenians pledge to never surrender to the Persians on the grounds of their duty to the Greek people, which is defined as "one race speaking one language, with temples to the gods and religious rites in common, and with a common way of life" (8.144). The Athenians then defined nationhood by shared blood, language, religion, and customs. As Martin Aurelio has argued, this is a powerful working definition of nationhood which remains valid to this day.[72] The Greeks would define "Greece" as being wherever Greeks happened to live. Being inhabited by Greeks, Sicily is described as "a large portion of Greece" (7.157). Similarly, the soldier-philosopher Xenophon traveled with his army along an attractive portion of the Black Sea coast, he said he wanted to settle there as "it would be a fine achievement to found a city and acquire extra land and resources for Greece" (*Anabasis*, 5.6.15-22).[73]

The rulers of the Persian Empire were often posed with the problem of the ethnic loyalties of their highly diverse subjects. The Phoenicians on one occasion would not attack their daughter-city of Carthage: "The Phoenicians, however, refused to obey; they were bound by solemn oaths, they said, and it would be wrong for them to attack their own sons" (3.19). During Persia's invasions of Greece, both Greeks and Persians often commented on the reticence of the Persians' Greek subjects to fight against their co-nationals.

---

[72] Martin Aurelio, "The Four Elements of National Identity in Herodotus," *Counter-Currents*, June 15, 2016.

[73] One may also make a seemingly banal observation: Herodotus notes that the social and national fact is so important that humans tend to name regions after the peoples inhabiting them, as opposed to say purely geographical criteria. He says: "Egypt is the whole land inhabited by Egyptians, just as Cilicia or Assyria are the countries where Cilicians or Assyrians live" (2.17).

At the same time, ethnic intermarriage is a common feature in the world of Herodotus. His characters are often obsessively proud of their genealogies. However, any concerns about purity were often thrown by the wayside in the face of the drive to procreate. Herodotus has many tales of men happily kidnapping and/or marrying foreign women, individually or *en masse*, thus founding mixed populations.[74] Indeed, this seems to have been common for at least some Indo-European groups that originally consisted of male war bands who would take wives and concubines from the conquered population. This ethnocentric world was evidently a genetically porous one.[75]

Herodotus is generally skeptical of claims of racial purity and observes on various occasions that Greek populations have mixed ancestries: that Ionian Greeks of Asia Minor had mixed with the neighboring Carians (possibly a fellow Aryan people; 1.146); that Athens included Hellenized Pelasgians (the indigenous pre-Greek inhabitants of the Greek peninsula; 1.54-56, 8.44),[76] contradicting Athenian claims of racial purity as having autochthonously 'sprung from the soil;' and that Ionians in the Peloponnese had become culturally assimilated

---

[74] E.g., Herodotus claims that when the Scythian men left their womenfolk for many years while on a foreign war, the woman took the extreme measure of marrying their own slaves in order to have children. The men of Babylon are supposed to have killed their own wives and children in order to hold out longer during a siege, and similarly had to import foreign women *en masse* to form families again.

[75] I would note that more generally, these cases of intermarriage reflect the fact that different parts of a given race or nation have genetic interests which do not fully overlap. Individual male conquerors for instance may have an interest in spreading their seed far and wide across foreign nations, even though this may be conflict with the narrower interests of their tribe.

[76] Andrew Hamilton has written on Herodotus' discussion of the Athenians and the Pelasgians, the former sometimes seeming to have an instinctive racial pride over the latter. Andrew Hamilton, "Ethnic Cleansing in Ancient Attica & Lemnos," *Counter-Currents*, April 15, 2014.

Dorians (the Greek ethnic group associated with Sparta, 8.73). Herodotus himself came from Halicarnassus, a Dorian city with partly Carian heritage, with many of the Greeks there having names of Carian origin. The learning of a particular ethnic group's language is frequently the marker of assimilation.

These observations of intermarriage and mixed ethnic backgrounds do not, I would argue, invalidate the relevance or evolutionary adaptiveness of cultural chauvinism and ethnic solidarity. Marxist scholars have often argued that nations are arbitrary, socially-constructed collective hallucinations with no underlying biological reality or even cultural identity. The Ancients certainly did not see things this way. The various Greek populations were not completely identical—there was variation in ancestry, regional dialects, religious worship, and lifestyle—nonetheless, Greek civilization was a perfectly identifiable bioculture, a cluster of peoples whose members on the whole clearly shared these traits with one another more than they did with barbarians.

I would argue that Herodotus' observations are eminently compatible with a scientific and evolutionary perspective on race/genetics and ethnicity. Race is, especially in geographically-contiguous land masses, typically a clinal phenomenon, with gradual change in genetic characteristics (i.e. allele frequencies) as one moves, for instance, from northern Europe to central Africa. While intermarriage tends to spread genes, gene flow is slowed by geographical and ethno-cultural boundaries, leading to significant racial-genetic clumping and differentiation.

The birth of a nation, *ethnogenesis*, occurs when linguistic, cultural, and possibly genetic drift leads a particular population to acquire an ethnic identity distinct from its neighbors. Cultural chauvinism and ethnic sentiment work together in this, magnifying one another: cultural traits such as language and customs become more and more similar within the in-group, while differences with out-groups become more and more marked. Thus, a point on the genetic cline is hardened into a more-or-less discrete ethno-cultural node and genetic cluster: a nation. The degree of nationhood is defined by the population's level of genetic and cultural commonality, and distinctness from other groups.

This perspective recognizes the powerful but not exclusive role of culture in the formation of ethno-national identity. Cultural elites can actively contribute to the formation or preservation of ethno-cultural identity (such as by spreading a common language and customs) and genetic identity (such as by discouraging miscegenation). Conversely, as in the West today, cultural elites can seek to suppress cultural chauvinism and ethnic solidarity, for example by glorifying foreign cultures and shaming native ethnic pride. Such nations are unlikely to survive long however.[77]

One does not need a population with an absolutely "pure" lineage for ethnocentrism to be evolutionarily adaptive. On the contrary, one needs only sufficient genetic and cultural

---

[77] The suppression of ethnic sentiment is a constant struggle because such sentiment is an in-born human drive to identify and be solidary with perceived kin. This natural sentiment can however be partially suppressed, magnified, and/or channeled in various ways by culture. Cultural influence over the sex drive is exactly analogous: traditional Christianity could never eliminate the sex drive, but it could promote monogamy and make adultery taboo, thus channeling that powerful instinct into an arguably pro-social direction. I would argue the nation-state was an institution which similarly channeled the ethnocentric instinct in such a pro-social direction, helping to fashion a solidary body of citizens.

The historical and scientific evidence suggests that a common language and race (by which I mean intra-continental genetic proximity) are minimum requirements for the formation of a common ethno-national identity. That humans have an evolved, hard-wired tendency to identify ethnic kin according to language and race is suggested by studies which have shown that infants as young as six months discriminate against foreign accents and races. "Racial bias begins in infancy, new insight on cause: Kang Lee's studies show babies favour own race as early as six months of age," University of Toronto press release, April 11, 2017. "Five-month-old babies prefer their own languages and shun foreign accents," *Phenomena National Geographic blog*, June 14, 2009.

similarity for the members of the community to form a common identity and become a solidary in-group, and there must be greater average genetic similarity among individual in-group members than there is between individual in-group members and the members of out-groups they come into conflict with.[78] In any event, in the world of Herodotus, the importance of kinship, both familial and ethnic, is fundamental and pervasive across both Greek and barbarian nations.

The Greeks in Herodotus are fiercely proud of their heritage. True, the sentimental love for Hellas was often overridden by personal or political interests. Prominent Greek leaders and cities frequently collaborated with the Persians, either because the alternative was oblivion or simply for profit. Nonetheless, one is struck by the pervasiveness of pan-Hellenic discourse and expressions of Greek pride. The Athenians and Spartans invariably cite their sacrifice to defeat the Persians and save Greece as their greatest glory, their great claim to legitimacy as regional powers. At the war's conclusion, one Greek tells the Spartans: "The god has allowed you to earn more fame than anyone else we know of, for saving Greece. What you need to do now is follow up this achievement, to enhance your reputation even more and to make any foreigner in the future think twice before committing obscene crimes against Greeks" (9.78).

PERSIAN VIRTUE: A PERSIAN GROUP EVOLUTIONARY STRATEGY?

The people described in most detail by Herodotus is in fact not the Greeks, but their enemies the Persians, a fellow Aryan people. Herodotus speaks a great deal about Persian culture, often very positively. For instance, he says that "the Persians

---

[78] Conversely, if two genetically-close nations fight each other, thus empowering a more genetically-distant third nation, this would be a case of maladaptive ethnocentrism. Sadly, as shown by the Greek fratricide of the Peloponnesian War and the European fratricide of the World Wars, this phenomenon is only too common in Western history.

are normally the last people in the world, to my knowledge, to treat men who fight bravely with disrespect" (7.238). The historian is far more critical of individual arrogant Persian rulers, such as Cambyses and Xerxes, than he is of Persia as such.

Herodotus claims that the Persian Empire — which in his day stretched from Greek Asia Minor in the west to India in the east, and from Egypt in the south to the edges of Scythia in the north — had grown through "customs" of monarchic power and conquest. These led every Persian king to expand the empire, at least until this led to unnatural excess and to their downfall.

Persian culture, as described by Herodotus, is in many respects highly adaptive. He says that among the Persians:

> After bravery in battle, manliness is proved above all by producing plenty of sons, and every year the king rewards the person producing the most; they think that quantity constitutes strength ... they study only three things: horsemanship, archery, and honesty. (1.136)

Thus the Persians put a supreme value on martial valor, reproduction, and trust.[79] The Persians, like other conquering Aryan peoples such as the Greeks and Scythians, glorified warriors and looked down on manual labor.

---

[79] Herodotus also says of the Persians: "The most disgraceful thing, in their view, is telling lies, and the next most disgraceful thing is being in debt; but the main reason (among many others) for the proscription of debt is that, according to the Persians, someone who owes money is obliged to tell lies as well" (1.138).

The Persians are not the only people described as having a martial culture. The Scythians are said to have customs and a way of life worthy of Conan the Barbarian: human sacrifice, worship of the war-god Ares, drinking the blood of one's first kill, keeping the heads of one's kills to confirm them and be rewarded on that basis, making coats from scalps, using the tops of skulls as cups . . . In an annual ceremony, all Scythian men who have killed enemies may drink, while the others are gravely shamed (4.66). Many of Herodotus' verifiable observations about the Scythians – such as the use of hemp and the burial of their chieftains in mounds with their horses – have been subsequently confirmed by archaeology.

The Persian Empire itself is presented as a kind of ethnocracy. Before the rise of Cyrus, the rulers had been the Medes—an ethnic group perhaps related to the modern-day Kurds—who greatly feared being ruled the Persians, presented as a foreign ethnic group. The Median king's advisers clearly express both their fear of being ruled by another group and the idea of sharing in the king's rule by virtue of being members of the same people:

> My lord, it's true that the prosperity of your rule is very important to us as well, because the alternative is for power to fall into foreign hands. If it devolves on to this boy [Cyrus], who is Persian, we Medes will be enslaved by the Persians and will become worthless outcasts. But you are one of us. As long as you are king, then, power is partly ours too, and we have important standing in society thanks to you. We are bound to do all we can to look out for you and your rule. (1. 120)

When Cyrus took power from the Medes, he is indeed supposed to have granted special privileges to Persians, protected their interests, exempted them from taxes, and given them command of the multiethnic Persian army (3.75, 3.97, 7.96).

The Persians culturally reinforced their own group solidarity through various practices. The overthrowing of the Medes was the most important day in the Persian calendar (3.79) and the Persians feared a return of Median power. The Persians cultivated their feeling of oneness through prayer. A Persian, Herodotus says, "is not allowed to exclude others and pray for benefits for himself alone; he prays for the prosperity of the king and the whole Persian race, since he is, after all, a member of the Persian race himself" (1.132). Conversely, one of the signs of the madness of Cambyses was his abuses against his own people. An adviser warned him: "you are killing your own countrymen ... If you go on behaving like this, you had better watch out or the Persians will rise up against you" (3.36).

The Persians, like the Greeks and Romans, did not however make a religion of racial purity. There was no indiscriminate mixing of ethnic groups in their empire, the army for instance was divided into units along national lines, but the Persian elite allowed for some intermarriage with members of other groups (Herodotus cites cases of half-Greeks and half-Medes in the Persian elite).

THE BANALITY OF RACE WAR

One of Herodotus' characters laments the tragedy of war: "no one is stupid enough to prefer war to peace; in peace sons bury their fathers and in war fathers bury their sons" (1.87). Yet, war is inevitable, whether willed by the gods, the clash of cultures, scarce resources, the arrogance of men, or simply old hatreds for past atrocities.

A nation is only free to pursue its existence and determine its own destiny if it can defend itself militarily. In the ancient world, defeat frequently meant enslavement or extermination. Indeed, as so often, ethnic cleansing was a grim but logical consequence of ethnic solidarity: wars between states were actually wars between peoples. Physical liquidation of the enemy population meant eliminating a potential source of rebellion, securing their land and other resources for oneself, and sending a message to other would-be rebellious subjects.

The Persians could be quite tolerant rulers but did not hesitate to be outright genocidal towards those who resisted their power. Cyrus directly comments on this topic to his adviser Croesus, the former king of Lydia, a country he had conquered. The Lydians were causing trouble because they were still attached to their former king, who was "more than a father to the Lydians" (1.155). Cyrus wondered whether he should simply enslave all the Lydians. He said: "I've behaved like someone who has killed the father but spared the children" (1.155).[80]

Herodotus records numerous instances of ethnic cleansing committed by the Persians and other peoples. This was

---

[80] Similarly, among the Scythians: "The children of people executed by the king are not safe either: he has every male child killed, although he leaves the females alone" (4.69).

commonly done either at the conclusion of military conquests or to punish rebellions. After being conquered by the Persians, the important Greek island-city of Samos was depopulated: "The Persians 'trawled' Samos and handed over to Syloson [a Greek collaborator] an uninhabited island." (3.149). On one occasion the Persians seemed to wish to inflict the worst possible biological damage on the defeated Ionians: "they picked the best-looking boys and castrated them, cutting off their testicles and turning them into eunuchs; they also took the most attractive girls and sent them to the king as slaves" (6.32). The inhabitants of the Greek city of Barca on the Libyan coast were enslaved and deported to Bactria in Central Asia (4.204). During the Persian invasion of Europe, several entire Thracian tribes (living north of Greece) were "uprooted from their native land and taken to Asia" (5.15). Following the failure of the Ionian Revolt, the Persians destroyed the important Greek city of Miletus:

> Most of the male population was killed by the Persians ... their women and children were reduced to slavery, and the shrine at Didyma — both the temple and the oracle — was plundered and burned ... Those Milesians who remained alive were [relocated] on the Red sea.... . So Miletus was left empty of Milesians. (6.19-22)

During the invasion of mainland Greece, the city of Eretria was punished for siding with the Athenians by deporting them *en masse* to central Persia (6.119). The island-city of Naxos was burned to the ground by the Persians and, while the population fled into the wild, all those who were caught were enslaved (6.96). The Persians were by no means alone in resorting to ethnic cleansing. One on occasion, Croesus as king of Lydia threatened to wipe out an uncooperative city "as if they were a pine tree" as "the pine tree was the only tree which produced no shoots after it had been cut down, so that it was utterly destroyed, with no hope of regeneration" (6.37). Following an atrocious ethnic conflict with the native Pelasgians of Lemnos, the Athenians expelled the island's inhabitants (6.137-40).

Entire peoples could also decide to move of their own accord in order to escape being conquered. Half of the population of Phocaea, an Ionian city, fled rather than submit to Persian rule (1.164). There was also a proposal for all Asiatic Ionians to emigrate to Sardinia rather than submit to Persia. The Scythians for their part were able to avoid and defeat their enemies through superior mass-mobility. Herodotus says:

> Although in other respects I do not find the Scythians particularly admirable, they have come up with the cleverest solution I know of to the single most important matter in human life ... how to prevent anyone who attacks them from escaping, and how to avoid being caught unless they want to be detected. (4.46)

MALADAPTIVE CULTURE: HERODOTUS ON LUXURY, EFFEMINACY, AND DECADENCE

Living in a dangerous world, the Ancients considered the maintaining of martial virtue and hardiness to be a supreme imperative. Like Homer and Plato, Herodotus has much to say on the perils of luxury, effeminacy, and decadence. Herodotus is acutely aware of the fragility and transience of nations and civilizations. He says at the beginning of the *Histories*:

> I will cover minor and major human settlements equally, because most of those which were important in the past have diminished in significance by now, and those which were great in my own time were small in times past. I will mention both equally because I know that human happiness never remains long in the same place. (1.5)

Herodotus suggests a cycle of rise and fall of civilizations: as one becomes wealthy and powerful, it tends to lose over the generations the manly virtue which made this possible, becoming at once effeminate and arrogant. This cycle of decadence, which was later famously analyzed by the Andalusian historian Ibn Khaldun, is a common feature of human history. Moderns are apt to forget that until quite recently primitive and nomadic virile barbarians periodically conquered more culturally advanced but decadent sedentary civilizations. One need only mention the ancient Germans, Huns, Vikings, Arabs, Turks, and Mongols.

Herodotus' characters repeatedly comment on the debilitating effects of luxury and effeminacy, in a word, of being over-civilized. The Persians' rise to power in the century prior to Herodotus' writings is explained by their initial Spartan-like ruggedness and simplicity, while their decline is due to their indulgence in comfort and wealth since the passing of Cyrus the Great in 530 BC. Overly rich and arrogant empires seeking ever-more land repeatedly come to grief by attacking impoverished but still-manly free peoples.[81]

The Greeks are famously said to be a free people though "poverty" is always with them, overcoming their enemies through courage, intelligence, and adherence to law (7.102). The Spartans, who had an extremely simple diet whose staple was a black broth, are said to have laughed upon being shown a magnificent Persian meal. The Spartan king Pausanias is supposed to have said: "how stupid the Persian king is. Look at the way he lives and then consider that he invaded our country to rob us of our meager portions!" (9.82). For the Greeks, freedom was synonymous with the manly virtue necessary to secure it against hostile powers. Conversely, the Ionian Greeks under Persian rule are repeatedly shamed for their supposed effeminacy, making them fit to be slaves rather than free men.

---

81   Examples include:

The wealthy of kingdom of Lydia's disastrous attack on the virtuous Persia of Cyrus's early reign, whose food consisted "of what they can get, not what they might want, because of the ruggedness of their land" (1.71).

The Persian attack on the Massagetae, a Scythian people who would defeat and behead Cyrus: "a Persian-style good life and anything approaching real luxury is, I hear, something with which the Massagetae have no acquaintance or familiarity" (1.207).

During Cambyses' failed invasion of Ethiopia, the Ethiopian king gave the Persian king a longbow saying: "When the Persians can draw bows of this size as easily as I do now, then he can march against the long-lived Ethiopians" (3.21).

Interestingly, Herodotus explicitly mentions a case of a hostile ruling elite consciously promoting maladaptive, feminizing culture among their subjects in order to reduce their power of resistance. Fearing that Cyrus would completely destroy his rebellious Lydian subjects, their former king, Croesus, advised the following:

> You can be lenient towards the Lydians and still issue them a directive to ensure that they never rebel and are no threat to you. Send a message that they are forbidden to own weapons of war, that they are to wear tunics under their coats and slippers on their feet, to raise their sons to be retailers. Before long, my lord, you will see them become women instead of men, and so there will be no danger of them rising up against you. (1.155)

Cyrus agreed to these measures. Thus, the conqueror might not necessarily exterminate the conquered biologically, but ruin them culturally.

Significantly, Herodotus concludes his *Histories* with a flashback warning from Cyrus the Great. The King was advised to move away from his current rugged territory to one of the gentler regions of the Persian Empire. Herodotus says:

> Cyrus was not impressed with the proposal. He told them to go ahead — but he also advised them to be prepared, in that case, to become subjects instead of rulers, on the grounds that soft lands tend to breed soft men. It is impossible, he said, for one and the same country to produce remarkable crops and good fighting men ... they chose to live in a harsh land and rule rather than to cultivate fertile plains and be others' slaves. (9.122)

The message could not be clearer: a prosperous and civilized people is precisely the most vulnerable to creeping weakness. Herodotus says elsewhere, though admittedly in a context referring to oracles and religious omens: "There are invariably warning signs given when disaster is going to overwhelm a community or a race" (6.27).

CONCLUSION: KING NOMOS' CHILDREN

The *Histories* deliver a bounty of information on the ancient world eminently compatible with an evolutionary perspective. We comfortable moderns can never be reminded enough of the violence and desperation of the struggle for existence in past times. A man's livelihood was his land, stability and law were often nowhere to be found, and one lost battle against foreign invaders could make the difference between freedom and slavery, life and extermination. If one were not exterminated, being conquered meant, at the least, the end of a people's self-determination, their ability to decide their own way of life. In this context of constant struggle, one would expect peoples with maladaptive cultures—cultures which do not promote one's survival and reproduction—to be gradually replaced by peoples with adaptive cultures.

What, however, are the traits of an adaptive culture? I propose that an adaptive culture must:

- Hold a powerful sway over the society;
- Be able to maintain itself in the face of both time and foreign influence;
- Put a supreme value on kinship, both familial and ethnic, as reflecting relative genetic similarity;
- Create a solidary in-group (with eventual assimilation of genetically-close, reciprocating, and compatible out-groups);
- Promote reproduction;
- Promote martial prowess and manliness.

By this definition, many of the traits of traditional cultures can be identified as evolutionarily adaptive. Reverence for ancestral tradition, cultural chauvinism, in-group loyalty, familial and ethnic solidarity, a religious duty of reproduction, and the shaming of effeminacy in males are extremely common among traditional cultures across the world, not least in the cultures described by Herodotus. Much of what liberals and Marxists condemn as purely arbitrary and oppressive is revealed to have an evolutionary logic in that much in these

87

cultures clearly promoted the survival and flourishing of the peoples who bore them.

With Herodotus, we see that circumstances change but certain fundamental laws remain. Tribalism and love of kin are as old as humanity itself. The history of the human species is that of the rise and fall of nations and civilizations — more prosaically, the spread and recession of genetic and cultural memes. At the very beginnings of recorded history, Herodotus himself is acutely conscious that values and habits of weakness can lead to the fall of one's people. The struggle within a people's soul between manly virtue and luxurious decadence goes back at least to the dawn of civilization.

HERODOTUS II
HELLENIC FREEDOM & UNITY
IN THE PERSIAN WARS

If the struggle, rise, and fall of nations and cultures is a great theme in Herodotus' *Histories*, center stage is given to the wars between Persia and the Greeks (499-449 BC). Writing years after the events related, in the early stages of the Peloponnesian War between Athens and Sparta, Herodotus self-consciously recorded and commemorated the triumph of Greek unity and freedom that had been achieved just a generation before, within living memory. The *Histories* begin thus:

> Here are presented the results of the inquiry carried out by Herodotus of Halicarnassus. The purpose is to prevent the traces of human events from being erased by time, and to preserve the fame of the important and remarkable achievements produced by both Greeks and barbarians; among the matters covered is, in particular, the cause of the hostilities between Greeks and barbarians.

In addition to giving us an encyclopedic view of the cultures and conflicts of the ancient world, Herodotus then provides a portrait of the Greek city-states in action in their successful struggle for survival against Persia.

Indeed, Herodotus himself takes up a self-consciously "Helleno-centric" viewpoint. The *Histories* are full of expressions of Greek pride in their race and civilization: individuals and cities justify their action *for the sake of Greece*, a supreme good, and are rewarded with glory and reputation *in the eyes of Greece* as an ethno-cultural entity, a supreme prize. This nationalistic discourse is surprisingly pervasive but is often merely rhetorical. While Greek patriotic sentiment was widespread and there were episodes of actual Greek solidarity, the political reality of Greek division between city-states was tragically common. As we shall see, pan-Hellenic sentiment was by no means limited to Herodotus, but was found across

Greek civilization, both in terms of time and space.

The *Histories* are also a celebration of the Greek tradition of civic freedom, in contrast with Persian Empire and "slavery," which Herodotus claims was the underlying cause of the conflict: in an escalatory cycle, the Persian custom of imperial expansion came crashing against the Greek custom of free civic self-government. In this respect, Herodotus considered hierarchical and disciplined Sparta to be as much an exemplar of freedom as democratic and dynamic Athens. The triumph of the Greeks is essentially the outcome of the successful collaboration of these two, often rival, poles of Greek civilization.

PERSIAN IMPERIAL CONQUEST

The Persians had in their struggle for power with other nations acquired a formidable culture of empire. War was integral to their way of life. On one occasion, a Persian advised the King to undertake a new military adventure so as to keep his own subjects busy instead of conspiring against him (3.134). Xerxes claimed that Persia had constantly been at war with other nations and thus, in moving to conquer Greece, was remaining faithful to national tradition (7.8). One Persian official observed: "We conquered the Sacae, the Indians, the Ethiopians, the Assyrians, and plenty of other important races, and we now hold them in slavery. Why? Not because they did us any wrong, but just because we wanted to increase our dominion" (7.9).

Persia's conquest of Lydia in 546 BC led to control of the latter's Ionian Greek subjects in Asia Minor. Apparently, the Spartans early on opposed the Persians' expansion into Europe, warning them "not to harm any settlement on Greek soil, since the Lacedaemonians would not tolerate it" (1.153). Herodotus' memorable (however implausible) account of Cyrus' reaction shows that the Greeks were quite aware of the uniqueness of their civic way of life on the margins of a great empire:

Cyrus' response to this message was reputedly to have asked some Greeks in his entourage who on earth

Lacedaemonians were, and how numerous they were, that they addressed him in this way. Once he had been told about them, he is supposed to have replied to the Spartiate agent as follows: "I have never yet had occasion to fear the kind of men who set aside a space in the middle of their town where they can meet and make false promises to one another. If I remain healthy, their tongues will be occupied with events at home rather than those in Ionia." This was intended by Cyrus as a slur against Greeks in general, because they have town squares where they buy and sell goods, where it is not Persian practice to use such places at all and the town square is entirely unknown to them. (1.153)

The great conflict between the European Greeks and Persia would however only begin in earnest later in a classic case of escalatory geopolitical and ethnic conflict. The proximate cause was the Ionian Revolt of 499 BC, in which the Asiatic Greek cities tried to liberate themselves from Persia. The Ionians sought support from the European Greeks. Aristagoras of Miletus tried to convince the Spartan king Cleomenes to support the rebellion, promising an easy victory over weak barbarians and the gain of the untold wealth of Asia. Aristagoras also appealed to their shared blood and gods:

> This is the situation: the sons of the Ionians are slaves, when they should be free. But it isn't only we Ionians who should feel the terrible ignominy and pain; more than anyone else, you should feel it too, because you are the champions of Greece. I beg you, by the gods of the Greeks, to liberate your kinsmen in Ionia from slavery. (5.49)

The cautious Spartans however refused to come to their aid. Aristagoras then went to Athens, reputedly a weaker state, making the same promises. He appealed to yet closer ties of kinship, "point[ing] out that Miletus was an Athenian colony ... therefore it was reasonable to expect Athens to use its considerable power to protect them" (5.97). The Athenians were convinced and thus sent 20 ships to assist the Ionians.

Herodotus is quite negative about the episode and considers the Athenians to have made a mistake in supporting their kinsmen. He makes the antidemocratic observation: "It seems to be easier to fool a crowd than a single person, since Aristagoras could not persuade Cleomenes of Lacedaemon, who was all alone, but he succeeded with thirty thousand Athenians" (5.97). The sending of the Athenian ships was for Herodotus "the beginning of misfortune for Greeks and barbarians alike" (5.97). The Athenians encouraged the Ionians in a doomed rebellion which would lead to the destruction of Miletus and provoke the Persians to invade Europe. The Athenians evidently felt some attachment for their daughter-city: when the poet Phrynicus organized a play entitled *The Fall of Miletus*, the emotion was such that the authorities felt the need to ban its performance (6.21).

Xerxes would later justify the invasion of Greece as a retaliatory and preventive action:

> I am sure the Athenians will do something if we do not; to judge by their past moves, they will certainly mount an expedition against our country, since these are the people who burned down Sardis [a Persian city] and invaded Asia. It is impossible for either side to withdraw now; the only question at stake is whether or not we actively take the initiative. And in the end either all Persia will be in Greek hands, or all Greece will be in Persian hands; there is no middle ground in this war. (7.11)[82]

The King's ambition was great, telling his men: "we will make Persian territory end only at the sky so that the sun will not shine on any land beyond our borders. With your help I will sweep through the whole of Europe and make all lands into a single land" (7.8).

In describing the Persian invasion of Europe, Herodotus is keen to contrast the patriotic Greek citizen-soldiers and Xerxes' diverse "slave" soldiers, so recalcitrant they must be driven by

---

[82] Xerxes' alleged concerns about a Greek conquest of Persia may seem hyperbolic given how small and divided the Greeks were as a people. As things turned out, Alexander the Great's Greco-Macedonian forces would indeed conquer Persia one century later.

whips. The Persian army formed "a confused mass of soldiers, with all the different peoples and tribes indiscriminately mixed up together" (7.40). The Persians commanded their forces divided into various national regiments. These included the Ethiopians who "were dressed in leopard skins and lion pelts, and were armed with bows made out of palm fronds" (7.69). In the face of these subjects would stand free Greek citizen-soldiers, as embodied above all the hoplite, with his heavy equipment and perfect organization within the phalanx.

HELLENIC FREEDOM: AN ETHNOPOLITICAL, COMMUNITARIAN, & VIRILE TRADITION

The Greeks had a very keen sense of the uniqueness of their way of life and a tremendous pride in themselves as a people. Throughout their history, the Greeks considered Eastern barbarians to be effeminate, luxurious, and slavish, in self-conscious contrast to their own manly virtue, poverty, and freedom. The Greeks were at once community-oriented and notoriously competitive as individuals. It was said to be "typically Greek to envy success and hate being outdone" (7.236). The Greeks thought of themselves as being "distinguished from barbarians by being more clever and less gullible" (1.60). Greek thinkers developed scientific theories to explain reality, such as the regular flooding of the Nile river, "motivated by a desire to enhance their reputation as clever people" (2.20). Whereas the Semitic Phoenicians and Egyptians had a reputation for being money-grubbing,[83] the Persians were supposedly alarmed that the Greeks "ma[de] excellence rather than money the reason for a contest!" (8.26). The shaming of effeminacy and softness as unworthy and even un-Greek is a recurring theme in Greek history, expressed as much

---

[83] The Semitic Phoenicians are often presented as avaricious in Greek literature. In Homer, the Phoenicians appear consistently as seafaring traders, sometimes unscrupulous ones. In the *Republic*, Plato has Socrates say: "the love of money . . . one might say is conspicuously displayed by the Phoenicians and Egyptians" (436a, trans. G.M.A. Grube, rev. C.D.C. Reeve).

by laymen as philosophers.[84] The contrast between Oriental servitude and the Greek love of freedom was most stark in the Greeks' horror at the Persian practice prostration before their King, as though he were a god not a man (7.136). Greeks were supposed to be civilized and pious, reflected in such practices as respect for the corpses of the fallen (9.79).[85] These Greek conceptions about themselves and foreigners, however stereotypical they might be, reflected both their tremendous national pride and the uniqueness of the Greek tradition of citizenship.

For Herodotus, there was no doubt that the Greek way of life of freedom in the *polis*, embodied in such different states as Athens and Sparta, was a tremendous source of strength. Greek soldiers fought with more enthusiasm and vigor because they, unlike the Persians' "slaves," fought for themselves as a solidary community. Demaratus, a former Spartan king who had joined the Persian court, is supposed to have told Xerxes: "There has never been a time when poverty was not a factor in the rearing of the Greeks, but their courage has been acquired as a result of intelligence and the force of law" (7.102). Intelligence and conscientiousness, psychological virtues, are thus emphasized as far more important to the well-being of a people than mere economic conditions. Later, Herodotus in his own voice argues that the Greek hoplite warrior as a type of soldier was particularly effective against the Persians, defeating the Persian light infantry through superior skill and armor (9.62-63).

According to Herodotus, civic freedom empowered both

---

[84] During Xenophon's later expedition in Persia, a Greek is shamed for his effeminate appearance: "'Actually, he doesn't belong in Boeotia or anywhere in Greece: he has both ears pierced, Lydian-style – I've seen them.' This was true, and they evicted the man from their company" (*Anabasis*, 3.1.29-38).

[85] One has the impression that such stereotyped claims, such as a purported Greek respect for corpses, were also exhortatory: a speaker would seek to convince his fellow-Greeks to engage in good behavior (such as respecting the bodies of the fallen) by appealing to national pride.

Athens and Sparta, albeit in different ways. Sparta was a military aristocracy under a strict, all-encompassing basic law. This did not entail 'individual freedom' or refer to a purely procedural 'rule of law' as moderns understand them. Rather, the semi-legendary lawgiver Lycurgus had bestowed upon Sparta a stern way of life, combining systematic hierarchy and rigorous training. This had welded the Spartans into a powerful martial community. As Demaratus told Xerxes:

> [The Spartans] are as good as anyone in the world when it comes to fighting one on one, but they're the best when it comes to fighting in groups. The point is that although they're free, they're not entirely free: their master is the law, and they're far more afraid of this than your men are of you. At any rate, they do whatever the law commands, and its command never changes: it is that they should not turn tail in battle no matter how many men are range against them, but should maintain their positions and either win or die. (7.104)

Like most ancient thinkers, Herodotus is ambivalent about Athenian democracy, and seems, like Aristotle and Thucydides, to have preferred a moderate regime.[86]

---

[86] In the famous "Persian debate" Herodotus reports a purported conversation on the re-founding of the empire by Darius, in which the Persian leaders debate the merits of democracy, aristocracy, and monarchy. In fact, the discussion reflects contemporary Greek Sophistic political debates. Herodotus defines democracy as a regime of accountability, decision by the people, and election by lot: "it has the best of all names to describe it – equality before the law [isonomia]" (3.80). The Persians however reject democracy noting that "knowledge and the masses are incompatible" (3.81) and "corruption is inevitable in a democracy. . . . This kind of thing goes on until someone emerges as a champion of the people and puts an end to these corrupt politicians" (3.82). They conclude: "Let us leave democracy to Persia's enemies" (3.81). In the end, the Persians choose to follow their traditional way, as though incapable as barbarians of civic self-government: "we should not abolish our ancestral customs, which serve us well" (3.82). Similarly, Herodotus says "[t]he Egyptians found it impossible to live without a king" (2.147).

Nonetheless, Herodotus is clear that the rise of democracy had empowered the Athens by giving each citizen a stake in the polity:

> Athens flourished ... the advantages of everyone having a voice in the political procedure are not restricted just to single instances, but are plain to see wherever one looks. For instance, while the Athenians were ruled by tyrants, they were no better at warfare than any of their neighbors, but once they had got rid of the tyrants they became vastly superior. This goes to show that while they were under an oppressive regime they fought below their best because they were working for a master, whereas as free men each individual wanted to achieve something for himself. (5.78)[87]

For Herodotus, there was no doubt that both aristocratic Sparta and democratic Athens embodied, by their sovereignty and distinct civic ways of life, freedom. We cannot stress enough that the Greek notion of freedom was virile and communitarian, one could say 'illiberal,' and thus completely incompatible with effeminate weakness or individualist solipsism. Herodotus shames the Ionians at some length as soft and effeminate, traits which explain their failure to throw off Persian domination. He says:

> The Scythian opinion of Ionians is that they make the worst and most cowardly free people in the world, but that if they were to think of them as slaves, they would have to say that no master could hope to find more loyal and submissive captives. That is the kind of insult Scythians have hurled at Ionians. (4.142)

During the Ionian Revolt, the rebel leader Dionysius of Phocaea equated hierarchical self-discipline with collective freedom:

---

[87] One is struck at the similarity of Alexis de Tocqueville's statements on the dynamism of American democracy. See Guillaume Durocher, "The Eternal Anglo: Tocqueville's Prophetic History of the United States," *Counter-Currents*, July 28-31.

We can remain free or we can become slaves — and runaway slaves at that. If you are prepared to accept hardship then in the short term there'll be work for you to do, but you will defeat the enemy and be free; if, on the other hand, you choose softness and lack of discipline, I am quite sure that you'll be punished for rebelling against the king. (6.11)

Apparently, this was too much for the Ionians however. After a week of hard labor, defeatist thoughts are supposed to have spread among them: "Anything in the world is better than this misery, even so-called slavery in the future, since it's slavery we're enduring at the moment" (6.12). For the Greeks, freedom did not mean self-gratification, but quite the opposite: having the self-discipline to, among other things, delay gratification.

That effeminacy and cowardice were incompatible with Hellenic citizenship is no surprise, if we consider that the foundation of a *polis* was a military act as well as a religious one. A new *polis* was whatever territory a solidary group of men, a band of brothers, succeeded in imposing their military power and sovereignty over, typically in the face of hostile native states and tribes. The community would endure so long as there were enough courageous men among the citizens to protect against hostile outsiders. The colonial expeditionary force which was typically sent to found a new city was also a military force.

The Greeks thought of military and colonial expeditions as similar undertakings. During the Peloponnesian War, the Athenian general Nicias explicitly compared his army of some 6,000 men in Sicily to a colonial expedition:

You should think of this as like an expedition to establish a colony in an alien and enemy country, when the prime need is to win control of the territory on the very day of landing, in the knowledge that failure will mean a hostile environment at every turn. (Thucydides, 6.23)

Later, while leading the Athenians in this ill-fated expedition, Nicias sought to instill confidence in his forces by comparing them to a city: "You should have in mind that wherever you settle you form an immediate city, and no other city in Sicily will easily resist your attack or dislodge you, once established" (Thucydides, 7.77).

The military nature of the *polis* is also evident in Xenophon's *Anabasis*, his memoir of how he with Ten Thousand other Greek mercenaries fought for a pretender to the Persian throne and, after many adventures, successfully returned to Greece. Following the death of their pretender at the Battle of Cunaxa (401 BC) and the treacherous massacre of the Greek army's generals by the Persians, Xenophon tells of how this motley army was reorganized into a coherent 'marching republic.' We see a kind of summary of the emergence of the *polis* and its communitarian ethics. During their travails, the Ten Thousand must learn to have fruitful political debates, enforce discipline, and impose unity for the sake of the group. The *Anabasis* even concludes with Xenophon's reflecting that "it would be a fine achievement" to convert the wandering army into a new city on the Black Sea (5.6.15-22).

Given the military nature of the *polis*, the Greeks considered that those who performed military service, typically as armored hoplites, were naturally the state's citizens. Indeed, why should anyone be made a citizen of a community if he is unwilling to fight and sacrifice for its very existence? Conversely, even aristocratic Athenians could concede that illiterate workers could be thought entitled to citizenship, insofar as they were necessary to man the navy critical to the city's survival.

A certain manly and martial virtue was then central to the Greek tradition of citizenship. The citizen-soldier's freedom was inseparable from the manly courage necessary to defend it. For Plato, freedom and self-control were impossible without *thumos*, or spiritedness, an innate drive for self-assertion and recognition. Speaking of *andreia*, meaning manliness or courage, Aristotle said that the "courage of the citizen-soldiers" is "most like true courage" (*Nicomachean Ethics*, 3.8).

Finally, while the Greek freedom emphasized the well-being of the community, there was also an individualist strain, insofar as each citizen sought, in a competitive manner, to prove their excellence and worth in the eyes and for the sake of the community. This was a legacy of the Greeks' aristocratic *philotimia*, meaning ambition or literally "love of honor." As Lynette Mitchell notes:

> While the Greeks had a strong sense of community, at the same time in their social actions they also had a strong sense of individualism reflected both in their tendency to compete at both state and individual levels, and in the value they placed on *philotimia*, an individualism which finds its origins in an aristocratic heritage. Indeed, in the classical period *polis* ideology was composed of both elite and egalitarian strands held in tension with each other (so that, for example, Alcibiades can boast that he has competed in the chariot race at the Olympic games, and that the city benefits from his glory).[88]

As Paul Cartledge has observed, pan-Hellenism itself was marked by this ethos, being "a competitive as much as it was a co-operative ideological signifier," even friendly sporting or cultural events were opportunities to compete for excellence and glory.[89]

Philotimia also had a dark side however, for proud men were apt not only to be bold to defend the community, but also to tear it apart, as most memorably recounted in the *Iliad*. As Mitchell observes:

> In the context of the *polis*, "love of honor" directed at the common good of the community was part and parcel of patriotism … Ambition is only useful to the community when it is directed at the common good. Otherwise, it could be a dangerous and destructive force.[90]

This was the competitive, aristocratic, and manly spirit of citizenship which the Persians would come crashing against

---

[88] Mitchell, *Panhellenism and the Barbarian*, 646 (numbers for this work refer to the e-book's reference numbers).

[89] Paul Cartledge, *Ancient Greece: A History in Eleven Cities* (Oxford: Oxford University Press, 2009), p. 201.

[90] Mitchell, *Panhellenism and the Barbarian*, 290.

during their invasion of Greece. The spirit of individual and civic ambition no doubt contributed to the Greeks' incessant internal conflict. But we must never lose sight of the fact that this aggressive spirit was also critical to the Greeks' dynamism: their exploration, their conquests, and especially their unrivalled accomplishments in politics, the arts, and philosophy.

Philotimia, self-assertion for the sake power and excellence, also operated at the level of the collective. The Greeks not only had a strong sense of their own identity but were unabashed about their belief in their own superiority and their right to impose themselves upon others in the struggle for survival. The orator Isocrates expressed this in characteristically frank fashion, observing that the Greek city-states of Europe and Asia had been founded when the Greeks set forth to conquer new lands to overcome their own poverty and internal strife:

> [The Athenians] saw that the barbarians held most of the land, that the Greeks were shut into a small part and that, because of the meagerness of the land, they plotted and made campaigns against each other, and were being destroyed by lack of daily needs and by war, and, consequently, not being able to overlook these things, our city sent our leaders to the other cities, who enlisting the neediest and setting up generals at their head, conquered the barbarians in war and founded cities on both continents [Europe and Asia], settled colonies in the islands, and saved both those who followed and those who remained. (Isocrates, 4.34-5)

'Might is right' was of course the rule of all Bronze Age tribes. However, Greek rule over barbarians was also justified in terms of the Greeks' supposedly unique capacity for freedom. Aristotle was the most famous exponent of this doctrine, meaning that Greeks had a natural right to enslave foreigners, the European barbarians being too savage and the Asian barbarians too womanish for freedom. The enslavement of foreigners provided the Greeks with the leisure to actualize their own potential for freedom. Aristotle, as so often in his politics, was in this respect merely reflecting existing Greek practice and attitudes.[91]

These beliefs may appear arrogant, but one must admit that no other people in the ancient world so engaged in free self-government and rational philosophy. The Greek contributions to politics, culture, science, and philosophy have proved unique and enduring in human history, being referred to and built upon to this very day by nations across the world.[92] The fruits of Hellenic civilization are all around us, down to our very vocabulary. Given this, one cannot equate Hellenic power with a merely punitive and extractive lordship. Rather, the brutalities of Hellenic power, which are typical of human history, also enabled uniquely great political and cultural accomplishments.

An obsession with kinship and ethnicity is very common across human societies. The Greeks were unique however in combining familial and ethnocentric imperatives with a spirited, competitive, and communitarian practice of republican politics, producing an unrivalled biopolitical tradition. Theirs was a distinctly ethnocentric, communitarian, and virile notion of freedom.

PAN-HELLENISM: GREEK IDENTITY & SOLIDARITY

The Greeks fought and sacrificed against the Persians to preserve their freedom, that is to say their independence and civic self-government. This was far from the only reason however. The Greeks also justified their struggle in the name of

---

[91] In the play of the same name, Euripides has Iphigenia say: "It is right for Greeks to rule barbarians, but not, mother, for barbarians to rule Greeks. For the former are slavish, but the latter free" (*Iphigenia in Aulis*, 1400-1). A century later, Demosthenes claimed: "it is right for barbarians to be subject to Greeks" (3.24).

[92] This was of course true of Aristotle himself, whose leisure enabled him to make pioneering work of ethics, biology, physics, and much else which proved influential for centuries. One can ask: would the race have been better served if Aristotle had been unable to dedicate himself to philosophy and science, but instead had been forced by economic necessity to be a potter or a merchant?

the gods and the Greek nation itself. At the height of the conflict, after their city had been evacuated and burned to the ground by the Persians, the Athenians pledged to the Spartans that they would continue the struggle on the grounds of being part of the same people:

> [W]e are all Greeks—one race speaking one language, with temples to the gods and religious rites in common, and with a common way of life. It would not be good for Athens to betray all this shared heritage. So if you didn't know it before, we can assure you that so long as even a single Athenian remains alive, we will never come to terms with Xerxes. (8.144)

The Greeks' kinship circles extended from family, to clan, to city, to all of Greece herself. R. F. Stalley observes that the Greeks had a strong sense of both their common identity and their superiority to barbarians:

> The Greeks believed that they shared a common ancestry. They also shared a loose cluster of beliefs and myths about the gods and heroes which could accommodate local traditions and practice while also allowing them to recognize certain common religious shrines and festivals. But clearly what contributed most to their sense of unity was the possession of a common language (albeit with significant variation of dialect) ... According to this way of thought the Greeks were not just different but better—more intelligent and inventive and more competent in military and other matters.[93]

It seemed natural to the Greeks that, in principle, they ought to be gentle with one another, on the grounds of Herodotus' famous fourfold definition of nationhood: shared blood, language, culture, and gods.

Greek identity was not merely a Herodotean obsession. The ubiquity of pan-Hellenic sentiment from the earliest Greek

---

[93] R. F. Stalley, Introduction, in Aristotle, *Politics*, trans. Ernest Barker and R. F. Stalley, (Oxford: Oxford university Press, 1995), xv.

history is made clear by Lynette Mitchell in her comprehensive work dedicated to the subject.[94] Mitchell summarizes: "the chief themes of Panhellenism that were current from the archaic period to the mid-fourth century [were] community through cult, through kinship and friendship, through joint action in a war against the barbarian, and through shared culture and common values."[95] Greek ethno-cultural pride was a powerful and widespread sentiment not restricted to any particular Greek city or time period. As Mitchell observes, pan-Hellenism was itself "a panhellenic phenomenon" which "was a vibrant, flexible, and coherent collection of themes and representations that brought the Hellenic community to life."[96]

Greek identity, if only in the enumeration of places and peoples considered Hellenic, is evident in the earliest Greek literature, whether in the *Iliad*, the Homeric *Hymn to Apollo*, or the Hesiodic *Catalog of Women*. By these poems and hymns, the Greeks affirmed that they shared in a great war, in gods, and in descent. As early as the seventh century BC, the Olympic Games were already attracting participants from across the Greek world. Mitchell says on "the vitality of Panhellenism" throughout Greek history: "One of the more surprising and exciting elements about Panhellenism is the way it perpetually worked (and still works) to regenerate the Hellenic community."[97]

The ancient Greeks, like traditional peoples in general, were obsessed with kinship and genealogy. It was widely assumed that ties of kinship ought to entail solidarity and that inherited qualities ran in the blood of families and nations. Being a Hellene was assumed to be in part a matter of blood. Claims of kinship or of racial superiority were of course frequently politicized to opportunistically suit particular interests. Cities and royal families imagined common ancestors to justify a contemporary political alliance. Peoples on the edge of the

---

[94] Mitchell, *Panhellenism and the Barbarian*.
[95] *Ibid.*, 59.
[96] *Ibid.*, 48, 662.
[97] *Ibid.*, 652.

Greek world had an interest in claiming Greek ancestry, in order to share in its socio-political relations and prestige. The most obvious example of this are the Macedonian kings, who successfully argued that they were descended from Heracles and thus entitled to participate in the Olympic Games (their Macedonian subjects were nonetheless generally considered by the Greeks to be barbarians).[98]

As is often the case, the Greeks became acutely aware of their own ethnic identity through contact with other peoples. The Greeks of Naucratis, in Asia Minor, built a common cult center known as the Hellenion, probably in the 570s. Mitchell notes that "it is probably significant that it was the *Greeks of Asia Minor* that made this strong statement identity," being on the political and cultural edge of the Greek world.[99] Mitchell claims that "the poem that has come down to us as the *Iliad* with its strong Panhellenic agenda almost certainly went through a significant phase in its development in Asia Minor."[100] While there was mixing with the local Carian communities in Asia Minor, Mitchell observes: "It is striking that, despite the apparent levels of cultural assimilation that occurred in Caria between Hellenes and Carians, the two communities asserted cultural separateness."[101]

The Greeks developed new myths and reinterpretations old ones in ways that resonated with their powerful psychological feelings of shared identity and kinship. The Athenian orator Lysias in his *Olympic Oration* claimed that Heracles, the paradigmatic mythical Greek hero, founded the Olympic Games to promote peace, friendship, and competition among the Hellenes:

---

[98] There is a parallel here with the modern era, in which groups wishing to benefit from the social and economic achievements of northwestern European societies had an interest in claiming to be valid fellow citizens: either by claiming to be White or by arguing that Western ethnic/racial identities are irrelevant.

[99] *Ibid.*, 214.

[100] *Ibid.*, 267.

[101] *Ibid.*, 219.

[Heracles] first assembled this contest out of goodwill for Hellas. For up till this time the cities were estranged from each other, but when this man put an end to tyrants and prevented the violence, he instituted a contest for the body, the ambition of wealth, and display of intellect in the fairest of Hellas, so that we might join together for the sake of all these things alike, both for what we would see and hear. For he considered that the assembly here would be the beginning for the Greeks of friendship towards one another. (Lysias, *Olympian Oration*, 33.1-2)

The Games were accompanied by a sacred truce within Olympia to enable participants to safely attend. Lysias argued that membership in the Greek community entailed reciprocal ties of friendship and lawfulness, the violation of which, as in the case of a warmongering tyrant, was grounds for exclusion.

Similarly, the Trojan War as depicted in the *Iliad* came to be seen as an exemplar of Hellenic unity in the face of Eastern barbarians. Mitchell says: "Homeric epic and what became its 'barbarian war' was an important expression of and a defining moment for Hellenism in the Panhellenic imagination."[102] For Thucydides, the Trojan War was the first "enterprise taken in common by Greece" (Thucydides, 1.3). In time, the Persian Wars themselves, notably as recorded by Herodotus, also came to be seen as a paradigmatic case of Greek unity.

The epic patriotic narratives of the Trojan and Persian Wars—expressing values of honor, glory, and heroism in service of the community—were not mere nostalgia, but were meant to glorify and actualize a living and actual Greek unity: the epics "tell stories for that [Greek] community of it acting as a community in order to justify its existence."[103] A major example of this is Aeschylus' patriotic play *Persians*, which soon after the war commemorated the Greeks' decisive victory over Xerxes. *Persians* is the oldest play in world history that has come down to us intact and, significantly, was partly financed by Pericles and won first prize at the state-sponsored Dionysia

---

[102] *Ibid.*, 176.
[103] *Ibid.*, 67.

festival in 472 BC. While the play displays considerable compassion for the defeated enemy and Persia's suffering widows and fatherless daughters, the Persians are also portrayed as wealth-clutching and weepingly incontinent. Through contrast Aeschylus then emphasizes, much like Herodotus, the Hellenic virtues of austerity, self-control, and virility necessary to civic freedom. *Persians* culminates with Athens' triumph at the Battle of Salamis to the battle cry: "O sons of Greece, go on! Free your fatherland, and free your children, your wives, and the shrines of your paternal gods, and the tombs of your ancestors! Now the struggle is for all!" (*Persians*, 401-05). The political significance of *Persians* political significance was such that one historian goes so far as to call the play "the charter of the Delian league," the anti-Persian alliance of cities which the Athenians established by liberating the Asiatic Greeks.[104] *Persians* was also later performed at Syracuse to celebrate victories over the Carthaginians and Etruscans, a fact suggestive of the play's pan-Hellenic appeal.

The poet Pindar similarly glorified the Sicilian Greeks' struggle against the Semitic Carthaginians, comparing it with the more famous war against the Persians. Plato's *Letters* — written to his friends in Sicily, explaining why his attempts to advise the Syracusan tyrants had failed — present a cogent program for unifying the Sicilian Greek states and expelling the Carthaginian barbarians. The politician Demosthenes, at the twilight of Athenian democracy, later famously urged the Greeks to unite to resist the domination of Philip of Macedon, on this occasion considered a barbarian power. Mitchell observes that an external opponent was central to the ideology of Hellenic unity: "the barbarian as a natural enemy had become an important rhetorical figure, and was raised to the level of ideology."[105]

If war against barbarians appeared natural, one conversely finds Greek writers and orators condemning again and again

---

[104] Thomas Harrison, *The Emptiness of Asia: Aeschylus' Persians and the History of the Fifth Century* (London: 2000), p. 64.

[105] Mitchell, *Panhellenism and the Barbarian*, 425.

conflict among Greeks. Herodotus, Thucydides, Plato, and Isocrates all compared war among Greek states to civil war (*stasis*). In his comedic play *Lysistrata*, Aristophanes has the women of Greece engage in a sex-strike until their husbands put an end to the intra-Greek Peloponnesian War and thus "save Hellas together" (*Lysistrata*, 39-41). In that play, Aristophanes reproaches the Greeks for fighting one another despite "sprinkling altars with the same holy water like kinsmen at Olympia, Pylae, and Pytho" (*Lys.*, 1128-34).

The pan-Hellenists also made practical proposals, urging their fellow-citizens to serve common Greek interests. Aristotle reports an argument paralleling civic and national loyalty: "If an individual should care for your reputation, citizens, then you should all care for that of the Greeks" (*Rhetoric*, 2.23). The sophist Gorgias argued in his *Olympic Oration*, probably delivered in 408 BC, for concord among Greek cities, that they should stop envying each other's possessions and conquer barbarian lands instead. Isocrates, who lived during the tumultuous period between the beginning of the fratricidal Peloponnesian War and the rise of Alexander the Great as Greek hegemon, is a remarkable figure in representing in many ways the culmination of pan-Hellenic sentiment, complete with an ambitious geopolitical program. In speech after speech, Isocrates urged Greek unity under the leadership of some hegemon, whether Athens or Macedon, joined together through a common crusade against Persia, so as to liberate the Asiatic Greeks and seize the untold wealth of Asia. He went so far as to argue that war against the barbarian was "more like a sacred mission than a military expedition" (Isocrates, 4.181-85). He thought it disgraceful that Asia was wealthier than Greece and argued that Greece's excess humanity, whether political exiles or impoverished masses, should be sent there.

The pan-Hellenist project would to a certain extent by actualized by Alexander the Great's stunning victories against Persia in 334-330 BC. Alexander made the Greeks one of the more privileged nations of his empire and his conquests spread Hellenistic civilization from Egypt all the way to India. The youthful world-conqueror deployed substantial pan-Hellenist propaganda to justify his wars and brutalities: in razing the rebellious city of Thebes, he cited that state's collaboration with the Persians generations earlier, while the conquest of Persia was justified by the liberation of the Asiatic Greeks and retaliation for the previous Persian invasions. The monarchies which succeeded Alexander's vast empire would also appeal to Hellenic freedom in their propaganda.

PAN-HELLENIC SENTIMENT & UNITY IN THE PERSIAN WARS

Pan-Hellenic sentiment was particularly present during the Persian Wars. One cannot exaggerate the pervasiveness of the rhetoric of kinship and pan-Hellenic identity throughout the conflict. Again and again in Herodotus, various parties demand others to sacrifice or justify their own sacrifice in the war on grounds of kinship. The Athenians were convinced by one speaker to resist the Persians because then they would be "remembered as long as there are people alive on this Earth" and would become "the leader of Greece" (6.109). The Spartans said that in general it was wrong for any "Greek state" to collaborate with the Persians (8.142). On grounds of kinship, the Athenian leader Themistocles urged the Ionian Greeks serving in the Persian army to defect, be neutral, or fight beneath their best: "Men of Ionia, it is wrong of you to fight against your ancestral line and to enslave Greece" (8.22). At the end of the war, the Asiatic Ionians appealed to the allies: "I urge you to rescue us, Greeks like yourselves, from slavery and to fight back against the foreign invaders" (9.90). The kind of Macedon said he risked giving secret information to the allies on grounds of his Greek ancestry: "I wouldn't be telling you this if I didn't care so deeply for Greece as a whole. My family background makes me a Greek myself, and would hate to see Greece lose its freedom and become enslaved" (9.45). Xerxes himself allegedly argued to Argos that the Persians were descended from Perseus, and hence were related to them.[106]

---

[106] Xerxes said: "we are descended from Argive stock. It follows that it would be wrong for us to make war on you, since you are our ancestral line, and it would be wrong for you to take up arms against

Pan-Hellenic rhetoric also extended into the later periods documented by Thucydides and Xenophon. During the Peloponnesian War, the Spartans justified their war against Athens in the name of the freedom of the Greek city-states in the face of an overbearing hegemon.[107] During that war, rhetoric surrounding kinship between cities and intra-Greek ethnic groups was pervasive.[108] Pan-Hellenic rhetoric is similarly pervasive in Xenophon's *Anabasis* and *Hellenica*, the latter being a history covering roughly Sparta's later hegemony and fall. The Spartan commander Lysander killed an Athenian general for having executed Andrian and Corinthian prisoners at sea, saying: "What do you deserve for having been the first to act like a criminal towards your fellow Greeks?"[109] The Asiatic Greek city of Cebrene, under Persian control, would surrender to the Spartans saying: "the Greeks were opposed to the actions of their commander; they themselves would rather be on the side of their fellow-Greeks than on that of the foreigners."[110]

These professions of Hellenic loyalty may be considered merely opportunistic propaganda, and no doubt they often were. Nonetheless, the fact that claims of Hellenic kinship were so present in the propaganda of Greek city-states is significant in itself, showing that they believed ethnic rationalizations for their actions would resonate emotionally with both themselves and others.

The Greeks occasionally avoided conflict and encouraged collaboration with one another on grounds of their shared Hellenic identity. The oracle of Apollo at Delphi, which was frequently consulted on decisions such as whether to undertake military or colonial expeditions, seems to have

---

us by siding with others" (7.150).

[107] According to Thucydides: "The general feeling among the Greeks was very much in favor of the Spartans, especially since they had proclaimed that they were liberating Greece" (Thucydides, 2.8).

[108] See Maria Fragoulaki, *Kinship in Thucydides: Intercommunal Ties and Historical Narrative* (Oxford: Oxford University Press, 2013).

[109] Xenophon, *Hellenica*, 2.1.32.

[110] *Ibid.*, 3.1.18.

encouraged Greek solidarity. Xenophon reports that "it was an ancient and established principle that Greeks should not consult the oracle with regard to a war waged against Greeks."[111] On one occasion, the oracle "urged all Greek states to help the Cyreneans in their project of colonizing Libya" in the face of the hostile natives (4.159).

While the Greeks often enslaved their co-nationals, there was often the feeling, expressed in Plato, Xenophon, and Aristotle, that such behavior should be reserved for barbarians. After the failure of the Ionian Revolt, Dionysius abandoned his position as admiral to begin a career in piracy: "he headed straight for Phoenicia, just as he was, where he made himself rich by sinking merchant ships. Then he went to Sicily and set himself as a pirate with his base there; he used to attack Carthaginian and Tyrrhenian [i.e. central Italian] ships, but left Greek shipping alone" (6.17). Much later, the Spartan commander Callicratidas refused to make slaves of captured Methymnaeans and Athenians, as "no Greek should be sold as a slave, if he could help it."[112]

The Persians were often concerned about the ethnic loyalties of their Greek subjects. They would occasionally try to isolate Greeks from one another and avoid situations in which their Greek subjects would need fight to against their co-ethnics. On one occasion, the King was urged to separate the Ionian rebel leader Histiaeus, who had once served the Persians, from his fellow Greeks (5.23). On another, the King was warned that the Ionians would be unreliable soldiers in Greece, despite having long been a part of the Persian Empire:

> In my judgment, you shouldn't lead the Ionians against their Athenian fathers, even though the Ionians have been tribute-paying subjects of Persia ever since Cyrus the son of Cambyses ... if they come with us they'll either have to reduce their mother city [Athens] to slavery or help her win her freedom. In other words, they'll have to choose between committing a terrible crime and behaving with integrity.

---

[111] *Ibid.*, 3.2.22.
[112] *Ibid.*, 1.6.14.

(7.51)

The effects of such ethnic loyalties during the war appear to have been slight however. At the later naval battle at Artemisium, "some of the Ionians in the Persian fleet, who were pro-Greek and had joined the expedition against their will, were very concerned at the sight of the Greeks being surrounded" (8.10). However, "[a]ll the others, though, were delighted with the situation" and eager to seize Athenian vessels. Herodotus says only a single Greek commander, Antidorus of Lemnos, defected to the Greek allies on that occasion (8.11).

Later at the more decisive battle of Salamis, Herodotus says that despite the urging of the Athenian leader Themistocles, "only a few of the Ionians ... deliberately fought below their best; the rest of them fought as normal" (8.85). At the final decisive battle of Plataea, Herodotus says that the non-Boeotian (i.e. non-Theban) Greeks on the Persian side "deliberately fought below their best" (9.67).[113] Thus, while ethnic loyalty could make itself felt and was often a headache for the Persians in managing their subjects, this was rarely a major impediment.

THE CHALLENGE OF HELLENIC UNITY

There was undeniably a strong feeling of shared national and cultural identity among the Greeks. However, if one looks at the sweep of ancient Greek history, one is struck by the disconnect between a pervasive rhetoric expressing pan-Hellenic sentiment and the political reality of division and often brutal wars among Greeks. Pan-Hellenism, however powerful emotionally, was often politically inoperative. As Mitchell notes: "despite the common peace treaties and numerous calls for unity and war against the barbarian from Panhellenists such as Isocrates and Demosthenes, the Greek states were almost continuously at war with each other in one context or another until the mid-fourth century and Philip II of

---

[113] Herodotus' consistent portrayal of Thebes as a collaborator state would greatly anger the later Boeotian historian Plutarch, who would call his predecessor "the father of lies."

Macedon's 'League of Corinth' was formed in 337."[114]

The *polis*' demand of total loyalty from its citizens meant that there were few qualms about annihilating fellow Greeks, if this was in the city's immediate interest. Furthermore, it is often difficult to determine the degree to which patriotic sentiment actually underpinned the Greek states' resistance to the Persians, as opposed to merely being eloquent rationalizations for narrowly political interests, such as Athens and Sparta's desire not to be dominated by any foreign power, Greek or not. Indeed, Herodotus says that one city, Phocia, opportunistically sided with the allies purely because its traditional enemy, Thessalia, sided with the Persians (8.30). The collaboration of individual politicians[115] and cities with the Persians was common. Indeed, the city of Delphi itself medized. In short, as so often in our history, broader ethnic and civilizational interests were ignored in the face of narrow state or personal interests. One is struck at how tenuous and exceptional was the Greek allies' unity. While they may have called themselves "the Greeks," they in fact only made up about one-in-ten continental Greek cities, the rest remaining neutral or collaborating. All that said, the allies' unity ultimately proved sufficient to repulse the invaders.

Though far less discussed than the *polis*, the Greeks did have a quite venerable tradition of confederalism, that is to say, of forming leagues of city-states. The league—combining joint temples, a common council, arbitration, military alliance, and coinage, with greater or lesser degrees of central authority—was a common feature in Greek political history. Shared ethno-regional identity was a common basis for the formation of a league of cities, as in Arcadia, Boeotia, Crete, and Ionia. Sparta and later Athens each led their own military alliances as hegemonic cities.

The league projected the basis features of the familial

---

[114] Mitchell, *Panhellenism and the Barbarian*, 107.

[115] For example. at the end of the wars, the Spartan general Pausanias collaborated with the Persians and was rumored to wish to become "the tyrant of all Greece" (5.32).

religion beyond the city to a regional commonwealth: shared blood and gods sealed the alliance of cities in a league, including notably a shared holy sanctuary, just as the family household and the *polis* were sacred spaces. However, the league was typically not a true federal state or sovereign federation, but a coalition of cities each with their own army and jealous of their civic sovereignty. The confederal league then never had the solidity of the *polis*. The various leagues tended to fluctuate in their effectiveness as the necessity of unity (typically to acquire military scale) was in constant tension with the centrifugal tendency caused by each city's desire for autonomy. In practice, a league tended to do well if it had a hegemonic city which could impose decisive leadership or, if led by two cities, if these leader-cities were in basic agreement. Rebellion and subjugation of cities was common. The Greek leagues failed to scale beyond small regions and it is not surprising that they eventually fell to the far larger powers that were Macedon and Rome. The ancient Greek leagues in their fragility were not unlike later fractious confederations of sovereigns, such as the Hanseatic League, the *antebellum* United States, the German Confederation, or the European Union.

Given the fragility of the league, moderns will be less surprised to learn that despite the Greeks' strong sense of identity, it rarely occurred to them to seek to achieve *political* unity. This was not so much due to lack of imagination — Plato and Isocrates did make concrete proposals for Greek unity at the expense of barbarians — but due to the sheer impracticalities of federalism in an age before telecommunications. In the premodern world, as Montesquieu later remarked, scale was only possible for monarchies, not for republics.[116]

External threats were perhaps the most important driver of

---

[116] With the rise of modern telecommunications, polities were able to expand to their natural optimal size: the nation-state. If a polity expanded beyond a single a single ethny, the natural sensitive pride of each constituent nation made keeping together such multinational states difficult, often leading to secession. The development of national pride itself was facilitated by the telecommunications and mass education of the modern era.

Greek unity. Prior to the Persian conquest, the twelve Ionian cities of Asiatic Greece were united in a loose league. These Ionians met together to worship Poseidon, compete in sports, and hold council at a joint sanctuary known as Panionion. During the Ionians' brief independence between Lydian and Persian overlordships, the philosopher Thales of Miletus—famous for his feats of mathematics, astronomy, and engineering—proposed that the twelve kindred cities should unite into a genuine political federation and "establish a single governmental council, that should be in Teos (because Teos is centrally located in Ionia), and that all the other towns should be regarded effectively as demes [i.e. districts]" (1.170). Ionia however lacked any city with the preponderance to be a natural leader, as Athens and Sparta were in mainland Greece, and proved too fractious to resist the Persians. Another proposal, not carried out, was that instead of accepting Persian rule "the Ionians should pool their resources, set sail for Sardinia, and then found a single city for all Ionians," with the goal of establishing a powerful and independent mercantile state.

Interestingly, Herodotus often has the Persians complaining about the disunity and fractiousness of the Greeks. One Persian governor "sent for representatives from the [subjugated] states and forced the Ionians to submit their disputes to arbitration instead of raiding and plundering one another" (6.42). Mardonius, one of the leading Persian generals during the second invasion, was amazed at the Greek propensity for infighting and said: "What [the Greeks] should do, since they all speak the same language, is make use of heralds and messengers to settle their differences, since anything would be preferable to fighting" (7.9).

Herodotus himself laments Greek disunity. In the context of divisions between cities in the Greek alliance, he uses the expression *stasis*—a term usually used for civil strife or war within cities—and more specifically *emphylo stasis* or "intra-tribal conflict." He says: "internal dissension is worse than a united war effort to the same degree that war is worse than peace" (8.3). Herodotus' expression suggests that Greek ethnic unity should have been the natural state of affairs.

In practice, Greek unity during the Persian Wars was often tenuous. During the first Persian invasion in 492-90 BC, in which the Persians secured Thrace, Macedon, and the Cyclades, Athens alone won the battle of Marathon against Xerxes, the famously pious Spartans having apparently been held up due to a religious festival (6.109). During the second invasion of 480-79 BC, Xerxes achieved titanic feats such as digging a canal at the isthmus of Mount Athos and sending perhaps 200,000 soldiers and 600 warships. The resisting Greek states formed an alliance called the Greek League and held a congress of the 70 participating members at Corinth, but had no governmental apparatus as such. These states represented only about a tenth of the 700 Greek cities in the mainland. These patriots, a critical minority, assumed ultimate authority over their nation as a whole and were to have a decisive impact on its destiny. The allies swore an oath promising to punish those who had betrayed their Greek nationality:

> These peoples were the object of an oath sworn by those of the Greeks who resisted the Persian invasion to the following effect: that after the successful conclusion of the war all those who had surrendered of their own free will to the Persian, despite being Greeks, were to have a tenth of their property made over to the god of Delphi. (7.132)

The allies shared plunder and could annihilate collaborator states. Although, one must say, the Greeks did not need pan-Hellenic justification to raze each other's cities. The allies justified their authority as representing "[a]ll the Greeks who had the best interests of Greece at heart" (7.172). The Spartans later proposed depopulating collaborator-states and resettling them with the Ionians of Asia Minor (9.106; the Athenians however objected to both Spartan interference in Ionian affairs and to the evacuation of the Asian cities).

The Spartans were given supreme command on land and the Athenians at sea. The Greek League was a fractious alliance however, and by no means a state, dependent for its survival ultimately on the good will and relations between the two leading cities: Athens and Sparta, who did have divergent interests. Athens was in Attica, closer to Persian power, and thus was burned down. Sparta was in the Peloponnesian peninsula and had an interest in delaying fighting until the Persians made their way south and even considered abandoning Athens to merely fortify the Peloponnesian isthmus. Both Athens and Sparta had to show goodwill: the Athenians in not coming to terms with the Persians despite the torching of their city, the Spartans in risking battle at Thermopylae before they were directly threatened in the Peloponnese.

The ability of political interests to override ethnic ones is clearly visible in the case of Syracuse. The Greek allies had sent messengers across the Mediterranean—to Sicily, Corcyra, and Crete—to ask various Greek cities to join their alliance: "The idea was to try to find a way to unite the whole of the Greek world—to get everyone to think and act in concert—on the grounds that all Greeks were equally threatened by the imminent danger" (7.145). Syracuse was a Greek city-state in Sicily which under a series of tyrants had risen to great power, ruthlessly destroying cities and rearranging populations on the island (including moving them to Syracuse and making them citizens). The allies asked the tyrant Gelon for assistance as a fellow Greek: "your rulership of Sicily means that quite a large portion of Greece is in your hands, so we are asking you to support those of us who are fighting for the freedom of Greece and join our struggle" (7.157). According to Herodotus, Gelon was open to helping the allies, offering them hundreds of ships and tens of thousands of troops. However, this came to nothing for reasons of petty-politics and prestige: Gelon asked to be given supreme command of the overall Greek forces, something which the Spartans rejected. Gelon then offered to be made commander only at sea, but the Athenians rejected that. So much for the politics of prestige ...

THE TRIUMPH OF GREEK FREEDOM

Despite lack of Syracusan support, Athenian and Spartan unity and combined naval and land power proved sufficient to defeat the Persians. The legendary sacrifice of King Leonidas and his 300 Spartans at Thermopylae in 480 BC was less significant militarily than in showing Sparta's willingness to fight and die for her allies and indeed Greece. Without this sacrifice, perhaps Athens would have come to terms. The Athenians for their part at the same time fought the Battle of Artemisium at sea, sinking hundreds of Persian ships. Herodotus says: "In both cases the Greeks' rallying cry was to stop the foreigners entering Greece" (8.15).

That same year, the largely-Athenian fleet defeated the Persians at sea at Salamis. Finally, in 479 BC the Athenians and Spartans defeated the Persians together on land at Plataea. A Greek praised the Spartan Pausanias for his victory at Plataea in the following words:

> The god has allowed you to earn more fame than anyone else we know of, for saving Greece. What you need to do now is follow up this achievement, to enhance your reputation even more and to make any foreigner in the future think twice before committing obscene crimes against Greeks. (9.78)

In fact, the conservative Spartans showed little interest in retaliating against Persia following the collapse of Xerxes' great project. The Athenians however boldly counter-attacked, began liberating Asiatic Greek cities, and established their own Delian League, which would gradually become an Athenian empire. This league was justified on grounds of the unity needed to ward off the Persians and the shared Ionian kinship of most of its constituent states. Greece would enjoy a half-century of peace before the onset of the Peloponnesian War between Athens and Sparta. Some Greeks believed that the gods themselves had been angered by the arrogant Persian ambition of intercontinental world-government. As the Athenian leader Themistocles said: "the gods and the heroes [divinized ancestors] did not want to see a single man ruling both Asia and Europe" (8.109).

By their triumph in the Persian Wars, the Greeks preserved their sovereignty and identity, setting the stage for the Golden

Age of Athenian power and philosophy. The Greeks triumphed because of the winning combination of their culture of civic freedom and solidarity, and the successful alliance between Athens and Sparta, which required both cities to adopt a conciliatory attitude. Herodotus' *Histories* are a poignant commemoration of the fragility and value of Greek unity. Whether in the Athenians' retreat *en masse* from their city rather than surrender or in the fight to the death of Leonidas and his 300 at Thermopylae, the Greeks' struggle against Persia provides an exemplar of unity and sacrifice for national freedom which has resounded throughout the ages. As Mitchell notes: "the Persian Wars became the basis for a utopian vision of the symbolic community, which the Greeks then looked back on as the ultimate example of not only what the Hellenes should achieve but also what the Hellenic community should be."[117] The later Greco-Roman historian Polybius bestowed the highest praise on Herodotus and other historians for having given future generations such powerful inspiration for their own struggles:

> Those who preserved and passed on to us records of the Persian invasion of Greece ... have enormously helped the Greeks in their struggles on one another's behalf for independence, because if someone bears in mind the part played by the extraordinary and the unexpected on those occasions, and remembers how many myriads of men were, for all their fearlessness and their armament, destroyed by the resolve and the resources of those who faced danger intelligently and rationally, he will not be dismayed by immense quantities of supplies and weapons, and hordes of troops, into abandoning all hope and failing to fight for his land and the country of his birth. (Polybius, 2.35)

In the Persian Wars, the Greeks showed that a small and scattered people could, with luck, skill, and determination, triumph even over the greatest empire of the day. This example can still inspire us today and discredit all defeatism. In their

---

[117] Mitchell, *Panhellenism and the Barbarian*, 275.

victory, the Greeks were able to pass down an enormous political, cultural, and scientific heritage to all generations ever since. No wonder John Stuart Mill could claim: "The Battle of Marathon, even as an event in British history, is more important than the Battle of Hastings."

The Greeks were acutely aware their shared ethno-cultural identity and their difference from barbarians. Pan-Hellenic sentiment and idealism runs as a shining thread across the entire Greek tradition—in Homer and Herodotus' commemoration of pan-Hellenic wars against Eastern enemies, in Plato and Aristotle's biopolitical philosophies, and in Isocrates and perhaps Xenophon's dreams of a pan-Hellenic conquest of Persia, later realized by Alexander the Great. Pan-Hellenic ideas and sentiment were also expressed by many others: the playwrights Aeschylus and Aristophanes, the orators Lysias, Gorgias, and others. Tremendous pride in their shared race and civilization is one of the most striking characteristics of the ancient Greeks.

The idea of Greek freedom against Asiatic slavery has also been a common theme in later times, especially with the modern rise in republican and democratic self-government. There has been a tendency, notably among neoconservatives, of equating Western civilization with the values of freedom and democracy. There is truth to this of course insofar as a high degree of individualism and civic government are to a large extent Western phenomena. Even so, the *reduction* of Western identity to demoliberal values is absurd, if one only considers our long history in the eras of hunter-gathering, barbaric tribes, the Roman Empire, the feudal Middle Ages, or the absolutism of the Enlightenment, to not speak of modern experiments in authoritarian government. Western civilization is not synonymous with liberal democracy or the latest ever-more individualist and egalitarian iterations of 'human rights,' nor with Western liberal establishments' quest to impose these as the sole ruling ideology across the entire world.

Certainly, the pursuit of freedom is central to Western civilization and to the very being of European man. However, this must be well understood: The Greek conception of freedom was fundamentally communitarian, ethnocentric, and virile. For Herodotus, Sparta as a military aristocracy was as "free" as democratic Athens, for the Spartans adhered to a holistic rule of law. Athens for its part was dynamic, powerful, and marked by an exceptionally fertile cultural and intellectual life, but her democratic excesses were often lamented. The Greek notion of freedom was fundamentally ethnopolitical: civic life did not mean defending mere 'values' as such, let alone imposing them on outsiders. Rather, Hellenic freedom meant participating in the collective flourishing of an organic community defined by shared blood and gods.

ARISTOTLE
THE BIOPOLITICS OF THE CITIZEN-STATE

The texts that have come down to us from Antiquity were written for a time and place very different from our own. Their very origins are often mysterious, and yet, their concerns often speak to us very directly. We do not even know how Aristotle's *Politics*, his main political treatise, were edited. They appear to be the philosopher's fossilized lecture notes, which he would have used when teaching in his Lyceum, or were perhaps drafted to enable students not present to read them privately.

By their nature, the *Politics* are an excellent introduction to ancient Greek political practice and philosophy, and one which can be fruitfully read even by young minds. Aristotle's pedagogical method, presenting the apparent data (*phainomena*) and various opinions of learned men (*endoxa*) is particularly helpful: he provides an almost encyclopedic overview of the opposing viewpoints which were prevalent and of the practices of the various ancient city-states. We get a strong sense of the issues and debates which were already agitating our people. Aristotle's insights concerning the nature of responsible citizenship and the dangers of excessive egalitarianism and diversity remain relevant to this day.

Aristotle's political thought—at least in the surviving works—does not soar to the eugenic and spiritual heights of Plato. However, Aristotle's moderate and pragmatic brand of politics is much more palatable to someone raised in modern liberalism, while at the same time being a better introduction to the communitarian and aristocratic political ethics of the ancient Greeks. What was really unique about the Greek experiment of the city-states was the practice of citizenship. Never before and rarely since, even within the Western world, has a substantial body of the people been so involved in their own collective self-government. We would be mistaken however in equating citizenship in the ancient *polis* with that of the republicanism of the Enlightenment, let alone that of the postwar liberal democracies.

In his *Nicomachean Ethics*, a companion piece to the *Politics* dedicated to his son Nicomachus, Aristotle argues that one should have as much respect for unreflective views won from practical experience as for abstract arguments: "we ought to attend to the undemonstrated sayings and opinions of experienced and older people or of people of practical wisdom not less than to demonstrations; for experience has given them an eye they see aright" (6.11). Aristotle's politics were conventional for an upper-class Greek:[118] support for a moderate regime based on the rule of law and a sizable middle-class of citizen-soldiers. However, as we shall see, he also rationalizes traditional Greek politics in biological terms with novel scientific foundations and philosophical ends.

Aristotle embraced the ethnocentric, communitarian, and virile traditions of the Greek *polis*. For the Greeks, the ideal of citizenship meant neither a guarantee of a set of arbitrary 'inalienable rights' as ends in themselves nor the privilege of simply doing as one pleased. Rather, they believed that the good of the individual necessarily depended upon the good of the whole, to which all had to sacrifice when necessary. Citizenship meant not rights, but *participation in the setting and enforcement of duties*. As Aristotle eloquently puts it, citizenship is "to rule and be ruled in turn." In the Greek city-state, this meant varying degrees of participation in the Assembly, the courts, and political and military offices. For Aristotle, as for the Greeks in general, citizenship was incompatible with egalitarian excess, decadence, and effeminacy.

In considering the possible structures of government discussed by Aristotle, we ought to bear in mind the sheer diversity of Greek polities scattered around the Mediterranean: the commercial-democratic imperial metropolis of Athens, the agrarian and austere military aristocracy of Sparta, the

---

[118] Perhaps we would have a different impression if Aristotle's dialogues had survived, in which he might have allowed himself more artistic and paradoxical flair in the vein of Plato.

multiethnic tyranny of Syracuse, traditional monarchies, the democratic federations of Boeotia and Arcadia, tribal confederacies ... the Ancients were certainly far more tolerant of diversity in forms of government than postwar Moderns are.

The Greek city-state could indeed be extremely intrusive. By modern liberal standards, it was not just authoritarian but 'totalitarian,' not recognizing a private life wholly free from politics and seeing the state as having a decisive role in the formation of culture. Aristotle himself recognized that law and culture were thoroughly intertwined, as "laws resting on unwritten custom are even more sovereign, and concerned with issues of still more sovereign importance, than written laws" (1287a32). The state's role included the definition and enforcement of positive cultural norms and customs. Economic, family, and religious life could be sharply regulated, so that all would acquire healthy habits promoting the common good. The *polis'* unique system of government was possible because of the intimacy of the city—generally not numbering more than 50,000 people, with far less citizens. The citizens were bound together by ties of kinship, personally knew the leading politicians directly, and participated on a day-to-day basis in civic life, whether as jurors, assemblymen, or soldiers. Thus for Aristotle, citizenship would not be possible if the whole Peloponnesian peninsula were a single state or indeed if the super-city of Babylon were a republic.

In practice, ancient Greek politics was defined by the choosing of office-holders, the deciding of policies, the holding of trials, and the more-or-less amicable debates surrounding these. Depending on the kind of regime, hereditary kings, elected councils, or even the entire citizenry gathered in assembly would decide on such matters. In domestic affairs, the state would regulate and supervise the marketplace, countryside, and marriages, spend on public works, organize military forces on land and sea, decide on immigration, define the legally-recognized classes of citizens, and censor or promote various forms of culture. The more ambitious cities, such as Sparta, sought to regulate reproduction, systematically educate the youth, and organize the citizens' common meals, gymnastics, and military training.

In foreign affairs, the state would decide on war and peace, the formation of alliances and confederations, economic embargoes, the subsidizing of allies, the extermination or enslavement of enemies, the establishment of puppet regimes, and overseas colonization. The stakes were high: failure to maintain goodwill among citizens often led to gruesome civil wars and conquest by invaders, including fellow Greeks. The *polis* as a system of government was a demanding one which was eventually superseded by the great universal empires. Nonetheless, it served the Greeks well for centuries, enabling their expansion across the Mediterranean and unprecedented experiments in self-government. The *polis* allowed for an astonishing diversity of forms of governments and corresponding achievements, from the martial prowess and stability of Sparta to the economic, political, and cultural dynamism of Athens.

ARISTOTLE'S BIOPOLITICAL FOUNDATIONS

If Aristotle's politics appear broadly conventional, his justification for the *polis* is novel and sophisticated: he grounds that splendid society on a surer foundation—nature—and a higher end—reason. For Aristotle, as for the ancient philosophers in general, ethics is founded upon the recognition of the inequality, unity, and nature of things. In brief: the better should lead the worse, all should recognize that each plays a role as a particular part of wider whole, and one must respect the nature of each thing.

Uniquely, Aristotle's politics are, to a surprisingly 'modern' degree, grounded in biology. For if Aristotle was not a spiritual leader in the mold of Plato, he was an outstanding scientist, and indeed the first to leave us a massive corpus of empirical data, analysis, and theory, notably in the field of biology. As D'Arcy Wentworth Thompson observed:

> The influence ... of scientific study, and in particular of Biology, is not far to seek in Aristotle's case. It has ever since been a commonplace to compare the state, the body politic,

with an organism, but was Aristotle who first employed the metaphor ... Just as in order to understand fishes, he gathered all kinds together, recording their forms, their structure, and their habits, so he did with the Constitutions of cities and states.... . But whatever else Aristotle is, he is the great Vitalist, the student of the Body with the Life thereof, the historian of the Soul.[119]

Aristotle had a teleological view of nature and biology: every species is naturally fitted for a particular end, fulfilling a particular role in the cosmic order. What is 'natural' to an organism is that which allows it to actualize that species' potential and final end. One's nature is both one's existing condition and one's end: the nature of a flourishing acorn is to become a mighty oak.

Aristotle's ethics and politics aimed at human *eudaimonia*, meaning "happiness," or rather "flourishing" and "well-being" in this very specific sense: that human beings fulfil their potential as a rational and social species.[120] As species differ in character and end, it follows for Aristotle that there is "a different philosophic wisdom about the good of each species" (*NE*, 6.7). For Aristotle, to respect one's nature, in fact meaning

---

[119] D'Arcy Wentworth Thompson, *On Aristotle as Biologist* (Oxford: Clarendon Press, 1913), p. 25.

[120] In *The Descent of Man*, Darwin seems to endorse a eudaimonic ethics:

In the case of the lower animals it seems much more appropriate to speak of their social instincts, as having been developed for the general good rather than for the general happiness of the species. The term, *general good, may be defined as the rearing of the greatest number of individuals in full vigour and health, with all their faculties perfect, under the conditions to which they are subjected.* As the social instincts both of man and the lower animals have no doubt been developed by nearly the same steps, it would be advisable to take as the standard of morality, the general good or welfare of the community, rather than the general happiness; but this definition would perhaps require some limitation account of political ethics. (Darwin, *The Descent of Man*, p. 145)

our biological nature, is to realize that an organism does not prosper in every circumstance: just as an oak tree does not thrive in every soil or climate, so humans do not flourish under just any set of laws. Aristotle makes his the conventional pagan conception of human happiness:

> Gentle [i.e. aristocratic] birth, a wide circle of friends, a virtuous circle of friends, wealth, creditable offspring, extensive offspring, and a comfortable old age; also the physical virtues (e.g. health, beauty, strength, size, and competitive prowess), reputation, status, good luck, and virtue. (*Rhetoric*, 1.5)

Aristotle's is a remarkably holistic and biological view of human flourishing. There is that naïvely pagan and aristocratic assumption that happiness would indeed mean that we would wish ourselves and our posterity to be as beautiful and healthy as possible. Aristotle's *unabashed* ethics are typically Hellenic: there is no egalitarian consolation for the ugly and the misbegotten, there is no pretense that *all* human beings can be happy and actualized. Rather, Aristotle, like the Greeks in general, celebrates excellence.

Aristotle claims that what makes humans unique relative to other animals is our capacity for *reason*, that highest part of us. As individuals, we must "so far as we can, make ourselves immortal, and strain every nerve to live in accordance with the best thing in us" (*NE*, 10.7). As a society, the pursuit of excellence is understood as creating the conditions for man to exercise his reason, both in terms of rational civic self-government and philosophical and scientific inquiry. For Aristotle, human societies should not be organized for 'individual happiness' but rather must be organized so as to achieve collective excellence.

This vision is in fact unabashedly communitarian and aristocratic: Firstly, the human species cannot flourish and fulfill its natural role unless it survives and reproduces itself in the right conditions; secondly, the society must be organized so as to grant the intellectually-gifted and culturally-educated minority the leisure to exercise their reason.

The state's purpose is then to fulfill our nature, not merely by securing the existence of the community, but enabling the gifted minority to engage in rational activity. Aristotle famously said that "man is by nature a political animal" (1253a2), by which he meant that he can neither lead a civilized life outside of a community, nor fulfill his nature as a rational being outside of a *polis*. As politics is humanity's ultimate exercise in the self-determination of its destiny, Aristotle considered it to be the highest branch of ethics and indeed "most truly the master art" (*NE*, 1.2). Politics was then for Aristotle a noble undertaking grounded in human biology: the *polis* is at once "a certain number of citizens" (1274b38), "the most sovereign of all [human associations]," and, therefore, "directed to the most sovereign of goods" (1252a1), and "the final and perfect association" (1252b27).

Aristotle's premises about inequality, unity, and nature have profound implications for his biopolitics. They demand that the city be rationally and hierarchically organized, with individual interests yielding to the collective interests of the community as an organic whole. This includes regulation of reproduction and education. The implications are perhaps made clearest by the philosopher's biological analogies:

> [I]t is clearly natural and beneficial to the body that it should be ruled by the soul, and again it is natural and beneficial to the affective part of the soul that it should be ruled by the reason and the rational part; whereas the equality of the two elements, or their reverse relation, is always detrimental. (1254b2)

> [T]here must necessarily be a union or pairing of those who cannot exist without one another. Male and female must unite for the reproduction of the species—not from deliberate intention, but from the natural impulse, which exists in animals generally as it also exists in plants, to leave behind them something of the same nature as themselves. Next, there must necessarily be a union of the naturally ruling element with the element which is naturally ruled, for the preservation of both. The element which is able, by

virtue of its intelligence, to exercise forethought, is naturally a ruling and master element; the element which is able, by virtue of its bodily power, to do the physical work, is a ruled element, which is naturally in a state of slavery, and master and slave have accordingly a common interest. (1252a24)

If politics is aimed at the good of the city, then this means policy should seek to improve the citizenry, which Aristotle understands in both a biological and cultural sense, for again, "a city is a certain number of citizens." Hence, Aristotle considers education and population policies to be of fundamental importance and are practically the first duties of the state. Aristotle's communitarian ethos is made particularly clear in his comments on education. He writes: "All would agree that the legislator should make the education of the young his chief and foremost concern" (1337a11). Furthermore:

> The city as a whole has a single end. Evidently, therefore, the system of education must also be one and the same for all, and the provision of this system must be a matter of public action. It cannot be left, as at present, to private enterprise, with each parent making provision privately for his own children, and having them privately instructed as he himself thinks fit. Training for an end which is common should also itself be common. We must not regard a citizen as belonging just to himself: we must rather regard every citizen as belonging to the city, since each is a part of the city, and the provision made for each part will naturally be adjusted to the provision made for the whole. (1337a21)

ARISTOTLE'S REPUBLIC OF VIRTUE

From these biopolitical premises, Aristotle wholeheartedly agreed with the communitarian ethos which the Greeks took for granted. As the philosopher explains: "the goodness of every part must be considered with reference to the goodness of the whole" (1260b8) and "[a] whole is never intended by nature to be inferior to a part" (1288a15). Indeed, Aristotle's definition of a community-centered notion of justice may well be incomprehensible to many Moderns: "The good in the sphere of politics is justice; and justice consists in what tends to promote the common interest" (1282b14). How many political discussions today — whether about abortion, gay marriage, immigration, economic policy, or whatever — refer to the *common* good rather than to solipsistic arguments about *individual* or *sectoral* 'rights' and 'fairness'?

Aristotle is decidedly more 'bourgeois' and less spiritual than Plato. He has far less to say about the role of religion in the good society, being practically an afterthought. He seems to hope for, at best, a stable and moderate regime, one respecting the interests of both rich and poor, founded upon an enlightened citizenry composed of independent landowners and responsible citizen-soldiers. But Aristotle too had an elevated notion of what politics should be about. He contradicted those who already then believed that the state exists only as a kind of contract between individuals, meant only to guarantee their security or to enable them to chase after coin.

For Aristotle, man fulfills his nature as a rational being through philosophical contemplation and active citizenship. But only a minority have the intellectual gifts necessary to do this and furthermore, as a practical matter, the work of servile subalterns is necessary to secure the needed leisure to pursue philosophy and politics. Hence, Aristotle notoriously endorses a doctrine of natural slavery: barbarians and the morally defective are incapable of freedom and are only fit to be slaves of better men, thus enabling the latter to fulfill our human potential. Natural slaves are those who, either as individuals or as entire peoples, are so poorly endowed in reason that they may only participate in it as the servants of superior men. Aristotle observes: "what difference, one may ask, is there between some men and the beasts?" (1281b15). The recognition of inequality, enabling the creation of a just community and hierarchy, is no less central to Aristotle's ethics and politics than those of Plato.

Aristotle advocates a kind of restricted democracy or constitutional government. He generally believes a large number of people should have citizenship, limited by service in the army and a moderate property qualification. He argues for a mixed regime featuring democratic, oligarchic, and aristocratic elements, subject to a largely unchanging basic law, the latter embodying and stipulating a way of life. Aristotle, like Plato, is greatly concerned with ensuring solidarity among the citizens, for he says that friendship (*philia*) "is the chief good of cities" (1262a40) and "seems to hold states together" (*NE*, 8.1). This friendly solidarity is guaranteed by both common ethno-cultural identity and by our more conventional notions of justice, namely reciprocity: "it is by proportionate requital that the city holds together" (*NE*, 5.6).

Aristotle is no egalitarian however. In his ideal state, a citizen's participation in decision-making should be proportional to their goodness of character and their contribution to the community:

> Those who contribute most to this association have a greater share in the city than those who are equal to them (or even greater) in free birth and descent, but unequal in civic excellence, or than those who surpass them in wealth but are surpassed by them in excellence. (1281a2)

The inegalitarian foundations of Aristotle's thought are in practice moderated by his empiricism and pragmatism. We all should in principle agree that the best should rule. But as Aristotle notes: "it is not as easy to see the beauty of the soul as it is to see that of the body" (1254b27). How then can we identify the best and ensure they come to power? There are no easy answers to this question.

As a partial solution, Aristotle's ideal government, which he calls *politeia* (strangely, the generic word for civic government), grants citizenship only to those who would exercise their powers moderately and wisely. His is a middle-class regime of citizen-soldiers, independent farmers, and family fathers, who have neither the conspiratorial tendencies of the rich nor the instability of the poor. Aristotle's state seeks to give a critical mass of residents a stake in the perpetuation of the regime, with checks to represent the interests of each class, thus ensuring the rich are secure and the poor are treated reasonably. A degree of democracy is desirable for, Aristotle says, the people as a whole, including the elite, has more wisdom than does the elite alone.

It is significant that none of Aristotle's arguments for moderate democracy are founded on 'rights,' but rather, are based on what benefits the community as a whole. Aristotle's citizens rule and are ruled in turn, this reciprocity fostering a spirit of friendship between social classes. The soldiers in particular should have a say in the government for, as Aristotle observes, they guarantee the existence of the state.

Aristotle's pragmatic and empirical approach is attractive. His empiricism leads him to reject any one-size-fits all solution: all the cities and peoples of the world being different, the regime suited to each will differ accordingly. A city with a truly exceptional royal family then might be rightly ruled by a king. A city with a vicious and uncultured population of working poor might be unfit for democracy. Aristotle's pragmatism also leads him to rejects communism. Already in ancient times, private property and economic inequality were sometimes blamed for the existence immorality and social conflict. Aristotle's arguments against communism and for private property regulated in the public interest have stood the test of time:

> What is common to the greatest number gets the least amount of care. (1261b32)

> [A]lthough there is a sense in which property *ought* to be common, it should in general be private. When everyone has his separate sphere of interest, there will not be the same ground for quarrels; and they will make more effort, because each man will feel that he is applying himself to what is his own. (1263a21)

Aristotle is clear however that private property is not a *right* enabling individuals to be as capricious and selfish as they please, but merely a sensible way of producing wealth, whose aim must ultimately be the well-being of the community.

Aristotle's high-minded teleology conversely leads him to reject consumerism, capital accumulation, and usury as unnatural. Man should only acquire sufficient wealth to secure his livelihood and leisure as a rational being. Anything beyond this is unnatural. Usury, which abuses both the use of currency and man's end, is then denounced:

> The trade of the petty usurer is hated with most reason: it makes a profit from currency itself, instead of making it from the process which currency was meant to serve ... of all modes of acquisition, usury is the most unnatural. (1258a35)[121]

For Aristotle, we should never lose sight of man's nature and potential as a rational social animal.

THE ENSLAVEMENT OF BARBARIANS

As we have seen, Aristotle believed that superior men required natural slaves in order to have the leisure necessary to engage in contemplation and civic life, and thus fulfill their nature as rational beings. This begs the question: who should be slaves? Those incapable of self-government. Aristotle speaks of "foolish people ... who by nature are thoughtless and live by their senses are brutish, like some races of the distant barbarians" (*NE*, 7.5). Aristotle then believed not only certain individuals but entire peoples could be incapable of self-rule. And just as superior men should lead lesser men, so superior peoples should lead lesser peoples. Aristotle then recommends that barbarians be enslaved by Greeks. It is not entirely clear whether Aristotle believes barbarian incapacity for self-government is due to congenital inability, historical trajectory, or geographical and climatic conditions.

One might dismiss Aristotle's views as merely

---

[121] See also Aristotle's scornful comments in the *Nicomachean Ethics*:

> [Some] exceed in respect of taking by taking anything and from any source, e.g., those who ply sordid trades, pimps, and all such people, and those who lend small sums and at high rates. For all of these take more than they ought and from wrong sources. (*NE*, 4.1)

rationalizations for the chauvinism and unjust social system of his time. While few ancient authors contested the ethics of slavery, moderns may accuse Aristotle of resorting to a chauvinistic compromise, reserving slavery for foreigners whom the Greeks naturally had less sympathy for. The underlying *principle* is however an important one.[122] One should also remember that the Greeks were exceptional in their pursuit of reason and practice of citizenship, in stark contrast with the wild barbarism of northern illiterate tribes or the divinely-sanctioned despotism of Middle-Eastern god-kings. Aristotle is willing to give credit to the Carthaginians, a seafaring Semitic people, who had also developed a sophisticated civic government.

Aristotle asserts that neither the wild Europeans nor the slavish Asiatics were capable of self-rule, unlike the Greeks who represented a happy mean between the two. He says Asiatics are less attached to freedom than Europeans: "these barbarian peoples are more servile in character than Greeks (as the peoples of Asia are more servile than those of Europe); and they therefore tolerate despotic rule without any complaint" (1285a16). The Europeans however were still at a barbaric level of culture, notably due to lack of communications and harsh climate. Aristotle says:

> The peoples of cold countries generally, and particularly those of Europe, are full of spirit, but deficient in skill and intelligence [or understanding, διάνοια]; and this is why they continue to remain comparatively free, but attain no political development and show no capacity for governing others. The peoples of Asia are endowed with skills and

---

[122] One may observe that even many of those who disown slavery are implicitly acting according to the principle that the enlightened and self-governed must impose their will on the unenlightened and ungoverned in international relations. One thinks of the innumerable wars to spread liberal-democratic values and Western pressure to protect endangered species in the Third World, done either in the name of these values as such (thus 'forcing them to be free') or in the name of the whole (global public goods such as the environment).

intelligence, but are deficient in spirit; and this is why they continue to be peoples of subjects and slaves. The Greek stock, intermediate in geographical position, unites the qualities of both sets of peoples. It possesses both spirit and intelligence, for which reason it continues to be free, to have the highest political development, and to be capable of governing every other people—if only it could once achieve political unity. (1327b18)[123]

The last line, dreaming of Greek unity and world-hegemony, betrays Aristotle's powerful ethnocentric sentiments. The dream of course would be realized by the Kingdom of Macedon's unification of most of Greece and Alexander the Great's conquest of the enormous Persian Empire all the way to India. Aristotle, who served as Alexander's tutor, is said by Plutarch to have advised the conqueror to rule over the Greeks as peers and the barbarians as slaves (Plutarch, *Moralia*, 329b).

Aristotle's principles also had implications for the morality of war. Certain peoples being incapable of self-government, and the acquisition of slaves and territory through war being necessary for men to fulfill their nature as rational beings, Aristotle argued that war was a natural and potentially just activity:

> [T]he art of war is in some sense a natural mode of acquisition. Hunting is a part of that art; and hunting ought to be practiced, not only against wild animals, but also against human beings who are intended by nature to be ruled by others and refuse to obey that intention, because that sort of war is naturally just. (1256b15)

All this will naturally shock the modern liberal sensibility. We must understand Aristotle's views in the context of their time and seek to separate what is only relevant to the past and

---

[123] The underdevelopment of northern Europe was often attributed to its harsh climate. Herodotus says: "I think that it is the cold that has stopped people from settling in these northern regions" (Herodotus, 5.10).

what is of enduring importance. We would certainly not endorse, both for reasons of civil peace and of ethnic integrity, reliance on foreign slaves in our lands. Furthermore, Aristotle explicitly states that if, by some magic, tools could operate themselves, slavery would be unnecessary:

> We can imagine a situation in which each instrument could do its own work, at the word of command or by intelligent anticipation, like the statues of Daedelus or the tripods made by Hephaestus, of which the poet relates that "Of their own motion they entered the conclave of gods on Olympus." A shuttle would then weave of itself, and a plectrum would do its own harp-playing. In this situation managers would not need subordinates and masters would not need slaves. (1253b23)

Aristotle then might well have conceded that in the age of automation the enslavement of foreigners is particularly unnecessary. There is also an important point of principle however. Insofar as a people genuinely is more enlightened and capable of reason than another—who perhaps is squatting on valuable resources—it follows from Aristotle's argument that the better people has a natural right to claim them, by conquest.

KINSHIP AND HOUSEHOLD RULE

If family and kinship were of supreme importance to the ancient Greeks, they also hold a major place in Aristotle's biopolitics at both the individual and collective levels. Citizens had a duty to respect their kin and form good families. The society as a whole was furthermore a group defined by kinship and was in fact an extended family. Aristotle perceptively observes that shared blood entails a common identity and is the cause of love within a same family:

> Parents, then, love their children as themselves (for their issue are by virtue of their separate existence a sort of other selves), while children love their parents as being born of them, and brothers love each other as being born of the same parents; for their identity with them makes them

identical with each other (which is the reason why people talk of 'the same blood,' 'the same stock,' and so on). They are, therefore, in a sense the same thing, though in separate individuals. (*NE*, 8.12)[124]

The common Greek view, and indeed this is virtually universal across human societies, was that crimes are more heinous when committed against close kin. Aristotle says that assault, homicide, fighting, and slander "when they are committed against father or mother or a near relative, differ from offenses against people who are not so related, in being breaches of natural piety" (1262a25). Bringing harm upon one's close kin was considered unnatural and impious.

Family and kinship play a fundamental role in Aristotle's account of the emergence of society and politics. Aristotle believes that the first and simplest societies were families or households. Then, as a family expanded into multiple households, they banded together into villages. The father rules the household by virtue of his kinship and experience, just as a king rules:

> The first form of association naturally instituted for the satisfaction of daily recurrent needs is thus the family ... The next form of association ... is the village. The most natural form of village appears to be that of a colony [or offshoot]

---

[124] Aristotle sees kinship as naturally leading to affection, whether among family members as in a race or species:

> Parent seems by nature to feel [friendship] for offspring and offspring for parent, not only among men but among birds and among most animals; it is felt mutually by members of the same race, and especially by men, whence we praise lovers of their fellow men. We may see even in our travels how near and dear every man is to every other. (*NE*, 8.1)

Aristotle defends conventional family-centered ethics. In giving, he says the good person will be discerning and "will refrain from giving to anybody and everybody, that he may have something to give to the right people, at the right time, and where it is noble to do so" (*NE*, 4.1) and that "it is not proper to have the same care for intimates and for strangers" (*NE*, 4.6).

from a family; and some have thus called the members of the village by the name of "sucklings of the same milk," or, again, of "sons and the sons of sons." This, it may be noted, is the reason why cities were originally ruled, as the peoples of the barbarian world still are, by kings. They were formed of people who were already monarchically governed, for every household is governed by the eldest of the kin, just as villages, when they are offshoots from the household, are similarly governed in virtue of the kinship between their members. (1252b17)

Aristotle elsewhere defines the *polis* as "an association of households and clans in a good life, for the sake of attaining a perfect and self-sufficing existence" (1280b29).

Within households, Aristotle argues that the father's rule is justified "because of the tie of blood and the benefits he confers; for the children start with a natural affect and disposition to obey" (*NE*, 10.9). The philosopher draws explicit analogies between the rule of the good father and that of the good king:

The relation of the male to the female is permanently that in which the statesman stands to his fellow citizens [i.e. of near-equals]. Paternal rule over children, on the other hand, is like that of a king over his subjects. The male parent is in a position of authority both in virtue of the affection to which he is entitled and by right of his seniority; and his position is thus in the nature of royal authority. Homer was right, therefore, to use the invocation "father of gods and of men" to address Zeus who is king of them all. A king ought to be morally superior to his subjects, and yet of the same stock as they are; and this is the case with the relation of age to youth, and of parent to child. (1259a37)

The father's household management, like the statesman's politics, is not aimed at the accumulation of material wealth or honors, but towards the moral improvement of his wards. Furthermore the tyrant, who does not rule legitimately, can nonetheless make himself more agreeable if he rules in "a spirit of paternal discipline" (1315a8). Thinkers throughout history have observed that political altruism can be achieved by, among other things, extending the feeling of familial solidarity to the society as a whole, something obviously infinitely easier to achieve if the members of that society are indeed kin.

The Greeks' kinship circles extended from family, to clan, to city, to all of Greece herself. While every citizen owed loyalty to their family and city-state, the common Greek identity was cultivated through sporting events and religious festivals, and there it was understood that Greeks owed each other a duty, very imperfectly followed, of fighting together against barbarian invaders. Here again, Aristotle is typical of the Greeks.

Finally, there is a tendency in Greco-Roman philosophy towards a kind of universal kinship, all men being thought of as related, both in a limited biological sense, and in sharing in reason and thereby a kind of kinship with the divine. The idea that man ought to follow nature and reason, both of which being universal, was increasingly interpreted as meaning one ought to be a citizen of the universe, a cosmopolitan.

Aristotle's philosophy of eudaimonic and naturalist ethics rejected such conclusions however. For him, reason, and in particular the political exercise of reason through citizenship, was only possible within the confines a particularistic and exclusionary *polis*. Though nature and reason are universal, human beings can only exercise that reason in particular communities, which must have both the natural endowment necessary for reason and have sufficient kinship ties and identity to enable the solidarity necessary for reciprocal citizenship. Insofar as a cosmopolitanism ignores the diversity and inequality of men, this undermines both the real foundations for the solidarity necessary to active citizenship and the achievement of the highest human potential. This for Aristotle would have been unnatural and unethical.

POPULATION POLICIES & EUGENICS

True to his communitarian foundations, Aristotle argues that population policies—notably concerning immigration, naturalization, and reproduction—are a fundamental element of statecraft and ought to serve the interests of the society as a whole. Aristotle observes very lucidly: "The prime factor necessary, in the equipment of a city, is the human material; and this involves us in considering the quality, as well as quantity" (1325b33). The city is defined not by mere geography, but above all by the population. Therefore: "To determine the size of a city – to settle how large it can properly be, and whether it ought to consist of the members of several races – is a duty incumbent on the statesman" (1276a24). The statesman then has a duty to decide who is fit to be a citizen and to ensure the biological reproduction and quality of the citizens, thus perpetuating the city.

In line with Aristotle's imagined foundation of the city as an extended family, the Greeks typically granted citizenship according to rules of descent. Aristotle observes: "For practical purposes, it is usual to define a citizen as one 'born of citizen parents on both sides,' and not on the father's or mother's side only; but sometimes this requirement is carried still farther back, to the length of two, three, or more stages of ancestry" (1275b22). Aristotle also defines a city in part by the possibility of intermarriage among its members. Naturalized citizens are clearly considered exceptional, Aristotle deeming them citizens "in some special sense" (1274b38).

The ancient Greeks were obsessed with their ancestry and lineage, following aristocratic and hereditarian assumptions. Aristotle says that "good birth, for a people and a state, is to be indigenous or ancient and to have distinguished founders with many descendants distinguished in matters that excite envy" (*Rhetoric*, 1.5).[125] Following the widespread Greek assumptions that both nature and nurture mattered, he writes that "it is likely that good sons will come from good fathers and that the appropriately raised will be of the appropriate sort" (*Rhetoric*, 1.9). Aristotle furthermore lists shared blood as one of the forms of friendship, an eminently adaptive view: "The species of friendship are companionship, intimacy, consanguinity, and

---

[125] Aristotle also says: "good birth is the reputation of one's ancestors" (*Rhetoric*, 2.15).

so on" (*Rhetoric*, 2.4).

At the political level, each Greek city-state was similarly quite conscious of having a distinct ancestral identity which persisted across generations. Aristotle evidently is describing a common view when he asks:

> Assuming a single population inhabiting a single territory, shall we say that the city retains its identity as long as the stock of its inhabitants continues to be the same (although the old members are always dying and new members are always being born), and shall we thus apply to the city the analogy of rivers and fountains, to which we ascribe a constant identity in spite of the fact that part of their water is always flowing in and part always flowing out? (1276a34)

Aristotle himself does not fully accredit this view, adding that the nature of the city evolves with changes in regime type.

There were debates about who should be citizens and there were instances of cities assimilating foreigners. The legislator had a role to play in cultivating a common identity among the citizens, sometimes mixing different Greek stocks together. The sophist Gorgias of Leontini likened the statesman to a demiurge or master craftsman: "As mortars are things which are made by the craftsmen who are mortar-makers, so Larissaeans [a people] are made by the craftsmen who are Larissaean-makers" (1275b22).

The lawmaker has a duty to ensure the existence and reproduction of a population of high quality in appropriate numbers. This is the reason for the institution of marriage:

> If we assume that the legislator ought, from the start, to see that the children who are brought up have the best possible physical endowment, it follows that his first attention must be devoted to marriage; and here he will have to consider what the ages of the partners should be, and what qualities they ought to possess. (1334b29)

Bearing and raising children (or not) is then a duty for all citizens, husbands and wives together. They "render public service by bringing children into the world" (1335b26). Both man and wife should be able to have children and children should be born in time to take over their parents' estate (but not sooner or later). Aristotle recommends men be married at the age of 37 and women at 18. He argues that adultery should always be a disgrace, but particularly at childbearing age, presumably because this means chaos for families. This should be "punished by a stigma of infamy proportionate to such an offense" (1335b38). Marriage is then not meant for the mere convenience or pleasure of two individuals, but to create children, and families in which they can be safe and educated. The Greek view then reflected what should be obvious: that the formation and quality of the next generation is an absolutely fundamental metric of the city's success and continuity, and thus a matter of critical public interest, according to which to citizens ought to be educated and regulated as appropriate.

Aristotle endorses the widespread Greek belief in heredity. He remarks on "[t]he resemblances between children and parents" (1262a1). High birth is identified as one of the criteria for being recognized as a citizen: "the descendants of better men are likely to be better, good birth means goodness of stock" (1283a23). At the same time, he recognizes that the luck of the draw was also a factor in each generation: "They [hereditarians] are claiming that just as man is born of man, and animal of animal, so a good man is born of good men. It is often the case, however, that nature wishes but fails to achieve this result" (1255a21).

Aristotle, unlike Plato, does not draw particularly radical eugenic conclusions from these premises. He seems to take the basic quality of the population as a god-given variable which cannot really be modified:

> It may be urged ... that just as the art of the statesman does not produce human stock, but counts on its being supplied by nature and proceeds to use her supply, so nature must also provide the physical means of subsistence—the land, or sea, or whatever it be. (1258a19)

Aristotle does urge some limited eugenic measures however. Husband and wife should both be neither too young (citing young mothers' health risks) nor too old. Aristotle apparently adheres to a proto-Lamarckian view of inheritance, urging pregnant women to exercise so that their children have strong bodies:

> Wives, as well as husbands, need the physical qualities of which we have just been speaking. Pregnant mothers should pay attention to their bodies: they should take regular exercise, and follow a nourishing diet. The legislator can easily lead them to a habit of regular exercise if he requires them to make some daily pilgrimage for the purpose of worshiping at the shrines of the goddesses who preside over childbirth. (1335b11)

Aristotle supports severe negative eugenics. The Greeks practiced infanticide through exposure of babies considered undesirable, most often because either their parents could not provide for them or the infant was congenitally deformed. Aristotle argues that, concerning overpopulation, it is better to prevent births in the first place, rather than kill infants. Concerning the congenitally deformed however, he urges mandatory infanticide: "There should certainly be a law to prevent the rearing of deformed children" (1335b19). This method was obviously supremely cruel for the infant but was considered salutary for the family and the community, as scarce resources could then be dedicated to healthy infants. The reasoning here is not fundamentally different from the widely-accepted modern practice of aborting fetuses suffering from severe congenital defects, such as Down's syndrome.

In addition to quality, there is the somewhat more straightforward issue of quantity. There was generally a trade-off: the larger a city's population, the more powerful that city tended to be, but the more the population grew, the more poverty there was. Depending on the context, the authorities might urge citizens to have more or less children. Lycurgus of Sparta encouraged fertility so as to have as many soldiers as possible:

> Anxious for the Spartans to be as numerous as possible, the legislator encouraged citizens to have as many children as

possible; they have a law that the father of three sons should be exempt from military service, and the father of four entirely free from all taxes. (1270a11)

The authorities might on the other hand attempt to limit fertility in order to prevent poverty (1265a38). In a world in which the economic security of households was largely defined by ownership of land, the Greeks understood that overpopulation led to poverty through the decline of land per person, leading to the impoverishment of households and the growth of the landless population. The urban proletariat was held in contempt by upper-class Greeks such as Aristotle, who considered them uneducated and unstable. Aristotle lists overpopulation as one of the leading causes of "faction" or civil strife (1302b33).

Aristotle strongly emphasizes that social and economic problems such as poverty cannot be separated from demographic realities and therefore from population policies: "Those who propose legislation ought not to forget, as they continually do, that regulation of the amount of property ought to be accompanied by regulation of the number of children in the family" (1266a31). He notes that a certain Philolaus produced "laws of adoption" for Thebes which aimed to keep family plots constant by limiting the production of children (1274a22). The Cretans for their part sought to limit births by encouraging the segregation of women and homosexuality among men (1271b40, Aristotle does not make clear whether he endorses the practice or not). Aristotle reports that Carthage successfully reduced poverty by exporting surplus population to new cities:

> The Carthaginians have a constitution which is in practice oligarchical; but they get away with this by an excellent means—from time to time a section of the populace is planted out among the dependent cities and thus grows wealthy. In this way they remedy the defects of the constitution and give it stability. (1273b18)

Aristotle criticizes such measures as depending on "chance" however and prefers that excessive births be prevented in the

143

first place.

Aristotle's discussion of population policy and eugenics reflects the view which the Greeks took for granted: that the biological reproduction and quality of the citizenry was a fundamental matter of public interest. The citizen had a duty to act and the lawmaker to regulate by whatever means necessary to achieve these goals.

DIVERSITY, CONFLICT, & CITIZENSHIP

If kinship was central to the foundation and solidarity of the Greek polis, diversity was a factor of conflict. Aristotle, like Plato, is very concerned about preventing the internal civil conflicts (*stasis*) which periodically plagued the Greek city-states: "Friendship, we believe, is the chief good of cities, because it is the best safeguard against the danger of factional disputes" (1262a40). He notes in another context that "every difference is apt to create a division" in the city (1303b7).

As a good empiricist, Aristotle meticulously documents all the instances in which diversity and a lack of common identity led to conflict and a loss of the much-cherished friendship (*philia*) among the citizens. The philosopher writes that one the most common causes of "faction" and civil war was the unhappy consequences of unassimilated immigration and the consequent loss of identity and solidarity. Aristotle's prose is perfectly clear:

> Heterogeneity of stocks may lead to faction—at any rate until they have had time to assimilate. A city cannot be constituted from any chance collection of people, or in any chance period of time. Most of the cities which have admitted settlers, either at the time of their foundation or later, have been troubled by faction. For example, the Achaeans joined with settlers from Troezen in founding Sybaris, but expelled them when their own numbers increased; and this involved their city in a curse. At Thurii the Sybarites quarreled with the other settlers who had joined them in its colonization; they demanded special privileges, on the ground that they were the owners of the

territory, and were driven out of the colony. At Byzantium the later settlers were detected in a conspiracy against the original colonists, and were expelled by force; and a similar expulsion befell the exiles from Chios who were admitted to Antissa by the original colonists. At Zancle, on the other hand, the original colonists were themselves expelled by the Samians whom they admitted. At Apollonia, on the Black Sea, factional conflict was caused by the introduction of new settlers; at Syracuse the conferring of civic rights on aliens and mercenaries, at the end of the period of the tyrants, led to sedition and civil war; and at Amphipolis the original citizens, after admitting Chalcidian colonists, were nearly all expelled by the colonists they had admitted. (1303a13)

Thus, immigration of different peoples was a common source of conflict, often leading to civil war and concluding with the ethnic cleansing of either the native peoples or the invaders.

The importation and enfranchisement of foreigners, whether by democrats or tyrants, was a common method of subverting the political process and destroy the existing constitution. Tyrants were often keenly aware of the fact that common identity and civic solidarity were threats to their personal power. Kathryn Lomas observes that "the use of itinerant populations to subvert the status of the *polis* is common to many tyrants and Hellenistic monarchs throughout the Greek world."[126] The case of Syracuse, that powerful Sicilian city governed by a string of tyrants, makes for a useful contrast with the homogeneous and free city-state. Paul Cartledge observes that Syracuse became

what Tyranny in essence was: an autocracy based on military force supplied by a personal bodyguard and mercenaries; and reinforced by multiple dynastic marriages,

---

[126] Kathryn Lomas, "The Polis in Italy: Ethnicity, Colonization, and Citizenship in the Western Mediterranean," in Roger Brock and Stephen Hodkinson, eds., *Alternatives to Athens: Varieties of Political Organization and Community in Ancient Greece* (Oxford: Oxford University Press, 2000), p. 182.

the unscrupulous transfers of populations, and the enfranchisement of foreigners.[127]

In contrast, the Greeks considered homogeneity to be a source of strength in a state. During the Peloponnesian War, the adventurous Athenian political and military leader Alcibiades argued that Sicily would be easy to conquer because its diversity meant its cities lacked solidarity and social trust. Instead of common civic action, the Sicilians were prone to individual selfish behavior in the form of corruption and emigration:

> Sicily may have large cities, but they are full of mixed rabbles and prone to the transfer of populations. As a result no one feels that he has a stake in a city of his own, so they have taken no trouble to equip themselves with arms for their personal safety or to maintain proper farming establishments in the country. Instead, individuals hoard whatever money they can extract from public funds by persuasive speaking or factional politics, in the knowledge that, if all fails, they can go and live elsewhere. A crowd like that are hardly likely to respond unanimously to any proposal or to organize themselves for joint action: more probable is that individual elements will go with any offer that attracts them … (Thucydides, 6.17)

Given that Alcibiades made these comments in a successful speech aimed at convincing the Athenian Assembly to invade Sicily, we can assume such arguments resonated with Athenian citizens in general. In the event, the Athenian invasion of Sicily proved to be a disaster. Nonetheless, as one might expect, the Athenians did find local allies among Sicily's diverse population, notably among the indigenous Sicels. Sicily's lack of unity however did not make up for the general riskiness of the enterprise. Spartan support for Syracuse and long Athenian supply lines were major factors in the failure of the Sicilian expedition.

Aristotle's ideal of citizenship, entailing great reciprocal

---

[127] Cartledge, *Ancient Greece*, p. 128.

civic duties and group solidarity, necessarily requires a strong common identity and a sharp differentiation between citizens and foreigners. Conversely, foreign mercenaries had no solidarity with the people, and were thus frequently used by tyrants to enforce their unjust rule:

> Kings are guarded by the arms of their subjects; tyrants by a foreign force. Ruling according to law, and with the consent of their subjects, kings have bodyguards drawn from their subjects: the tyrant has a [foreign] body-guard to protect himself against them. (1285a16)

> If a single man is entrusted with the command of these [foreign] mercenaries, he frequently becomes a tyrant ... and if the command is vested in a number of people, they make themselves a governing clique. (1306a19)

> The aim of a tyrant is his own pleasure: the aim of a king is the Good. Thus a tyrant covets riches; a king covets what makes for renown. The guard of a king is composed of citizens: that of a tyrant is composed of foreigners. (1310b31)

Thus, outsiders with no kinship ties to the local people were ideally-suited for persecuting the citizenry.

Aristotle also clearly expresses the idea that relatedness and shared identity enable the group solidarity that is needed to throw off tyrannical rule and defend a state. He advises against the use of mercenaries instead of native citizens, saying:

> Professional soldiers turn cowards, however, when the danger puts too great a strain on them and they are inferior in numbers and equipment; for they are the first to fly, while citizen-forces die at their posts, as in fact happened at the temple of Hermes. [At the battle of Coronea of 353 BC, Phocia's mercenaries fled before the Thebans, while the Phocian citizen-soldiers actually fought and won.] (NE, 3.8)

If identity and community made a people better able to defend their freedom, conversely Aristotle argues that a diverse population with no common identity is easier to enslave. If one has a population of slaves, Aristotle pragmatically argues that these should be ethnically diverse so as to be easier to subjugate:

> The class which farms ... should, ideally, if we can choose at will, be slaves — but slaves not drawn from a single stock, or from stocks of a spirited temperament. This will at once secure the advantage of a good supply of labor and eliminate any danger of revolutionary designs. (1330a23)

Thus, a mass of mongrels without identity is easier to rule than a self-conscious people, a truth which the hostile elites which rule many Western nations today seem to instinctively understand.

In any event, for Aristotle, solidarity and citizenship manifestly require a common identity, whereas the lack of this is a recipe for enslavement, civil conflict, and tyranny. The philosopher's grim observations are worth repeating: immigration without assimilation can only lead to conflict, conflict which can only end through separation, separation which can only occur through the expulsion either of the invaders or the natives from their ancestral lands.

LAW VERSUS DECADENCE

A last concern of Aristotle's which is of great relevance to our time is the prevention of decadence. For Aristotle, the good of the city is reflected in the virtue of the citizens. The citizens are educated and trained in virtue by adherence to the city's largely-unchanging basic law, set in place by an inspired lawgiver. The question becomes: how can the law ensure that virtue is maintained in perpetuity?

There are no easy answers. Nations tend to be victims of their own successes. As Aristotle notes: "People are easily spoiled; and it is not all who can stand prosperity" (1308b10). He speaks at length on how Sparta's morals were corrupted after that martial city defeated Athens and achieved hegemony in Greece during the Peloponnesian War. According to Aristotle, adherence to Lycurgus' law did not survive material wealth and the empowerment of women.

The Greeks were less prone to excess individualism than the

modern West has been, but they often yielded to the siren song of egalitarianism. Aristotle reports that many Greeks believed that if men were equal in some respect, such as being freeborn, they must be equal overall and certainly equally entitled to rule. Many took equality as a goal, leading them to seek to both make the citizens equal and to indiscriminately extend citizenship: "some thinkers [hold] that liberty is chiefly to be found in democracy and that the same goes for equality, this condition is most fully realized when all share, as far as possible, on the same terms in the constitution" (1291b30).

While Aristotle is indeed more 'bourgeois' than Plato, he too is contemptuous of egalitarian excesses, which manifest themselves in democratic extremism and selfish individualism. Aristotle, like Plato, argues at length that right equality or justice means that equals should be treated equally and unequals unequally (1287a1). And again, for him, justice means the interests of the community:

> What is "right" should be understood as what is "equally right"; and what is "equally right" is what is for the benefit of the whole city and for the common good of its citizens. The citizen is, in general, one who shares in the civic life of ruling and being ruled in turn. (1283b27)

Aristotle notes that some democracies are so extreme that they actually undermine the existence of their own state, and hence do not survive as long as a moderate democracy. He writes with great eloquence on that "false conception of liberty" which has so often seduced our people:

> In democracies of the type which is regarded as being peculiarly democratic the policy followed is the very reverse of their real interest. The reason for this is a false conception of liberty. There are two features which are generally held to define democracy. One of them is the sovereignty of the majority; the other is the liberty of individuals. Justice is assumed to consist in equality and equality in regarding the will of the masses as sovereign; liberty is assumed to consist in "doing what one likes." The result of such a view is that, in these extreme democracies, each individual lives as he

likes — or as Euripides says, "For any end he chances to desire." This is a mean conception [of liberty]. To live by the rule of the constitution ought not to be regarded as slavery, but rather as salvation. (1310a12)

Is this not a very neat summation of the ills of modern liberalism? Since the 1960s, liberals have expressed desire only for "equality" and "solidarity," all the while destroying the very foundations for these ends through zealous and short-sighted imposition of multiculturalism and open borders.

Aristotle observes that constitutions have a tendency to turn increasingly oligarchic or democratic over time. This perhaps reflects the structural tendency of a faction with power to take measures which gradually reinforce that power. Aristotle argues that Solon, the founder of the Athenian regime, inserted the democratic elements which gradually led that city to become an extreme democracy, something Aristotle believes Solon did not intend. (Just as, we might surmise, the American Founding Fathers established the system which led to our current regime, but did not intend this outcome.)

In the great slouch towards equality, Aristotle observes that foreigners were a favorite political weapon not only of tyrants but also of demagogues. He writes: "At Amphipolis someone by the name of Cleotimus introduced Chalcidian settlers and incited them after their settlement to make an attack on the rich" (1305b39). Aristotle says that naturalization of foreigners played a key role in Athens' shift towards an extreme form of democracy. He says of Cleisthenes: "after the expulsion of the tyrants he enrolled in the tribes a number of resident aliens, both foreigners and slaves" (1275b34). Aristotle says elsewhere that extreme democrats consolidate their regime by efforts to mix the citizenry (breaking down old identities) and stoking individualism:

Other measures which are also useful in constructing this last and most extreme type of democracy are measures like those introduced by Cleisthenes at Athens, when he sought to advance the cause of democracy, or those which were taken by the founders of popular government at Cyrene. A number of new tribes and clans should be instituted by the side of the old; private cults should be reduced in number and conducted at common centers; and every contrivance should be employed to make all the citizens mix, as much as they possibly can, and to break down their old loyalties. All the measures adopted by tyrants may equally be regarded as congenial to democracy. We may cite as examples the license allowed to slaves (which, up to a point, may be advantageous as well as congenial), the license permitted to women and children, and the policy of conniving at the practice of "living as you like." There is much to assist a constitution of this sort, for most people find more pleasure in living without discipline than they find in a life of temperance. (1319b19)

These measures appear in line with what Samuel Francis called "anarcho-tyranny": by weakening traditional group identities and the authority of family fathers, the population of "liberated individuals" is paradoxically reduced to an impotent mass, which can then be skillfully manipulated.

Aristotle offers some advice for preserving a constitution. The law should incite citizens to be on their guard against those living lives contrary to the spirit of the law and the citizens should be trained to use leisure appropriately. While Aristotle is emphatic in stressing that war is not an end in itself, but merely a means to a good peace, he nonetheless observes: "War automatically enforces temperance and justice: the enjoyment of prosperity, and leisure accompanied by peace, is more apt to make people overbearing" (1334a11). Aristotle advises against regular changes to the basic law, for the small benefits this might entail are likely to be canceled out by a loss of reverence for the law's authority. It goes without saying that daily life in ancient Greece was not constantly transformed by technological innovations as our lives have been for the past few centuries.

Ultimately, one must hope for a great lawgiver. There is a strong element of chance and destiny in this. For as Aristotle observes: "It is easy enough to theorize about such matters: it is far less easy to realize one's theories. What we say about them depends on what we wish; what actually happens depends on chance" (1331b18). Aristotle recognizes that the law cannot foresee all circumstances. If suddenly a superior individual, a hero would appear:

> There can be no law governing people of this kind. They are a law in themselves. It would be a folly to attempt to legislate for them: they might reply to such an attempt with the words used by the lions, in the fable of Antisthenes, when the hares were making orations and claiming that all the animals should have equal status. (1284a3)

In Antisthenes' tale, the lions ask the hares: "Where are your claws and teeth?" Ultimately, the exceptional man must not be constrained by law but must himself promulgate a new one:

> It is surely clear that [the one best man] must be a lawgiver, and there must be a body of laws, but these laws must not be sovereign where they fail to hit the mark—though they must be so in all other cases. (1286a21)

In conclusion, Aristotle provides a powerful rationale for a moderate constitutional regime of responsible citizen-soldiers constrained by an enlightened basic law. He was keenly aware of the solidarity enabled by kinship and the dangers posed by a lack of common identity. Aristotle's citizens are not obsessed with their 'rights' to imagined equality or maximal individual liberty, but participate in the regulation of the collective life of the city, which is to say the assigning and fulfilling of duties. The city being the citizens, Aristotle ascribes a fundamental importance to legislating to ensure the cultural and biological quality and perpetuity of the community, to be achieved through rigorous education and systematic population policies.

Aristotle's eudaimonic ethics and politics, grounded in the biological realities of human nature and aimed towards collective survival and flourishing, are eminently compatible with a Darwinian worldview. The ancient philosopher's system can be readily updated, if need be, with the discoveries of modern genetic and behavioral sciences. Aristotle gives us at once an elevated, practical, and responsible vision of politics, far removed either from the effeminacy and solipsism of our times, or shrill denunciations of a stereotyped 'totalitarianism.' Indeed, he did not believe that civic freedom was even possible without manly virtue. Aristotle's views on the ideal state are a synthesis and summary of wider Greek ones, acquired after hard experience and deep reflection: a balanced regime founded on a mix of aristocratic and popular elements, an inspired basic law, and an enlightened citizenry. His *politeia* shows that there is no contradiction between a muscular and holistic biopolitics and a civic politics characterized by the rule of law and open debate. The politics of the Greek city-state is nothing more than that of the assembled family fathers and soldier-citizens, perpetuators and guarantors of the social order, come together to fulfill their sacred responsibility to protect, discipline, and educate their kinsfolk towards the good.

ATHENS & SPARTA
AN ANALYSIS OF TWO ETHNOSTATES

This book has been chiefly about the ideas and values that possessed the ancient Greeks. It has been political history only to the extent that the history of states intersects with that of ideas and ideologies. In this chapter, I will deal with the character and historical trajectory of two great city-states, Athens and Sparta. This is necessarily a somewhat fraught endeavor. States, unlike philosophers, poets, and historians, do not leave a well-defined corpus of writings embodying their ethos and world-view. A state's work is left not in words but in deeds, in action upon societies, but these societies are long-dead, and we must of necessity rely upon the faint echoes left scattered in surviving historical writings and archaeological ruins.

Our textual sources for most ancient eras and states are so patchy and fragmentary—for instance, being forced to rely primarily upon a single historian for an entire period—that very little can be said with absolute certainty.[128] We must bear in mind that the default form of ancient writing can perhaps best be described to Moderns as 'historical fiction.' Even the Greek historians—whether Herodotus, Thucydides, Xenophon, Polybius, Arrian, or Plutarch—are ultimately tale-tellers, greatly concerned with the moral effect of their narratives and casually inventing plausible speeches for their historical actors. We must then read their histories also as literary critics—as concerned with their internal coherence, moral effect, and

---

[128] In the nineteenth century, the Prussian military theorist Carl von Clausewitz would choose for this reason to exclude ancient history from his monumental treatise, *On War*, using data exclusively from the era of modern warfare, as "the latest military history is naturally the best field from which to draw, inasmuch as it alone is sufficiently authentic and detailed." Carl von Clausewitz, (trans. J. J. Graham and F. N. Maude), *On War* (London: Wordsworth, 1997), 2.6, p. 135.

intellectual arguments as with their historical accuracy as such.

The broad sweep of the history of the ancient Greek city-states is nonetheless discernible, even if their origins and much detail must remain mysterious. We are concerned with the *adaptive culture and values* of the Ancients, that which made for their power and survival, and these are vividly reflected in the surviving histories.

The Persian Empire was driven by a certain logic, certain feedback loops pertaining to domestic conditions and foreign relations, which led to that great state's steady expansion.[129] The waves of this expansion were finally dashed on the rocks of Greek freedom, embodied in the city-states of Athens and Sparta.[130] Athens and Sparta themselves were each driven by their own logic, their own virtuous circles of power, which defeated the Persian logic in Europe. If Persian power was that of a multinational military monarchy, a culture of empire, Greek power was that of patriotic, fractious little republics, defined by civic freedom.

The particular form of civic freedom and the virtuous circle of power at Sparta were very different however than those at Athens. At Sparta, a rigorous communitarian discipline was maintained by the demands of lordship, the need for the society to be constantly militarily organized to guard against the threat of rebellion by the enslaved Helots. The result was centuries of stability and regional power. At Athens, the virtuous circle of international trade and naval power led to rapid and constant demographic and imperial expansion. The result was a short-lived empire which almost achieved hegemony in the eastern Mediterranean and a stunningly creative artistic and philosophical flourishing with few rivals in

---

[129] Yuval Harari has said that organisms can be likened to algorithms, complex mathematical formula. The same could be said for nations and states, which are highly-complex social organizations characterized by innumerable feedback loops.

[130] We will have to largely ignore the hundreds of other Greek city-states, either because they were too weak to be of interest to us, or because, like Syracuse and Thebes, the historical record is too patchy for us to say much of interest.

all human history. Athens and Sparta seem to embody a recurring dialectic in Western history: between sea-power, commerce, democracy, individualism, and technology on the one hand, and land-power, autarky, hierarchy, community, and discipline on the other.

"COURAGE IS FREEDOM"
ATHENS AS A SPIRITED & NATIVIST DEMOCRACY

The verdict of the philosophers and men of the Right has generally been harsh towards Athens: a regime characterized by excessive democracy, individualism, and belly-chasing. Nonetheless, the fact is that Athens was a uniquely dynamic and powerful state, and one which even as a democracy still honored and embodied many wider Hellenic virtues. The political works of Athens' great lawgivers and statesmen, such as Solon, Cleisthenes, and Pericles, are not without ethnopolitical content. Athenian democracy was founded on family, patriarchy, community, military courage, ancestry, and an intense patriotism. One scholar has gone so far as to argue that the role of ancestry was so pronounced that Athenian democracy was based on an early notion of "racial citizenship."[131]

The Athenian regime significantly evolved over time, fluctuating between tyranny and more-or-less democratic forms of republican government. In the early sixth century, Solon reformed the city and was later credited with establishing its democratic tendency. The Assembly (*Ekklesia*), which made day-to-day decisions with a quorum of 6,000 attendants, and the juries were opened to all free male citizens. Solon's regime was however a 'moderate' democracy, maintaining property qualifications and thus restricting certain political offices to the rich. Solon's poems emphasize law, community, balance between rich and poor, equality before the law, and frugality.

---

[131] Susan Lape, *Race and Citizen Identity in Classical Athenian Democracy* (Cambridge: Cambridge University Press, 2010), p. ix.

Solon also abolished existing private and public debts and banned usurious loans for which the penalty for defaulting was enslavement. In his poems, Solon condemns the nation-shattering effects of usury and poverty, which lead unfree citizens to wander the world, homeless:

> For if men injure their own people, they soon find their lovely city scarred and faction-torn. Among the people these evils roam at large, and many of the poor folk find themselves in foreign lands, sold into slavery, and bound in shameful bonds ...[132]

> And many to Athena's holy land I brought back, sold abroad illegally or legally, and others whom their debts had forced to leave, their speech no longer Attic [i.e. Athenian], so great their wanderings ...[133]

The abolition of debt and the struggle against usury were then integral to the founding of Athenian democracy, that early great experiment in participatory politics.

Solon's reforms were pursued further by Cleisthenes in the late sixth century, who really gave Athens her fully democratic character. Treasurers and members of the annually-rotating Council of Five-Hundred (*Boule*), effectively the city's government, enforcing the decisions of the Assembly, were chosen by lot, a measure aimed at reducing corruption and giving the people the most direct say possible. Generals however continued to be elected by the people, an electoral system which was said to favor the rich. The practice of ostracism was instituted, whereby a plurality of citizens could exile anyone for ten years, a measure which was supposed to increase stability by temporarily neutralizing potentially dangerous leaders. Cleisthenes also sought to reinforce a sense of common Athenian identity by replacing traditional family names with ten new purely-geographical district (*deme*) names.

The importance of familial and religious piety in the

---

[132] M. L. West, ed. & trans., *Greek Lyric Poetry* (Oxford: Oxford University Press, 1994), "Solon," 4.

[133] *Ibid.*, 36.

Athenian democracy, as in all Greek city-states, is apparent from the questions posed to those being considered for political office:

> When they are examined, they are asked, first, "Who is your father, and of what *deme*? Who is your father's father? Who is your mother? Who is your mother's father, and of what *deme*?" Then the candidate is asked whether he possesses an ancestral Apollo or a household Zeus, and where their sanctuaries are; next if he possesses a family tomb, and where; then if he treats his parents well, and pays his taxes, and has served on the required military expeditions. (Pseudo-Aristotle, *Athenian Constitution*, 2.2.14-55)

Thus, those who failed in their familial, religious, or military duties were not considered eligible to serve the state and the community.

Pericles, the most famous Athenian statesman, presided over the city's Golden Age as a democracy and an empire. Pericles was a great orator who was regularly reelected to serve as general. Something of a populist, he combined democratic, socialistic, and exclusionary policies. Pericles sought to educate the poor and increase their political participation by subsidizing theater tickets and jury-duty, which simple craftsmen would otherwise have found too costly to attend. Among the plays one could see was Aeschylus' *Persians*, a celebration of Athenian military victory and civic freedom.[134] Anyone who has perused some of the other surviving plays from this period will be struck at their remarkably high intellectual level and deep explorations of the human condition. Following the Persian Wars, Pericles used the wealth from Athens' newly-acquired maritime empire to finance a great public works program, which created ancient Greece's most iconic surviving architectural masterpiece: the Parthenon.

In the face of a massive wave of immigration driven by Athens' economic prosperity, citizenship was restricted to

---

[134] See above, chapter "Herodotus II," section "Pan-Hellenism: Greek Identity & Solidarity."

those with two Athenian parents. This restriction not only enabled Athens to provide more benefits to her citizens, but was also aimed at increasing group loyalty. As Melissa Lane observes: "While that measure might sound more restricting than democratizing, it was aimed at curbing the elite's habits of inter-city kin and friendship marriages, which, in the eyes of democrats, watered down elite allegiance to Athens to suspiciously low levels."[135]

The most eloquent defense of the Athenian regime is that given by Pericles in his famous and moving Funeral Oration. This speech, as recorded in an idealized version by Thucydides, was given in celebration of the war dead in the early days of the Peloponnesian War. The Oration affirms the democracy's virtues: rule in the interests of the majority, individual freedom, meritocracy without concern for wealth, a lively cultural and intellectual life of games and festivals, a relatively open society without secrecy or systematic eviction of foreigners, the importation of a huge variety of foreign goods, and free speech and debate. At the same time, Pericles stressed that these freedoms have not made the Athenians weaker than the more sternly-educated and austere Spartans, and that the country had maximal self-sufficiency.

Pericles proudly affirms the specificity of Athens' democratic way of life: "We are unique in the way we regard anyone who takes no part in public affairs: we do not call that a quiet life, we call it a useless life" (Thu., 2.40). At the same time, Pericles stressed that courage was an integral part of Athenian citizenship: "You should now seek to emulate these men [the fallen]. Realize that happiness is freedom, and freedom is courage" (Thu., 2.43). This simultaneously participatory and manly ideal of citizenship was, no doubt, a major source of Athens' power and dynamism.

Pericles also eloquently appeals to the biopolitical aspects of Athenian citizenship. The Oration in fact begins by honoring the ancestors who had built Athens and the empire:

I shall begin with our ancestors first of all. It is right, and

---

[135] Lane, *Political Ideas*, p. 102.

also appropriate on such an occasion, that this tribute should be paid to their memory. The same race has always occupied this land, passing it on from generation to generation until the present day, and it is to these brave men that we owe our inheritance of a land that is free. (Thu., 2.36)

Pericles praises the honor gained in war as far more valuable than individual wealth. He, strikingly, consoles the parents of those who have already fallen and then urges them to have yet more children as a social duty:

Those of you who are still of an age to bear children should hold firm to the hope of further sons. In their own lives some will find that new children help them forget those they have lost, and for the city there will be a double benefit — both maintenance of the population and also a safeguard, since those without children at stake do not face the same risks as the others and cannot make a balanced or judicious contribution to debate. (Thu., 2.44)

The final comment is an interesting one in asserting that the childless, having less responsibilities, are to that extent less fit for citizenship.

Athens then reflected the widespread Greek assumption that whomever sustained the community, notably biologically and militarily, could rightly claim to have a say in politics. The anonymous author of the fourth-century pamphlet the *Constitution of the Athenians*, conventionally named 'the Old Oligarch' in the English-speaking world, was highly critical of the Athenian democracy and empire. But he could concede that at Athens "the poor and the people generally are right to have more than the highborn and wealthy for the reason that it is the people who man the ships and impart strength to the city" (Old Oligarch, 1.2).

The sophist Protagoras, a friend of Pericles, could also rightly argue that all humans, besides the most sociopathic, have as social creatures *some* in-born tendency to temperance and justice in order to live as social creatures. Therefore, he claimed: "It is reasonable to admit everyone as an adviser on this virtue [justice], on the grounds that everyone has some share of it" (Plato, *Protagoras*, 323a). Democratic and republican regimes could claim to have a superior mode of decision-making, based on their citizens' collective wisdom, rather than that merely of a single man or a small clique.

Pericles said that he gave the Oration to the benefit both of citizens and to metics (mostly Greek resident foreigners), and claimed that "our city as a whole is an education to Greece ... That this is no passing puff but factual reality is proved by the very power of the city: this character of ours built that power" (Thu., 2.41). He presented Athens as a model to the wider Greek nation, something which had a certain reality, insofar as the city was indeed the cultural leader of Greece.

However, for all the talk of protecting, educating, and leading Greece, it seems never to have occurred to the Athenians to give their colonial subjects a say in government. Periclean Athens was a decidedly chauvinist democracy, meaning a particularly brittle empire, prone to collapse in a wave of secessionist rebellions. As Herodotus implied, Athens acquired a negative reputation due the empire and it was said that "the Athenians enslaved the Greeks ... they enslaved those who had fought against the barbarians and done great deeds" (Aristotle, *Rhetoric*, 2.22). The Athenians may have had something of a guilty conscience concerning their treatment of fellow Ionians and Greeks. Aristotle records the saying: "Privately to use only barbarians as slaves, but publicly to acquiesce in the enslavement of many of the allies" (*Rhetoric*, 3.9).

From fairly early on, Athenian democracy became tinged with what Susan Lape calls a "racial ideology."[136] Whereas Herodotus had argued that the Athenian population was the product of a mixing between Hellenic settlers and Pelasgian natives, the Athenians claimed to be racially pure in contrast with the other Greeks, having supposedly sprung from the Attic soil as true *autochthones*. As the fourth-century orator Isocrates said:

---

[136] Lape, *Race and Citizen Identity*, p. 59.

[I]t is admitted that our city is the oldest and the greatest in the world and in the eyes of all men the most renowned. But noble as is the foundation of our claims, the following grounds give us even a clearer title to distinction: for we did not become dwellers in this land by driving others out of it, nor by finding it uninhabited, nor by coming together here a motley horde composed of many races; but we are of a lineage so noble and so pure that throughout our history we have continued in possession of the very land which gave us birth, since we are sprung from its very soil and are able to address our city by the very names which we apply to our nearest kin; for we alone of all the Hellenes have the right to call our city at once nurse and fatherland and mother. (Isocrates, 4.23-25)

The Athenians, Isocrates insisted, "were not of mixed origin" (Isocrates, 12.124). Autochthony is also affirmed and questioned in the surviving fragments of Euripides' play *Erechtheus* and in Plato's dialogue *Menexenus*. While claims to autochthony must be considered merely mythical, this widely-held belief underpinned Athenian citizenship and patriotism. The myth of autochthony justified exclusion or participation in the benefits of Athenian democracy, exhorted the citizens to be worthy of their lineage and forefathers, and demanded sacrifice for what was thought to be their literal motherland. Athens' radical and unique experiment in direct democratic politics and citizenship was grounded in a strong racial identity and pride in one's lineage.

THE VIRTUOUS CIRCLE OF ATHENIAN POWER: TRADE, SHIPS, & EMPIRE

The particular combination of individual liberty, social mobility, manliness, and patriotism inherent in the ideal of Athenian democracy would give that city a fundamentally different foundation to her power than Sparta's. Athens' rise to hegemony began with the expansion of the Athenian fleet and the liberation of island-dwelling and Asiatic Greeks during the Persian Wars. Herodotus is clear that Athens played the greater role in defeating the Persians, fighting more battles both at land and at sea. He expresses "an opinion [which] will offend a great many people … the Athenians proved themselves the saviors of Greece" (Herodotus, 7.139.). These victories entrenched a powerful virtuous circle of commerce, sea-power, demographic expansion, and empire. Athens became *the* commercial, migratory, and cognitive hub of the ancient Mediterranean. The population swelled to 250,000, simply enormous for a Greek city.

Only Athens had the funds and population to create a self-sustaining critical mass of naval power large enough to police both the seas and the Aegean Greeks. The latter became dependencies of Athens, providing either ships or coin, further magnifying Athenian power.[137] A large percentage of Athenian citizens were employed in what was, in effect, a vast military-industrial complex, as administrators, jurymen, ship-builders, and public works men. Athens' alliance, the Delian league, gradually morphed into an Athenian empire in which membership was no longer voluntary and recalcitrant members were crushed. Athens' centralized empire was both more coercive and more administratively advanced in terms of taxes and the judiciary than Sparta's. We should not exaggerate the degree of individual freedom and equality in Athens: colonial subjects, slaves, house-bound women, and metics were deprived of political rights. Athens was also something of a

---

[137] The Old Oligarch writes on Athens' ability as a maritime empire to keep her subjects weak and divided:

> Someone might say that the Athenians' strength consists in the allies' ability to pay tribute-money; but the rabble thinks it more advantageous for each one of the Athenians to possess the resources of the allies and for the allies themselves to possess only enough for survival and to work without being able to plot defection. (Old Oligarch, 1.15)

> [S]ubject peoples on land can combine small cities and fight collectively, but subject peoples at sea, by virtue of being islanders, cannot join their cities together into the same unit. For the sea is in the way, and those now in power are thalassocrats. (Old Oligarch, 2.2)

caste society, albeit not to the same degree as Sparta.

Athens embodied the long-term superiority, in terms of power, displayed by dynamic, commercial, democratic-individualist, and technologically-advanced systems over static, austere, hierarchical-communitarian, and primitive ones. The democratic-individualists tend to be far more dynamic and expansive in peacetime. They endure to the extent that they are then able to adopt sufficient hierarchical-communitarian characteristics in wartime. Great Britain and the United States of America have been characterized by a similar liberal dynamism to that of Athens, one which has since overwhelmed Continental Europe, but which was likely only possible because these two nations were protected by the seas. In the Peloponnesian War by contrast, Sparta triumphed over Athens, tearing down her city walls and abolishing her empire. Pericles once asked rhetorically: "if we were an island, could any be more invulnerable than us?" (Thu., 1.143) To which the Spartans could no doubt have answered: "If …"

Athens' cognitive and cultural pull is evident from the numerous foreign philosophers and sophists who came to the city from the mainland, Ionia, Cyprus, the Black Sea Coast, southern Italy, and elsewhere: Anaxagoras, Democritus, Protagoras, Aristotle, Diogenes, Zeno, and Epicurus are just some of the great names who established themselves there, in both classical and later times. Athens' cultural leadership would long outlast her military-commercial empire.

Given Athens' relative freedom of speech and intellectual ferment as the Mediterranean's central cultural node, one can certainly understand those Athenians who were frustrated with the ever-critical philosophers, such as Socrates, who might have been told: "You did not choose to go to Sparta or to Crete, which you are always saying are well governed" (Plato, *Crito*, 53a). Only a handful of Athenians ever went to live in much-praised Sparta, namely Tyrtaeus, who became the Spartan national poet, and Xenophon.

Until quite recently, Western thinkers both ancient and modern have tended to be critical of democracy in general, that rare phenomenon which had so conspicuously existed at

Athens.[138] We must be aware and critical of democracy's flaws. At the same time, we must not be blind to the very real virtues of the Athenian regime, which after all combined dynamism, power, equality of opportunity, intellectual inquiry, and cultural fecundity to a degree rarely seen in all human history. Athenian democracy fostered, at the individual level, that spirit of experimentation and enterprise without which there can be no learning. If both Sparta and Athens made great and comparable political accomplishments, culturally there is no contest. The Golden Age of Greece as we know it was largely an Athenian phenomenon.

Democracy certainly presents risks, in terms of cultural decline, of rejection of necessary disciplines, of failure to recognize harsh truths, let alone higher Truth. In the contemporary postwar era, certainly, democracy seems to mean a slouch into varying degrees of obesity and effeminacy. Nonetheless, there is no denying the collective power and dynamism which flows, in the right conditions, from the willing, indeed democratic participation of the citizens. The challenge for republics is to secure the buy-in and collective wisdom enabled by widespread civic participation while guarding against the gradual leveling and slouching caused by excessive egalitarianism and individualism. Ideally, each citizen's degree of influence over the polity should be exactly that amount which promotes the common good. In general, a citizen's political influence would be proportional to his wisdom and virtue.

Athenian power derived from the city's particular combination of democratic dynamism and the wider communitarian, competitive, and spirited character of Greek society and culture. At Athens, individual freedom and direct democracy were inflected by a familial, religious, communal, martial, patriotic, and even racial ideal of citizenship which gave pride of place to parents and soldiers. In short, ancient

---

[138] See Jennifer Tolbert Roberts, *Athens on Trial: The Antidemocratic Tradition in Western Thought* (Princeton: Princeton University Press, 1994).

Athens' civic ideal was decidedly spirited and biopolitical.

"GIVING BIRTH TO MEN"
SPARTA AS THE FIRST ETHNOSTATE

If in Athens we have biopolitical aspects, insofar as the democracy was tempered by Hellenic virtue, in Sparta we have a state wholly dedicated to systematic organization of the society according to a biopolitical ideal. Sparta's mixed system of government and fiercely communitarian and hierarchical customs were supposed to have been created by the semi-legendary lawgiver Lycurgus, who perhaps lived in the ninth century B.C. Nothing can be said for certain about his life. Lycurgus was, in later ages, rumored to have traveled to Egypt, Ionia, Crete, and even India, where "he talked with the Gymnosophists,"[139] before establishing Sparta's constitution. What is clear, in any case, is that the basic law and way of life attributed to Lycurgus, and credited for Sparta's success, were emphatically biopolitical.

Spartan law and culture were obsessed with systematically ensuring good breeding, martial skill, and group unity. Spartan ethics and law considered that what was good was whatever was good for the community. During a debate as to whether a commander had abused his authority, the Spartan king Agesilaus argued: "The point to be examined ... is simply this: has this action been good or bad for Sparta?"[140] Kevin MacDonald has argued that the law instituted by Lycurgus—featuring in-group altruism and unity, relative egalitarianism, separation from out-groups, specialization in warfare, and communally-determined in-group eugenics—qualifies as a genuine "altruistic group evolutionary strategy."[141]

---

[139] Literally "naked wise men," which is what the Greeks called the Hindu and Buddhist ascetics they found in India. Plutarch, *Life of Lycurgus*, 4.

[140] Xenophon, *Hellenica*, 5.2.32.

[141] Kevin MacDonald, *A People That Shall Dwell Alone: Judaism as a Group Evolutionary Strategy, with Diaspora Peoples* (Lincoln, Nebraska:

Athens & Sparta: An Analysis of Two Ethnostates

We face an almost insurmountable problem in reconstructing the historical Sparta, given that the overwhelming majority of sources about that state are foreign and, in particular, Athenian. The problem is worsened by the fact that the authors whose writings survive often tended to idealize Sparta: great landowners who admired that oligarchy's stability, foreign Greeks who sought to emulate Spartan power, and philosophers who modeled their own ideal politics on Spartan government and education. The Spartans were famous and widely-admired for their military expertise. In one of Plato's dialogues, it is said that the Spartans' "sole concern in life is to search out and take up any skill which, once mastered and practiced, will give them the upper hand in war over others ... there are no Greeks who rate this kind of thing higher than the Spartans" (Plato, *Laches*, 182e-183a). In another dialogue, Plato has Socrates humorously mention "the Spartanizing cults in the other cities ... all these people getting their ears mangled aping the Spartans, lacing on leather gloves, exercising fanatically, and wearing short capes, as if Sparta's political power depended on these things" (*Protagoras*, 342c). Though a contemporary, Thucydides himself complains of his difficulties in acquiring information due to Spartan secrecy. We, at 2,500 years remove, are naturally in an infinitely worse position. Sparta comes down to us today only through the distorted echoes of foreigners and philosophers.

The main sources for Spartan government and society are Xenophon and Plutarch. Xenophon was not only a contemporary, but served Sparta and even sent his sons there to be educated in their manner. Xenophon is then a knowledgeable but biased source. Plutarch, a much later Greek historian writing under the Roman Empire in the first century A.D., speaks at greater length than Xenophon but his *Life of Lycurgus* is evidently more an exercise in philosophical idealizing, with a moral purpose in mind, than actual history. The sources then present a mixture of the echoes of Spartan historical realities and of the authors' idealizations. While fully distinguishing between these two is impossible, we can say based on the surviving 'myth of Sparta' that both the practice of Spartan politics and the ideal of ancient political philosophy were eminently biopolitical.

Few forms of government have so drawn the admiration of both liberals and 'totalitarians' as that of Sparta. Many republicans, both ancient and modern, have been impressed by the Spartans' 'mixed' system of government, with its combination of monarchic, aristocratic, and democratic elements, as conducive to social unity, stability, and the rule of law. The Founding Fathers of the United States sought to emulate the stability of Sparta's constitution and saw in it a precursor to their own system of checks and balances.[142] Thinkers of a more communitarian bent, such as Rousseau and Hitler, have for their part admired the city for its rigorous holistic organization.

The Spartan citizen body was made up of landowning males past the age of 30 who had completed their arduous military training and education. These Spartiates, know as *Homoioi* (roughly meaning 'Equals' or 'Peers') made up an uncertain, but no doubt small, percentage of the country's population. The Helots, Sparta's large population of agricultural serfs, provided the citizens with the leisure to specialize in military training. These slaves were fellow Greek-speakers although, as non-Dorian Achaeans, there was a certain degree of ethnic difference from the Spartiates. So-called 'Peripherals' (*perioikoi*), foreign residents engaging in various skilled crafts at the service of the Spartans, appear to have regularly accumulated

---

[142] John Adams wrote:

Representations, instead of collections, of the people; a total separation of the executive from the legislative power, and of the judicial from both; and a balance in the legislature, by three independent, equal branches, are perhaps the only three discoveries in the constitution of a free government, since the institution of Lycurgus.

John Adams, *A Defense of the Constitutions of the United States* (1787), Preface, on wikisource.org.

around the Spartan state.

The Spartiates were famous and admired by foreign aristocrats for not having to work, instead being free to specialize themselves in military matters.[143] According to Aristotle, "growing one's hair [is] noble among the Spartans, as a sign of a free man, since it is not easy for a long-haired man to perform any manual task" (*Rhetoric*, 1.9). Lycurgus is said to have encouraged Spartiates to grow their hair long as this "renders handsome men better looking and ugly ones more frightening."[144]

Sparta was presided over by two relatively weak kings, from two distinct royal families, who served as priests, generals, and occasionally judges. The Ephors, five powerful magistrates elected by all citizens for a non-renewable one-year term, were responsible for implementing decrees and had judicial powers to supervise and prosecute others, including the kings. The most powerful body was the *Gerousia*, a council made up of the two kings and 28 elders over the age of 60, who were elected for life. The *Gerousia* set the political agenda, debated issues, and presented the decisions open to the Assembly. The Assembly of Spartan citizens did not lead itself but could only decide on whatever was presented by the *Gerousia*. Through these institutions, the Spartan regime sought to conciliate the values of authority, stability, law, aristocracy, seniority, and community. When asked why he did not institute a democracy, Lycurgus is supposed to have answered: "Make your own household a democracy first."[145]

Spartan society was systematically organized by the regime to achieve social unity and martial prowess. Practically, among the elite Spartiate body of citizens, this meant the encouragement of births, the communal education of children according to an austere and militaristic way of life, and constantly sharing life experiences through common meals and training. Failure to live up to the city's demanding standards

---

[143] Plutarch, *Lycurgus*, 24.
[144] *Ibid.*, 22.
[145] *Ibid.*, 19.

was harshly punished. Citizenship was not an automatic right, but had to be earned, by passing one's training and paying one's dues to the mess hall. According to Xenophon, Lycurgus "gave an equal share in the state to all law-abiding citizens, without regard for physical or financial deficiencies. But Lycurgus made it clear that if anyone should shirk the effort required to keep his laws, then he would no longer be considered one of the Equals."[146]

Following such customs was in Sparta a sacred duty. Not only were Sparta's institutions and customs attributed to the wise Lycurgus, but these were said to have been approved by Apollo himself. This was significant as the Spartans appear to have been exceptionally pious, regularly engaging in common rituals and sacrifices. Herodotus says that for the Spartans "divine matters took precedence over human ones" (Herodotus, 5.63). Once again, we find religious piety being central to the foundations of custom and the enforcement of group norms. Xenophon unsurprisingly emphasizes Spartan martial prowess. However, it is after giving an account of the excellence of the Spartans' rituals while on campaign that he says: "if you witnessed this you would think that militarily others are amateurs, whereas Spartans alone are real masters of the craft of war."[147] For both Xenophon and Plutarch, the joint and pious fulfillment of ritual inspires confidence in men before battle.[148]

Spartan politics began with the rearing of children and their education in the martial and communitarian values of their society. Lycurgus is said to have "regarded the upbringing of children as the greatest and noblest responsibility of the legislator."[149] Young men and women performed sporting events in the nude, so as to encourage both physical fitness and

---

[146] Xenophon, *Spartan Constitution*, 10.

[147] *Ibid.*, 13.

[148] Polybius similarly went so far as to argue that Rome's extreme religiosity was what made her constitution "so markedly superior" to other states (Polybius, 6.56). See Guillaume Durocher, "Religious Piety in Sparta & Rome," *Counter-Currents*, January 18, 2018.

[149] Plutarch, *Lycurgus*, 14.

marriages. Lycurgus was emphatic that there was a *civic duty* to ensure that the next generation of citizens be not only be produced, but be the healthiest and best possible. Plutarch reports this while drawing a direct analogy with heredity in animals:

> First and foremost Lycurgus considered children to belong not privately to their fathers, but jointly to the city, so that he wanted citizens produced not from random partners, but from the best. Moreover he observed a good deal of stupidity and humbug in others' rules on these matters. Such people have their bitches and mares mounted by the finest dogs and stallions whose owners they can prevail upon for a favor or fee. But their wives they lock up and guard, claiming the right to produce *their* children exclusively, though they may be imbeciles, or past their prime, or diseased. They forget that where children are born of poor stock, the first to suffer from their poor condition are those who possess and rear them, while the same applies conversely to the good qualities of those from sound stock.[150]

Past a certain age, single men were severely stigmatized. Lycurgus also believed that "the production of children was the most important duty of free women," thereby making a fundamental contribution to the society which sustained their freedom.[151] Spartan women were not sedentary and trapped in the family home, as most Greek women were. As their husbands were training constantly away from home, Spartan women were unusual in managing their own households and often becoming wealthy in their own right. These women were discouraged from overeating and encouraged to participate in sports such as wrestling and javelin-throwing on health grounds:

> Thereby their children in embryo would make a strong start in strong bodies and would develop better, while the women themselves would also bear their pregnancies with

---

[150] *Ibid.*, 15.
[151] Xenophon, *Spartan Constitution*, 1.

vigor and would meet the challenge of a childbirth in a successful, relaxed way.[152]

It was apparently considered shameful for men to be seen with their wives at Sparta, making sex irregular and the sex drive strong. There was another primitive eugenic rationale behind these measures: young, healthy, active, lustful parents were believed to produce healthier and stronger children. Newborns which were "puny and deformed" were said to be thrown into an abyss, the Spartans "considering it better both for itself and the state that the child should die if right from its birth it was poorly endowed for health or strength."[153]

Lycurgus is supposed to have banned dowries and make-up: "So that none should be left unmarried because of poverty nor any pursued for their wealth, but that each man should study the girl's character and make his choice on the basis of her good qualities."[154] His concern for biological quality was so extreme he apparently even allowed for a bizarre official practice of 'eugenic cuckoldry.' An elderly husband could have children by introducing his wife to "any man whose physique and personality he admired."[155] Conversely, a wifeless man could, if "eager to have remarkable children," have them "by any fertile and well-bred woman who came to his attention, subject to her husband's consent." Plutarch claims that by this measure the Spartans succeeded in "planting in fruitful soil, so to speak, and producing fine children who would be linked to fine ancestors by blood and family."[156] These strange measures were eugenic and natalist in their objectives, and perhaps emphasize Spartans' supreme subjection of their personal and familial interests to the public good, ideally up to and including access to their wives! Xenophon, an eyewitness source, claims that by these methods, Sparta gained "men whose size and strength are … superior."[157]

[152] Plutarch, *Lycurgus*, 14.
[153] *Ibid.*, 16.
[154] Plutarch, *Sayings of the Spartans*, "Lycurgus," 15.
[155] Xenophon, *Spartan Constitution*, 1.
[156] Plutarch, *Lycurgus*, 15.

There was an enormous emphasis in Sparta, as in no other Greek city, on the truly *systematic* education and training of the citizens in order to shape a culture conducive to the public good. Spartan education was communal and austere. The children were taken from their families at age seven and would not complete their training until they were 29. At that point, if the young man had succeeded in this *agoge* training, he would be made a full citizen. Whereas wealthy Athenians might have a private slave tutor for their children, Spartan children had a single Trainer-in-Chief (a *paidomus*, literally a "boy-herdsman") and any citizen could discipline them.

Young Spartans would go bare-foot, have a single cloak to wear all year in hot or cold, and would be given a limited amount of food, measures all aimed at making them tougher. Youths were expected to steal from or even murder Helots. The Spartans in general appear to have treated their Helots with extreme cruelty, from humiliation through making them drunk to regular ritualized murder, measures evidently aimed at keeping this class firmly separate and subservient. Plutarch himself concedes that "there is nothing to match either the freedom of the free man at Sparta or the slavery of the slave."[158] Montesquieu later would sum up the conflicted feelings of many classical liberals concerning Sparta, saying: "Lycurgus, combining larceny with the spirit of justice, the harshest slavery with extreme liberty, the most atrocious sentiments with the greatest moderation, gave stability to his city."[159]

We must imagine Sparta an ordered, hierarchical, and pious state characterized by constant ritual and training, a cross between a military-athletic camp and a monastery. Plutarch says:

> Spartiates' training extended into adulthood, for no one was permitted to live as he pleased. Instead, just as in a camp, so in the city, they followed a prescribed lifestyle and devoted themselves to communal concerns. They

[157] Xenophon, *Spartan Constitution*, 1.
[158] Plutarch, *Lycurgus*, 28.
[159] Montesquieu, *L'Esprit des lois*, vol. I, 4.6.

viewed themselves absolutely as part of their country, rather than as individuals, and so unless assigned a particular job they would always be observing the boys and giving them some useful piece of instruction, or learning themselves from their elders.[160]

Concerning adolescents, Lycurgus "gave orders that even in the streets they should keep both hands inside their cloaks, should proceed in silence, and should not let their gaze wander in any direction, but fix their eyes on the ground before them."[161] Young adults were encouraged to be competitive in music, sports, and "manly gallantry."[162] This education succeeded, according to Xenophon: "The result has been that respect and obedience in combination are found to a high degree at Sparta [the system] turns out men who are more disciplined, more respectful, and (when required) more self-controlled."[163] By his laws, Lycurgus was said to have "done away with prudery, sheltered upbringing, and effeminacy of any kind."[164]

There is a sense in which all life for Spartan citizens was communal and hierarchical. Even once one had completed the *agoge*, Spartiates would eat together in common mess halls, again creating common feeling. The ages were mixed, so that the older could teach the young, and citizens were expected to discuss noble deeds. In the gymnasium, the oldest man would supervise and citizens were expected to train regularly. Xenophon claims that "it would certainly not be easy for anyone to find men healthier or more physically apt than Spartiates."[165]

Lycurgus reputedly had accompanied his basic law with a land reform giving each in the small citizen class an equal property, although economic inequality gradually accumulated over time. A positive consequence of the Spartans'

---

[160] Plutarch, *Lycurgus*, 24.
[161] Xenophon, *Spartan Constitution*, 3.
[162] *Ibid.*, 4.
[163] *Ibid.*, 2.
[164] Plutarch, *Lycurgus*, 14.
[165] Xenophon, *Spartan Constitution*, 5.

systematically communal lifestyle was an extremely high degree of trust among citizens. They shared each other's hunting dogs and horses, the latter being extremely valuable property in those days. Citizens even trusted others to beat their own children if they had done wrong, for "there was a sense in which everyone regarded himself as father, tutor, and commander of each boy."[166]

The entire society was oriented towards inculcating martial valor and unity. Cowards were severely stigmatized, to the extent that they could be beaten freely and that "the citizens considered an honorable death preferable to a life of disgrace."[167] Citizens were banned from working and instead "all their time was taken up by choral dances, festivals, feasts, hunting expeditions, physical exercise, and conversation."[168] At the same time, the society's general frugality meant "there was ... no need to amass wealth (with all the work and concentration that this entails), since riches were emphatically neither envied nor esteemed."[169] Music played a large role in Spartan society and their songs dealt with military heroism, sacrifice for Sparta, and the shaming of cowards. The result was an intensely communal ethos:

> Altogether [Lycurgus] accustomed citizens to have no desire for a private life, nor knowledge of one, but rather to be like bees, always attached to the community, swarming together around their leader, and almost ecstatic with fervent ambition to devote themselves entirely to their country.[170]

The supreme values of this society are suggested even by their burial practices: "Those who buried a dead person were not permitted to inscribe the name on a grave except in the cases of a man who had died on campaign or a woman who had died in labor."[171] The dead were buried within the city, so

---

[166] Plutarch, *Lycurgus*, 17.
[167] Xenophon, *Spartan Constitution*, 9.
[168] Plutarch, *Lycurgus*, 24.
[169] *Ibid.*
[170] *Ibid.*, 25.
[171] *Ibid.*, 27.

as to habituate the young to their sight.

Sparta was an exceptionally xenophobic society, sharply controlling population movements of both citizens and foreigners so as to maintain their unique customs. Xenophon says that "expulsions of foreigners used to occur and absence abroad was not permitted, so that citizens should not be infected by lax habits caught from foreigners."[172] Iron bars, worthless outside of Sparta, were the only legal currency in the state. Plutarch claims this also led to great benefits: "it was impossible to buy any shoddy foreign goods, and no cargo of merchandise would enter the harbors, no teacher of rhetoric trod Laconian soil, no begging seer, no pimp, no maker of gold or silver ornaments."[173]

Sparta's values of patriotism and sacrifice were apparently so ingrained in the society that Spartan women were among their fiercest enforcers. A Spartan mother reputedly handed her son a shield as he was leaving for battle saying: "Son, either with this or on this."[174] There are many stories of Spartan mothers rejoicing that their son died in battle or conversely, if he had returned by fleeing as a coward, killing him herself. Plutarch says:

> [T]he women came to talk as well as to think in the way that Leonidas' wife Gorgo is said to have done. For when some woman, evidently a foreigner, said to her: "You Laconian women are the only ones who can rule men," she replied: "That is because we are the only ones who give birth to men."[175]

As he left to fight and die at Thermopylae, Leonidas is supposed to have told his wife "to marry good men and bear good children."[176] When Xerxes proposed making Leonidas tyrant of Greece, he is supposed to have responded: "For me, it is better to die for Greece than to be monarch of the people of

---

[172] Xenophon, *Spartan Constitution*, 14.

[173] Plutarch, *Lycurgus*, 9.

[174] Plutarch, *Sayings of Spartan Women*, 16.

[175] Plutarch, *Lycurgus*, 14.

[176] Plutarch, *Sayings of the Spartans*, "Leonidas," 2.

my race."[177]

The Spartans were famous for their brief 'Laconic' sayings and sharp wit. Plato claimed that the "distinctive kind of Spartan wisdom" was found in "their pithy, memorable sayings" (*Protagoras*, 343c), which can be recalled easily and thus be borne in mind in our daily lives. Laconic brevity also reflected the Spartan concern with *doing well* rather than merely speaking or speculating like the verbose Athenians. Lycurgus is supposed to have forbidden his laws from being written as "the guiding principles of most importance for the happiness and excellence of a state would remain securely fixed if they were embedded in citizens' character and training."[178] When asked why the Spartans kept their laws on bravery unwritten, a Spartan king is said to have replied: "it's better for [the youth] to get used to acts of bravery rather than to study written documents."[179]

A number of Spartan sayings have come down to us, although their precise attributions to various historical figures are probably unreliable. The Spartans, like the Cynic philosopher Diogenes, came to be idealized across the ancient world as an example of perfect virtue and would then tend to be credited with proverbs reflecting this. Nonetheless, the *Sayings of the Spartans* collected by Plutarch do give us a feeling for the Spartan spirit, as in the following sample:

> When asked how anyone could rule the citizens safely without having a bodyguard, [King Agasicles] said: "By ruling them in the way that fathers do their sons." (Agasicles, 2)

> [King Agesilaus] watched a mouse being pulled from its hole by a small boy. When the mouse turned round, bit the

---

[177] *Ibid.*, 10. Interestingly, many of Plutarch's *Sayings of the Spartans* – which may have in fact been attributed in later years – contain expressions of pan-Hellenic patriotism, sentiments generally at odds with the more narrowly self-interested realities of Spartan foreign policy.

[178] Plutarch, *Lycurgus*, 13.

[179] Plutarch, *Sayings of the Spartans*, "Zeuxidamus," 1.

hand of its captor and escaped, he pointed this out to those present and said: "When the tiniest creature defends itself like this against aggressors, what ought men to do, do you reckon?" (Agesilaus, 9).

When somebody asked what gain the laws of Lycurgus had brought to Sparta, he said: "Contempt for pleasures." (Agesilaus, 20)

To the man who was amazed at how modest his clothes and his meals were, and those of the other Spartans as well, he said: "Freedom is what we reap from this way of life, my friend. (Agesilaus, 20).

Asked once how far Sparta's boundaries stretched, he brandished his spear and said: "As far as this can reach." (Agesilaus, 28)

When somebody else asked why Sparta lacked fortification walls, he pointed to the citizens under arms and said: "These are the Spartans' walls." (Agesilaus, 29)

When another person put the same question to him, his reply was: "Cities shouldn't be fortified with stones or timbers, but with the valor of their inhabitants." (Agesilaus, 30)

When someone inquired of him what children should learn, he said: "What they will also use when they become men." (Agesilaus, 67)

As [King Agis] was passing through the Corinthians' walls and observed their height and strength and great extent, he said: "What women live in this place?" (Agis son of Archidamus, 6)

When someone was presenting proposals for the liberty of the Greeks which, while not ignoble, were difficult to put into effect, he said: "My friend, your words need to be complemented by force and money." (Agis son of Archidamus, 13)

When asked how one should remain a free man, he said:

"By despising death." (Agis son of Archidamus, 18)

When somebody said that [the philosopher Xenocrates] was a wise man and one of those who search for virtue, [King] Eudamidas said: "And when will he make use of it if he is still searching for it?" (Eudamidas son of Archidamus, 1)

To the stranger who was claiming that among his own citizens he was called a friend of Sparta [King Theopompus] said: "It would be better for you to be called a friend of your fellow citizens rather than a friend of Sparta." (Theopompus, 2)

When a man from Megara was rather outspoken towards him in the general assembly, [Lysander] said: "My friend, your words require the backing of a city." (Lysander, 8)

When a Persian inquired what type of constitution met with his greatest approval, he said: "Whichever gives brave men and cowards their due." (Lysander, 11)

When someone was asking why they made the poet Tyrtaeus [an Athenian, whose poems provide some of the only surviving Spartan literature] a citizen, [Panthoidas] said: "So that a foreigner should never be seen as our leader." (Panthoidas, 3)

When amongst the spoils some people were amazed at the extravagance of the Persians' clothing, he said: "Better for them to be men of great worth rather than to have possessions of great worth." (Panthoidas, 5)

When [Governor Pedaritus] observed some effeminate person being nonetheless praised by the citizens for his fairness, he said: "Men who are like women should not be praised nor should women who are like men, unless some necessity forces the woman." (Pedaritus, 2)

When someone asked [King Charillus] which type of government he considered the best, he said: "The one in which the largest number of citizens are willing to compete with each other in excellence and without civil concord."

(Charillus, 4).

THE VIRTUOUS CIRCLE OF SPARTAN POWER: DISCIPLINE THROUGH LORDSHIP

The defining fact of Spartan life was the hard-won conquest of neighboring Messenia in the eighth century and the enslavement of its population as Helots. This victory had launched the virtuous circle of Spartan power. The subjugated Helots provided the Spartan citizen-soldiers with both the leisure and the imperative need to dedicate themselves to martial prowess in the face of a constant threat of rebellion at home. The entire social organization of Sparta came to reflect this state of affairs. Thucydides noted: "most Spartan institutions have always been designed with a view to security against the Helots."[180]

The system instituted by Lycurgus proved remarkably successful for centuries. At Sparta's height, the organization and training of around 8,000 Spartiate citizen-soldiers to suppress the Helots also translated into international military power, which in turn allowed Sparta to secure allies and thus yet more military power in the Peloponnese. Xenophon opens his account of the Spartan regime saying: "Sparta, despite having one of the lowest populations, had nonetheless clearly become the most powerful and most famous state in Greece."[181] The unsentimental Thucydides says of Sparta: "its system of good order is very ancient and it has never been subject to tyrants. The Spartan constitution has remained unchanged for somewhat over 400 years ... a source of strength, enabling their political intervention in other states" (Thu., 1.18).

Indeed, Sparta was hailed for her lack of civil wars among

---

[180] Thucydides, *History of the Peloponnesian War*, 4.80. Translation from Paul Cartledge, *Sparta and Lakonia: A Regional History, 1300 to 362 BC* (New York: Routledge, 2002), Annex 4, p. 299. The passage is somewhat ambiguous. Cartledge also provides an alternative translation: "as far as the Helots are concerned, most Spartan institutions have always been designed with a view to security."

[181] Xenophon, *Spartan Constitution*, 1.

citizens, a common cause of grief in the Greek world, and for having intervened to liberate other Greek cities from tyrants. Sparta's oligarchic government seems to have been better than Athens at securing consenting allies among fellow-Greek city-states. The Spartans seem to have been better at developing stable interpersonal ties with foreign elites,[182] whereas the Athenian democracy tended to a chauvinism serving her own citizens alone without regard for its imperial subjects. Thucydides has Pericles boast that Athens did not use undependable foreign allies in war but only Athenian residents, implying that Sparta in contrast had the assistance of more-or-less consenting allies.[183]

The great successes of Spartan social organization came at a

---

[182] The Old Oligarch argued:

[F]or oligarchic cities it is necessary to keep to alliances and oaths. If they do not abide by agreements or if injustice is done, there are the names of the few who made the agreement. But whatever agreements the populace makes can be repudiated by referring the blame to the one who spoke or took the vote, while the others declare that they were absent or did not approve of the agreement made in the full assembly. (Old Oligarch, 2.18)

[183] Pericles says: "The Spartans do not invade our land on their own, but they have all their allies with them" (Thu., 2.39). Earlier, Pericles had argued that the Spartans' need for their allies' agreement to take decisions would paralyze them:

In a single pitched battle the Peloponnesians and their allies are capable of resisting the whole of Greece, but they are incapable of maintaining a war against an opposition which differs from them in kind: as long, that is, that they continue without a central deliberative forum, for lack of which they cannot take any immediate decisive action, and as long as all the various tribal groups in a miscellaneous confederacy have equal votes, so each promotes its own concern – a system unlikely to produce any effective results. (Thu., 1.141)

This can be taken as an early argument for sovereign central government rather than divided confederal government. Perhaps the need to convince their allies was partly responsible for the supposed timidity and slowness of Spartan foreign policy (Thucydides, 8.96).

heavy price. The city was devoid of material culture, leaving precious few artifacts in the archaeological record. Even during its heyday, Thucydides observed that Spartan architecture was so unimpressive in comparison with Athens, that "if the city of Sparta were to become deserted, with only the temples and the foundations of buildings left to view, I imagine that with the passage of time future generations would find it very hard to credit its reputed power (Thu., 1.10). Alexander Hamilton wrote that "Sparta was little better than a well-regulated camp."[184] Sparta is unlikely to have had much intellectual culture either. If there were any Spartan dramatists and philosophers, there is virtually nothing that survives of them. There is little to suggest there was any Spartan equivalent of Athens' extraordinary theatrical and philosophical achievements, notwithstanding the idealizations and ironic paradoxes of the philosophers.[185] Indeed, the Spartans were

---

[184] Alexander Hamilton, *Federalist No. 6*.

[185] Plutarch states that "some . . . claim that devotion to the intellect is more characteristic of Spartans than love of physical exercise" (*Lycurgus*, 20) and, in a beautiful rhetorical flourish, concludes his *Life* saying:

> Lycurgus . . . brought into the light of day, not paper theories, but a functioning constitution which is quite unmatched. To those who suspect that it is impracticable for a theoretical structure to be centered upon a Sage, he has exhibited his whole city practicing philosophy" (*Lycurgus*, 31).

Such passages in Plutarch must be considered idealizations and inspiring exhortations to political philosophy, rather than realistic history.

In his *Protagoras*, Plato has Socrates ironically claim that "the Spartans have the best education in philosophy and debate" (342e). This is no place for a full commentary on this dialogue. However, given the context, it seems Plato is making a paradoxical and humorous comment praising certain Spartan virtues – namely discretion, Laconic wit, remembrance of wise sayings – as integral to the practice of philosophy. One of the great challenges in studying ancient Greek literature, is determining whether a text is ironic or is making some kind of in-joke. Herodotus, Socrates, Plato, and Xenophon have all been noted for their use of irony.

said to be "the least intellectual of men" (Aristotle, *Rhetoric*, 1398b).

Sparta was basically a caste society. Besides the solidary elite citizen body of Spartiates, there were also "fallen" Spartans who had lost their citizenship for reasons of poverty or dishonor, "neo-citizens" who had been naturalized (especially in the later years) to have more soldiers, the working Peripherals who gravitated around the city, and finally the Helots. This appears to have been, somewhat like ancient and medieval India, a largely static society. This was certainly a closed society in which, besides the rigid social order, foreigners were restricted from entry and regularly evicted to prevent the Spartans from being infected with foreign cultural influence. Furthermore, it appears that Sparta's power in the Peloponnese was based on its ability to retard urban development abroad: rival cities were broken up into villages and placed under the government of Spartan-friendly landowners.[186] Sparta has an air of stagnation, and while the appearance of eternity typically impressed the Ancients, we Moderns tend to feel that that which does not grow is already doomed. On the other hand, as we live in times of perpetual economic growth leading to cultural collapse and ecological exhaustion, the Spartan ideal of a socio-political steady-state may take on a new relevance.

By the yardstick of individual freedom, the ledger is perhaps not *quite* as much in Athens' favor as one might expect. In every premodern economy, the precious leisure necessary for culture and civic life is necessarily the purview of a select few. On the whole, Athens no doubt afforded more scope for individual merit, freedom, and political participation to a greater share of the population. But one also should not forget that democratic Athens itself was based on chattel slavery, subject colonies, and house-bound women. In the Spartan empire, women and allied states generally enjoyed more freedom than those of Athens. Furthermore, those who have tasted the monastic life may also suspect that the highly-

---

[186] Xenophon, *Hellenica*, 5.2.7.

regimented Spartan lifestyle, of constant training in community life, athletics, and self-restraint, may have offered citizens certain deep satisfactions not available with the demoliberal lifestyle.

Ironically, Sparta's greatest failing was precisely in the biological, and specifically in the demographic, sphere. Sparta, somewhat miraculously, defeated Athens in the Peloponnesian War but fell within decades due to the failure to maintain the population of citizen-soldiers. As Kevin MacDonald observes:

> It would appear that the system devised by the Israelite lawgiver [Moses] was in some sense a better strategy for maintaining long-term ethnic coherence than that designed by the Spartan lawgiver, since the Israelite strategy, arguably, continues today (see [*The Culture of Critique*], Ch. 8). The Spartan system was an excellent defensive system, but was ill equipped to administer an empire, and there were no provisions, such as the hereditary Israelite priestly class, that would have allowed it to survive being militarily conquered—a contingency that was all but inevitable in the ancient world and that certainly continues to some extent today.[187]

For MacDonald, "while the group strategy of the ancient Spartans was successful for a significant period, it was ultimately a failure."[188] In marked contrast with the Jews, who were able to survive through fanatical adherence to a dogmatic ethnocentric religion, the Spartans proved completely incapable of maintaining their identity and group evolutionary strategy in the absence of a supportive sovereign state. In this respect, the Spartans were sadly typical of Western peoples. There is furthermore little reason to believe that Sparta's primitive eugenic measures had any much positive effect.

We would be wrong to downplay the Spartan achievement. The other Greeks were enormously impressed by those four centuries of Spartan order and power, during which they

---

[187] MacDonald, *PSDA*, p. 395.
[188] *Ibid.*, p. 8.

played a major role in Greek affairs. Polybius would later give a balanced summary of the greatness and limits of Sparta through a useful comparison with the Roman Republic. He remarked that "the constitution so framed by Lycurgus preserved independence in Sparta longer than anywhere else in recorded history" (Polybius, 6.10). Furthermore:

> [T]he Lycurgan system is designed for the secure maintenance of the status quo and the preservation of autonomy. Those who believe that this is what a state is for must agree that there is not and never has been a better system or constitution than that of the Spartans. But if one has greater ambitions than that—if one thinks that it is a finer and nobler thing to be a world-class leader, with an extensive dominion and empire, the center and focal point of everyone's world—then one must admit that the Spartan constitution is deficient and the Roman constitution is superior and more dynamic. (Polybius, 6.50)

There is no doubt that there is a tendency to "slouching" in human history: every new generation balks at the unexplained disciplines and traditional rigors inherited from the past. If this is done for the sake of comfort and pleasure, as opposed to replacing a tradition with new practices because they are more conducive to the public good, we call this decadence. In Sparta alone, the citizens were able to maintain a fearsome degree of virtue, by the authority held by the elders, by the systematic education and training of the citizens, and by the threat of insurrection posed by the Helots.

The constitution of Lycurgus—with its stability, mixing of elitism and democracy, sovereignty, lawfulness, training, social unity, and sacrifice for the common good—may serve a model for all nations who truly wish to fight to determine their own destiny and maintain lasting adherence to certain values. The example of Sparta, like Prussia in the modern era, incidentally shows that smallness is no reason for defeatism, that all nations have, with effort, a chance at achieving freedom and greatness. No wonder that the law of Lycurgus and the sacrifice of Leonidas' 300 Spartans have inspired philosophers and statesmen throughout the ages, even in the face of terrible odds. Given the challenges facing Western and European nations in the twenty-first century—consider the sheer scale of the rising foreign superpowers, ecological threats, and demographic collapse—the Spartan experience in building a lawful, holistic, and biopolitical martial republic may yet help inspire our renewal.

THUCYDIDES' BITTER EPILOGUE: STATE OVER BLOOD IN THE PELOPONNESIAN WAR

As we have seen, Athens and Sparta were each sustained by a particular feedback loop, a virtuous circle, which sustained and reinforced their power over the years. Athens enjoyed a virtuous circle of commerce, sea-power, demography, and empire, while in Sparta lordship over a large slave class both made possible and required systematic military organization which enabled the city's regional hegemony. Both Spartan and Athenian power, in different ways, were doomed by being excessively leveraged and based on enormous disenfranchised classes of would-be rebels. Spartan power was based on the subjugation of the Helots, Athenian power on that of its imperial subjects. In both cases, a lasting collapse was a constant threat, as any successful rebellion or large-scale military defeat would mean the break-up of their empires. What Pericles told the Athenians regarding their empire was equally true of the Spartans concerning their Helots: "The empire you possess is by now like a tyranny—perhaps wrong to acquire it, but certainly dangerous to let it go" (Thu., 2.63).

Athens never fully recovered from her defeat in the Peloponnesian War, entailing the destruction of her city walls and the loss of her empire, although there was a short-lived revival in the fourth century, and the city remained culturally influential long thereafter. Spartan power, despite lasting for four centuries, proved even more leveraged and brittle. With Sparta's defeats at the hands of the Thebans in the first half of the fourth century, the Messenian Helots were liberated and the cities of Messenia, Mantinea, and Megalopolis were (re)founded as rival powers to contain the Spartans in the Peloponnese. When Spartan power fell, this proved to be surprisingly rapid and permanent. Sparta and Athens in fact were insufficiently ethno-statal in being ethnostates of too narrow a character: neither was able to give representation and buy-in to their subject classes, even though these were fellow Greeks and, in the case of Athens, often fellow Ionians.

Indeed, if Homer's *Iliad* and Herodotus' *Histories* are celebrations of Hellenic unity in great wars, Thucydides' *History of the Peloponnesian War* is largely a bitter chronicle of fratricidal slaughter, of how narrow state interests tragically took precedence over shared blood. As the nineteenth-century American philosopher John Fiske observed, particularist political loyalties overwhelmed the otherwise widespread attachment to Greek identity:

> Greek history, after the expulsion of the Persians, is the history of the struggle between the higher and lower patriotism—between the two feelings known to the Greeks as PanHellenism and Autonomism ... The mournful history of Thukydides tells us autonomism won the day entailing the moral and political failure of Greek civilization.[189]

Thucydides says of the scale of the destruction in the Peloponnesian War:

> This war far exceeded the Persian War in length, and over its course the suffering that resulted for Greece was unparalleled on such a timescale. Never before were so many cities captured and desolated, some by barbarians, others through internal conflict (and in some a change of population followed their capture); never so many refugees or such slaughter, both in the war itself and as a consequence of civil strife. (Thu., 1.23)

---

[189] John Fiske, *Outlines of Cosmic Philosophy: Based on the Doctrine of Evolution, with Criticism on Positive Philosophy* (London: 1874), 2.205.

As in the Persian Wars, there were constant appeals to kinship throughout the Peloponnesian War.[190] When a city would ask for assistance from or side with either Sparta or Athens, any existing colonial (e.g. between mother-city and settlement) and tribal (e.g. Dorian/Ionian) kinship ties would be cited as a justification. In addition to being a geopolitical war between Sparta and Athens as rival states, the conflict was also seen as an intra-Greek tribal conflict between sturdy but conservative Dorians and soft but dynamic Ionians. Both sides claimed to be serving the best interests of Greece: the Athenians arguing that they had earned their empire in the war against the invading Persians, the Spartans asserting that the overthrow of Athens would restore freedom to the Greek city-states.

For Thucydides, however, there is no doubt that such claims were overwhelmingly propagandistic or mere rationalizations. He is often considered the father of the 'realist' school of thought in international relations, stressing the amoral and ruthless interests of states over sentimental concerns. Indeed, Thucydides' *History* meticulously documents the familial, colonial, and tribal kinship ties between individuals and cities, only to better highlight how these bonds were frequently violated with the utmost brutality.

Concerning political leaders, Thucydides sarcastically tells of how "Pausanias of Sparta and Themistocles of Athens, the two most eminent Greeks of their time," (Thu., 1.139) who had led the fight against Persia, went on to ignominiously collaborate with the King after they had become unpopular at home. Concerning domestic politics, the geopolitical conflict between Athens and Sparta magnified the vicious class and ideological conflict existing in many Greek cities, between rich and poor, oligarchs and democrats. Hence, the religious and familial bonds within the city broke down, as Thucydides recounts in his famous passage on civil wars on the island of Corcyra and elsewhere across Greece:

---

[190] See Maria Fragoulaki, *Kinship in Thucydides: Intercommunal Ties and Historical Narrative* (Oxford: Oxford University Press, 2013).

Death took every imaginable form; and, as happens at such times, anything went—and then worse still. Fathers killed their sons; men were dragged out of the sanctuaries and killed beside them; some were even walled up in the temple of Dionysus and died there.

That is how savagely the civil war progressed, and it was the more shocking for being the first of the revolutions. Because later virtually the whole of the Greek world suffered this convulsion: everywhere there were internal divisions such that the democratic leaders called in the Athenians and the oligarchs called in the Spartans ... And indeed civil war did inflict great suffering on the cities of Greece. It happened then and will forever continue to happen, as long as human nature remains the same, with more or less severity ...

And indeed family became less close a tie than party. As partisans were more prepared to do the deeds without question. (Thu., 3.81-82)

Between states, each city's foreign policy tended to ignore kinship ties. Curiously, in the same speech in which he claimed the Sicilians are weak due to their lack of common identity, Alcibiades argued for a non-discriminating imperial policy:

This is how we and all other imperial powers have built up an empire, by readily responding to any request, Greek or barbarian, for our intervention. If we were all to sit tight or let racial discrimination dictate where we give support, we should add little to our empire and in fact run the risk of losing it altogether. (Thu., 6.18)[191]

No doubt such thinking has motivated the rulers of innumerable multiethnic empires, from Cyrus to Alexander, and beyond. Indeed, both Athens and Sparta repeatedly appealed to various barbarian nations, including the Persian

---

[191] Conversely, politicians in Sicily argued that the Sicilians ought to ally against outsiders despite their internal tribal differences (Thu., 4.61).

King, for support and the Spartans were quite happy to receive Persian subsidies, a critical factor in their victory over Athens.

The war's climax occurred with the Athenians' massive expedition to Sicily, sending over 200 ships and tens of thousands of men. Opposing forces from the Spartan and Athenian coalitions gathered from all parts of the Greek world to fight on the island. Thucydides carefully records the civic and tribal identity of the participants, to better show their irrelevance (and perhaps also as a conscious counter-point to the Hellenic unity commemorated by Homer's famous Catalog of Ships). Cities from the various Greek tribal groupings, and even colonies of either Athens or Sparta, could be found on both sides of the great battle:

> There was now gathered in contention for Syracuse what was certainly the largest number of nations ever to converge on a single city ... They had come to share either in the conquest of the country or in its rescue, but their particular alignment was not determined by any justifying cause or kindred loyalty so much as by purely contingent factors of self-interest or compulsion. (Thu., 7.56-57)

The Athenians' ultimate defeat at the hands of the Spartans after three decades of conflict is somewhat mysterious. With her enormous population, empire, and economic resources, Athens ought to have crushed the Spartans with relative ease. Athens, unlike Sparta, perhaps had the potential to unite the Greek world into a single Mediterranean empire, long before Rome's supremacy. One wonders whether the Athenians lost due a structural lack of mettle relative to the Spartans or because of the particular strategic blunders of their leaders, who avoided the kind of head-on battle through which the Thebans later triumphed over wall-less Sparta. The Athenians instead turned to fruitless economic blockades, peripheral interventions, and the bizarre and disastrous Sicilian expedition.[192] Spartan victory would probably have been

---

[192] Athens' strategy somewhat recalls that of the timid Anglo-French Allies in the first phase of the Second World War, in which

impossible without Athenian incompetence and Persian subsidies. The Athenians were also harmed early in the war by their status as a connected imperial metropolis: a devastating plague reached them through docks at the Piraeus, killing perhaps a third of the population, including Pericles.

Sparta's weaknesses became apparent almost immediately after her victory. Plato could parody and critique Periclean democracy as leading to a mindless, belly-chasing imperialism, persecuting other Greeks in order to gratify the common people's bottomless appetite.[193] There is no doubt much truth in this. But the Spartans, reputedly so 'virtuous,' proved equally unworthy of their empire, becoming just as greedy and unpopular as the Athenians had been. Xenophon, who had happily served Sparta for decades, bitterly recounts that the Spartans were gradually corrupted by their imperial wealth and power, becoming arrogant, vainglorious, and avaricious, and had forgotten their ancestral ways.

The smallness of the Spartiate ruling class, at least in later years, was astounding. During the first phase of the Peloponnesian War, when 420 Spartiates became stranded on the island of Sphacteria due to an Athenian blockade, this caused a national crisis within Sparta and led to serious peace overtures. After the war, Xenophon recounts a scene in which, at the public square in Sparta, there were about 75 Spartiates amidst 4000 people.[194] Sparta's victory and hegemony masked a catastrophic steady demographic decline in the Spartiate citizen-soldier class. Lycurgus' measures proved ineffective in the end.

The impoverishment of many Spartiates through steadily-increasing economic inequality meant many were unable to pay their mess dues. This contributed to the shrinking of the citizen class. Aristotle argues that this trend, which was apparently due to flawed inheritance laws, ought to have been countered "by maintaining an equal distribution of property"

---

bold Germany triumphed.
[193] Notably in *Gorgias*, 517b ff.
[194] Xenophon, *Hellenica*, 3.3.5.

(*Politics*, 1270a11). Aristotle also blamed Sparta's decline on the failure to regulate women as men had been. This resulted in women leading lives "full of every kind of license and luxury" and whose "inevitable result ... is the worship of wealth" (*Politics*, 1269b12). In any event, in the battle with the Thebans at Mantinea: "The city was unable to withstand a single blow and was ruined for want of men" (*Politics*, 1270a11).

The Greeks never recovered from the fratricide of the Peloponnesian War and the failure of either Athens or Sparta to create an imperial consensus across the Greek world. There appear to have been both cultural and technological reasons for this. The classical Greek political religion seems to have favored absolute loyalty to one city alone. The particular Greek custom of civic politics was only practicable on a small scale prior to modern telecommunications and automation. Ancient civic politics was necessarily localist and dependent on some kind of servant class to provide leisure for citizens. The *polis* could not scale. In these respects, the modern nation-state's superiority to ancient city-state is clear: the nation-state is a spectacular modern innovation which allows for the welding together, often with astonishing power, of an organic civic body numbering millions, often across vast geographical expanses.

In later Antiquity, the Greeks improved at creating workable regional federations as significant powers. Macedon and Rome would in time however achieve enormous scale and hegemonic power against which the old city-states and federations could not compete. Rome in particular would dominate the Mediterranean for centuries through a strategy of partially enfranchising her imperial subjects, although one should also note that the Roman Republic did not long survive her empire.

Both Athens and Sparta have much to teach us still. The contrast and conflict between these two cities embody the competing dialectical poles in Western history, between liberty and authority, individual and community, equality and hierarchy. There are times when democratic participation, individual experimentation, and free communication are

192

clearly conducive to growth and cultural ferment. At the same time, for any order to survive, there must also be positive norms of behavior and these are typically imposed through the authority of elites, which we hope are legitimate and enlightened. This is particularly clear in wartime, when democratic, liberal, and legal pretenses tend to fall by the wayside. Constraints may also be necessary in peacetime, especially wherever biological and ecological sustainability are at stake.

The individual liberty and social mobility which make for democracy's dynamism, if these are not to lead to a randomness and selfishness harmful to the common good, must in fact be informed by right values. For the Ancients, republican liberties had to be accompanied by strong patriarchal, religious, and patriotic values. Democracy's natural tendency towards hedonistic anarchy absolutely had to be checked. Polybius said of the moderate democracy practiced in the Achaean League of city-states of which he had been a citizen: "What we call democracy is a system where the majority decision prevails, but which retains the traditional values of piety towards the gods, care of our parents, respect for elders, and obedience to the laws" (Polybius, 6.4). There is a more general dilemma for all societies and governments: whereas free inquiry is often necessary to discover the good, authority is often necessary to enforce the good.

If the Peloponnesian War heralded the beginning of the end for classical Greek political life, it meant only the end of the beginning for Greek political thought and culture. Greek thinkers certainly learned from the tragedies of their history. The fratricide set the stage for the pan-Hellenic schemes of Isocrates and Xenophon, who urged the reconciliation of the Greek states so as to conquer Persia. Out of the ashes of defeat also grew the philosophy of Plato, a vast project for the biological, political, and spiritual renewal of the Hellenic nation, creating what would prove to be the highest ethno-statal philosophy until the age of Darwin.

PLATO

THE ETHNO-STATAL PHILOSOPHER

Plato came of age in one of the most traumatic times for Greece and his native city of Athens. The Greeks had brutally fought each other and laid waste to countless cities in the Peloponnesian War. Athens herself fell, losing her hegemony and empire, and succumbing to vicious dictatorship and civil war. Plato's own uncles, Critias and Charmides, had been among the Thirty Tyrants who had cruelly ruled the city after the fall to Sparta, and were to be killed in battle against the democrats. His beloved mentor, Socrates, died at the hands of the restored democracy.

And yet, Plato did not flee into despair or otherworldly speculation. He established the Academy not merely as a place for scholarly learning, but to practice a philosophical way of life. A select few would through rigorous logic, dialogue, and daily training, seek to overcome conventional assumptions and prejudices, so as to discover the truth. Armed with truth, this elite would return to politics to reform the city on a new, rational, and enlightened basis. Plato undertook a staggeringly ambitious spiritual project, one in which we are still engaged.

Plato immortalized Socrates' quest to overcome prejudice and ignorance, above all in his moving portrayal of his last days, choosing death in the name of the pursuit of truth. At the same time, Plato did not remain at the level of the *aporia*, or the admission of ignorance. Rather, based on philosophical questioning and rigorous logic, he constructed a grand and hard-headed political program for the Greek world which was biopolitical to the core. If Aristotle was a pioneering scientist, Plato was a great spiritual reformer. However, in contrast with many other spiritual leaders throughout the ages, in Plato we have something rare: the spiritual quest is never divorced from biological realities, the cultivation of the spirit and of the body go hand in hand.

The foundations, realism, and paradoxes of Platonic

political philosophy are perhaps most strikingly summarized in the *Statesman*. In this strange and relatively short dialogue, Socrates and a mysterious Visitor from Elea, a city in southern Italy seek, in a basic Platonic exercise, to define what is a statesman. The notion presented, already before Aristotle, is perfectly biopolitical. Statesmanship is not a craft dealing with inanimate matter but "is something nobler, which always has its power among living creatures" (*Statesman*, 261d). The ideal statesman is compared to a herdsman of animals, statesmanship being "knowledge of the collective rearing of human beings" (*Statesman*, 267d). The herdsman-statesman analogy was in fact common across the ancient world, unsurprising given the widespread use of livestock. The comparison is already present in Homer, as well as in Mideastern mythology. Interestingly, both Plato and Xenophon record Socrates comparing statesmen to herdsmen, arguing for rule-by-experts and mindful reproduction.

Plato observes the great diversity of every society's individuals, noting that these are highly unequal in wisdom, and he takes for granted that, ideally, the wisest should rule. The Platonic paradoxes posed by the idea of a perfectly wise leader are evident in the *Statesman*. If such a being were to exist, a perfectly wise statesman would be entitled to be an authoritarian law unto himself, unconstrained by inferior laws and shaping the culture as he sees fit, including systematic suppression of bad culture. Plato is cognizant that in practice such a perfect ruler is unlikely to exist. One should therefore rely on the rule of necessarily rough, inflexible laws as a "second best" choice (*Statesman*, 297e). In practice, the usually authoritarian Plato is willing to give democracy some credit in this dialogue: whereas autocracy can be the best or most vicious form of government, depending on the character of the ruler, democracy at least hews to a consistently mediocre or middling route. Democracies have less variance.

Plato paradoxically both glorifies Socratic free inquiry in pursuit of the truth and advocates for an authoritarian state to enforce that truth. In the *Statesman*, the normally censorious Plato recognizes that if free inquiry were eliminated from a state: "It's clear both that we should see all the various sorts of expertise completely destroyed, and that they would never be restored, either, because of this law prohibiting inquiry; so that life, which even now is difficult, in such a time would be altogether unlivable" (*Statesman*, 299e-300a).

Plato never provides a final answer to these dilemmas and indeed we are still wrestling with them to this day. Plato is a mystery, a vast *koan*. I am tempted to the see the answer to these riddles in the very life of Socrates: just as the good state will not hesitate to do what is necessary for the good, neither will the good man hesitate, including sacrificing his life to condemn a bad state. The good cannot be guaranteed through self-imposed limitations on the state and the good man should not feel entitled to 'rights.' Plato would not see either the good man or the good state be paralyzed by the potential abuses of lesser men. In each case, there is a chance to take, a price to be paid.

The statesman or the laws will guide the people towards the good, laws being needed "for all those herds of human beings that graze, city by city" (*Statesman*, 295e). The statesman ruthlessly purges the incurably bad from the city—this includes both undesirable populations and criminals to be executed or exiled by law.[195] Plato goes so far as to define a good government as that which institutes sound population policies on the basis of expertise:

---

[195] Plato assigns a crucial role in statesmanship to criminalizing the incurably anti-social:

> [W]hat is truly the art of statesmanship [will never] put together a city out of good and bad human beings. It's quite clear that it will first put them to the test in play, and after the test it will hand them over to those with the capacity to educate them and serve it towards this particular end. ... those of their pupils that are unable to share in a disposition that is courageous and moderate, and whatever else belongs to the sphere of virtue, but are thrust forcibly away by an evil nature in godlessness, excess, and injustice, it throws out by killing them, sending them into exile, and punishing them with the most extreme forms of dishonor. (*Statesman*, 308d-309a)

And whether [the rulers] purge the city for its benefit by putting some people to death or else by exiling them, or whether again they make it smaller by sending out colonies somewhere like swarms of bees, or build it up by introducing people from somewhere outside and making them citizens — so long as they act to preserve it on the basis of expert knowledge and what is just, making it better than it was so far as they can, *this* is the constitution which alone we must say is correct ... All the others that we generally say are constitutions we must say are not genuine, and not really constitutions at all, but imitations of this one; those we say are "law-abiding" have imitated it for the better, the others for the worse. (*Statesman*, 293d-e)

The statesman's duty is to bring harmony to the people's disparate elements. He refers to the opposition between manic and lethargic people, very roughly analogous to that between progressives and conservatives, saying: "this disagreement, of these classes of people, is a sort of play; but in relation to the most important things, it turns out to be a disease which is the most hateful of all for cities" (*Statesman*, 307d). However, "the expertise belonging to the king brings their life together in agreement and friendship and makes it common between them, completing the most magnificent and best of all fabrics" (*Statesman*, 311c).

The Platonic obsession with eugenics is also present in this dialogue. Whereas in the *Republic* Plato proposes a straightforward program of biological improvement through selective breeding, in the *Statesman*, he raises the problem of what we would call dysgenic assortative mating in relation to temperamental diversity. The spirited and the timid, he says, tend to mate with people of the same temperament, leading the population over time to increasingly be made up of overly aggressive and overly passive individuals, who will be both individually flawed and prone to conflict with one another (*Statesman*, 310d). Plato then suggests the spirited and the timid should be paired so as to achieve a happy mean which would lead to more balanced human beings and preserve the city from civil war.

The *Statesman*, we must believe, is making use of metaphor to make challenging and substantive points. The idea of the good king as a "shepherd of the people" was ancient and widespread, but it was up to Plato to spell out the implications of humanity's biological nature and indeed of in-born inequality. Plato never lets go of the importance of expertise in political leadership, of biological quality, of altruistic and disciplined virtue, and of the good of the whole. His politics, even before Aristotle, was founded upon the recognition of biological realities, as the craftsmanship dealing with the highest of "living creatures."

There is a profound unity to Plato's politics across his paradoxical works, uniquely expressed in each case according to the particular genre in question: whether the arguments made in the shorter dialogues (*Statesman, Protagoras, Gorgias*), the sublime heights in the *Republic*'s ideal state, the polities described in the famous myth of Atlantis (*Timaeus-Critias*), the practical proposals in the lengthy *Laws*, and his actual political activity as described in the *Letters*. Plato begins with the facts of human life, of humanity's character as a perfectible animal, of our sheer diversity as individual human beings, and works from there. Plato's political philosophy at once embraces an elevated idealism and the most steely-eyed hereditarian and political realism. *Comprendra qui voudra !*

As we shall see, the Platonic corpus offered a comprehensive cultural and biopolitical program for Greece: a great reform of convention grounded in reason and expertise, to transform Greece into a patchwork of enlightened, non-grasping city-states, cultivating themselves intellectually and culturally, reproducing themselves in perpetuity through systematic and eugenic population policies, avoiding fratricidal war and imperialism among themselves, and working together against the barbarians, under the leadership of the best city-states. Taken together, I dare say we can speak of a Platonic Group Evolutionary Strategy for Greece.

PLATO'S RACIAL *REPUBLIC*

Egalitarians have argued that notions of nation and race are largely modern constructs. Marxists in particular have often claimed that Western ruling classes invented these ideas to consolidate the power of bourgeois states or as a mere pretext to divide the working class along (supposedly imaginary) racial lines and to oppress their colonial subjects. It is then important to look at the actual record of discussion of tribe, nation, and race in our European tradition. In fact, hereditarian and ethnocentric themes have been present from the earliest days of Western civilization, to be found in our most ancient poems, histories, and philosophy. This is particularly true of Plato.

Plato is the first Western philosopher whose work comes down to us in a complete form, rather than mere fragments. Strikingly, hereditarian and ethnocentric themes are fundamental to Plato's great treatise of political philosophy, the *Republic*, a founding text for the entire tradition of Western thought. A number of striking biopolitical themes are present throughout the text:

- Inequality: the idea that men are created *unequal* is absolutely pervasive throughout the *Republic* and is foundational to its ethics. Plato asserts that individuals have in-born differences in physique, personality, and intelligence, in addition to differences due to upbringing.

- Heredity and eugenics: Plato notes that human differences are significantly heritable and so often refers to eugenic solutions to improve both society and elites, with explicit comparisons to animal breeding.

- Patriotism: Plato argues that patriotism is a social good and compares it with love for one's family.

- Greek racial/ethnic identity: Plato argues that "ties of blood and kinship" meant Greeks should not wage war on one another or enslave each other, reserving this for non-Greeks, and that their common identity should be cultivated through joint religious practices.

Plato's *Republic* presents a powerful vision of an *aristocratic* racially-conscious state. The ruling elite, known as the "guardians," and to a lesser extent the wider citizenry would steadily improve themselves both culturally through education and biologically through eugenics. The elite would reach for the truth through constant reflection and dialectic, while both elite and masses would be conditioned through (civil-)religious education, being taught to consider the pursuit of these cultural and biological goods as a sacred moral imperative.[196] Interestingly, Plato reproduced the traditional Aryan tripartite division of society as later described by the French historian Georges Dumézil: Plato's ideal state of Callipolis is to be made up of workers or laymen, soldiers (auxiliaries to the ruling class), and the ruling priest-like philosopher-kings.

One needs a certain spiritual sensitivity to appreciate the *Republic*. That was common enough when suffering, and the religious and philosophical practices to answer that suffering, were widespread even among the elites of our societies. Without such spiritual experience, certainly one cannot even begin to understand, let alone be sympathetic to, the discipline involved. Plato's ideal state can be understood as a kind of monastic state, ruled by an order of truth-seeking warrior-monks. Callipolis is a philosophical Sparta, where the Spartiates have been replaced by a Pythagorean-Socratic sect. The *Republic* is all the more striking and challenging in that its ideal politics are presented in the context Plato's wider argument for a kind of unconditional altruism. This has made it both an unavoidable and often indigestible text for later times: we find all at once the transcendence of the Buddha, the charity of Christ, and the vitalism of the Führer. One is

---

[196] Modern philosophers such as Schopenhauer and Tocqueville have made largely analogous arguments on the role of (civil-)religion in educating and moralizing the masses.

dumbstruck by the paradox and challenged to understand further.

Of course, one must be careful not to take everything Plato says in the *Republic* literally. After all, Plato dedicated an entire dialogue, by far his lengthiest, the *Laws*, to practical political proposals. The *Republic* is chiefly an exploration of human psychology and the nature of morality. The discussion of politics is presented as an analogy for the human soul: the ideal city-state is meant to serve as a macro-scale model to explore what the ideal human soul might look like. Some of Callipolis' more bizarre policies — wife-sharing among the ruling elite, the banishing of all children above ten at the city's foundation — must be understood as measures necessary to imagining this utopia. In particular, these measures ensure perfect unity among the elite (no longer being divided by family or property), mirroring the unity of reason in an individual, and perfect education of the new generation. For the modern reader, the *Republic* is perhaps best read as an intellectual exploration through thought experiment, analogous to science fiction. This imaginative utopia was also for Plato a way of making and illustrating very concrete points concerning in-born inequality, eugenics, patriotism, and Greek racial/ethnic identity.

NATURAL INEQUALITY & ARISTOCRACY

Plato takes in-born human inequality as self-evident. He writes:

When you distinguish people as naturally competent or incompetent in a particular context, don't you mean that some people find it easy to learn that subject, while others find it hard? And that some people start to do their own broadly speaking original work in the subject after only a little study, while others can't even retain what they've learned after even a lot of study and care? And that some people's bodies are sufficiently subservient to their minds, while others' are obstructive? Aren't these the features — there are more too — which enable you to define some

201

people as naturally competent, and others as naturally incompetent? (455b-c)

Plato refers to "stupid adults" (598c), "slow-witted people" (526b), "inferior members of the human race" (495c), and "inferior kinds of people" (545a). He notes that children are born without reason and that "I'm not convinced some of them ever acquire reason" (441a-b). Moral and intellectual inferiority was partly in-born and partly due to miseducation. Plato however asserts that even good education cannot undo congenital imperfection: "Education is not capable of doing what some people promise. They claim to introduce knowledge into a mind which doesn't have it, as if they were introducing sight into eyes which are blind" (518c).

Plato also recognized in-born physical and mental differences between men and women, considering women to be "the weaker sex in all respects" concerning warfare and statecraft (455e). Nonetheless, Plato argues that women should have equal opportunity to be guardians or have any other role in the community, so long as they have the ability. This meritocratic 'feminism' was quite radical in the patriarchal context of ancient Greece.

The recognition of human inequality for Plato was by no means intended to humiliate or harm the less gifted. Rather, the point was to organize society in recognition of these differences, as "different people are inherently suitable for different activities" (370a).

Mika Ojakangas has aptly described Plato's ideal state is a "bio-meritocracy" which "is not led by the descendants of traditional aristocratic families but by the descendants of the most superior men and women."[197] Callipolis as a bio-meritocratic regime is entirely oriented towards a cognitive and moral sorting of the people, with the best (defined as the most intelligent, courageous, and moral) being selected to form the ruling elite of guardians. Failure to recognize inequality and in

---

[197] Mika Ojakangas, *On the Greek Origins of Biopolitics: A Reinterpretation of the History of Biopower* (London: Routledge, 2016), p. 19.

particular the excellence of the moral elite means the latter "end up living a life which is inappropriate for them and which isn't true to their natures" (495c).

Recognition of the reality of inequality is then not only pervasive throughout the *Republic* but is central to the entire moral argument. Put simply: both a human soul and a society are made up of different, conflicting parts, some better than others; morality is when the better overcome the worse. Plato considered that this was achieved when a person or society was governed by reason, in alliance with nobler emotions, the latter subordinating mere pleasure and pain.[198]

Given all this, it is no wonder that Plato is contemptuous towards egalitarians. These are undiscerning and undiscriminating people who have bad taste, poor judgment, and low or no standards. Because egalitarian individuals (and the equivalent political regime, democracy) are unable to distinguish good from evil, Plato considers them among the most immoral, only one rank above a psychopath or a tyrant. His account of democracy is at once humorous and damning.

HEREDITY & EUGENICS

Plato recognizes that human inequality is not only in-born, but is substantially hereditary. This point is made on several occasions, sometimes quite strikingly. For example, if "a small, bald metalworker" happened to accidentally get rich and married "his master's daughter," their offspring would only be "second-rate half-breeds" (496a). Plato argues that philosophy "should be practiced by men of true pedigree, not by bastards" (535c). He also links physical beauty and mental goodness, arguing that his ruling class of philosopher-kings should be "within reason, people who are very good-looking" (535b). (This is perhaps a surprising statement given that Plato's mentor Socrates, who makes the point in the dialogue, was notoriously ugly.)

---

[198] As an example: an alcoholic may suffer immediate discomfort from lack of drink, even though his reason knows he should abstain. His pride might assist his reason in resisting temptation.

Given the reality of in-born and partially hereditary human inequality, Plato considers the decision as to who should reproduce to be a matter of public interest.[199] There is a public interest in the composition of the gene pool. As such, Plato makes a muscular argument for eugenics, both positive and negative. He makes an explicit analogy with animal breeding:

> I've seen lots of hunting dogs and fine birds in your house ... Isn't it true that although they're all pedigree creatures, some of them prove to be exceptionally good? ... So do you breed from all of them indiscriminately, or do you take care to choose the outstanding ones as much as possible? ... And wouldn't you expect the result of failure to follow this breeding program to be the deterioration of your strain of birds and dogs? ... We're going to need really exceptional rulers if the same principle applies to humans too. (459a-b)

Plato draws the conclusion: "sex should preferably take place between men and women who are outstandingly good, and should occur as little as possible between men and women of a vastly inferior stamp ... This is how to maximize the potential of our flock" (459d-e).

Similarly, Plato argues that exceptional men, particularly warriors, should be rewarded with more sex:

> And the main privilege and reward that any young men who are good at fighting or at some other activity ought to receive is the right to sleep with the women more frequently, so that as many as possible of the children are fathered by this kind of person ... (460b)

Many of these specific policies are so radical that Plato probably meant for them to be understood as utopian. Indeed, he explicitly states that the regime conceived in the *Republic* may not be realizable.[200] The point however is the principle:

---

[199] One can wonder: given the biological and genetic basis of human existence, how could the composition of the current and next generations' gene pools *not* be considered a matter of public interest?

[200] Given ongoing breakthroughs in biology however, it seems humane eugenics will become more and more practicable, I think in

given the reality of heredity, improving the gene pool (or the breed or the race) is a moral good. Plato thus argues powerfully for regulating sex and reproduction, and not leaving such matters to the animalistic whims of individuals: "undisciplined sex (or undisciplined anything for that matter) is a profanity, and the rulers won't allow it" (458d-e).[201] This program also justifies the state in drafting the youths it raises into the regime: "We've bred *you*" (520b).

Plato also argues for negative eugenics: children of the worst parents and those who are congenitally disabled should be segregated from the elite, "otherwise our breed of guardians will become tainted" (460c).[202]

Plato elsewhere notes that Asclepius, the Greek god of medicine, was "a public-spirited person" because

> he didn't try to use diet gradually to drain and fill bodies which were diseased to the core, and so be responsible for a person having a long and horrible life and in all probability producing children with the same afflictions ... Such a person does neither himself nor his community any good. (407d-e)

In line with ancient Greek practice, even to some extent in democratic Athens, Plato radically subordinates the interests of the individual to those of the community on which he depends:

> Socrates: These two practices [legal and medical] will treat the bodies and minds of those of your citizens who are naturally well endowed in these respects; as for the rest,

---

particular of the possibilities of embryo selection and gene editing.

[201] Plato incidentally seems to equate the profane with whatever is harmful to the community: "our next task is to ensure that marriages are as far removed from profanity as possible — which will happen if they contribute as much as possible towards the community's welfare" (458e).

[202] It is not clear whether the *Republic* endorses eugenic infanticide or merely separation from such infants. In the *Timaeus*, Plato presents a similar ideal state, in which "the children of the good parents were to be brought up, while those of the bad ones were to be secretly handed to another city" (*Timaeus*, 19a).

those with a poor physical constitution will be allowed to die, and those with irredeemably rotten minds will be put to death. Right?

Glaucon: Yes, we've shown that this is the best course for those at the receiving end of the treatment as well as for the community. (409e-410a)

Plato argues that enforcement of these eugenic measures could be achieved through religious education or myth. The parenting of low-grade children would become a religious taboo (my emphasis):

We'll say he has sinned against both gods and men by fathering a child who (if the matter goes unnoticed and the child is born) will not have been affected by the rites and prayers which the priestesses and priests and the whole community pray at each wedding-festival — *for every generation of children to improve on their parents' in goodness and value* — but will instead have been born under the influence of darkness and dire lack of self-control. (461a-b)

Plato's hereditarian observations strikingly prefigured modern biological science. As David Galton has noted: "Plato's methods to improve the genetic constitution of the ruling elite class are far more original than those of Aristotle and are in accord with modern genetic theory."[203] Starting from the common observance of heredity in human beings and other animals, Plato was forthright and rigorous in drawing out the eugenic ethics which logically flow from this, even if these might often be impracticable.

FAMILY & PATRIOTISM

The *Republic* meditates at length upon the problem of how to make people love their city-state and serve it disinterestedly. Plato argues that public-spirited government can be promoted through (civil-)religious education and appeal to family

---

[203] David Galton, "Greek theories on eugenics," *Journal of Medical Ethics*, vol. 24, 1998, p. 266.

sentiment/patriotism.[204] Plato, like ancient Greek society in general, took family extremely seriously. He lists among the tyrant's sins: "on his tongue and in his unholy mouth is the taste of the blood of a kinsman" (565e). In the *Republic*, Plato imagines a society in which members of the elite would be selfless because they all belonged to one single family (notably through the utopian institution of wife-sharing). The guardians would be selected from those children showing selflessness and patriotism:

> They have to demonstrate love of their community while being tested in both pleasant and painful circumstances, and make it clear that they won't shed patriotism whatever ordeals or fears they meet with, or whatever changing situations they endure. Anyone who is incapable of retaining it is to be excluded, whereas anyone who emerges from every test without impurities (like gold tested in fire) is to be made a ruler and given privileges and rewards in life and in death. (503a)

More generally, Plato argues that the entire society could be conditioned to think of itself as one extended family through the teaching of a religious myth:

> What I'm saying is … I'm not sure where to find the gall or the words to tell the story … I'll be trying above all to convince the rulers themselves and the military, and secondarily the rest of the community, that all the nurture and education we provided happened to them in a kind of dream-world; in actual fact, they were at that time being formed and nurtured deep inside the earth, and their weaponry and their equipment in general were also being made there. When they were finished products, the earth, their mother, sent them up above ground; and now in their policymaking they must regard the country they find

---

[204] There are striking parallels with Alexis de Tocqueville's arguments in *Democracy in America*. See Guillaume Durocher, "Tocqueville's Patriotic Republic: Nationalist Themes in *Democracy in America*," *The Occidental Observer*, July 20-21, 2016.

themselves in as their mother and their nurse, they must defend her against invasion, and they should think of the rest of the inhabitants of the community as their earth-born brothers. (414d-e)

Each guardian, a member of the ruling elite, does not see another guardian as a "stranger" but as "a father or a mother, a son or a daughter, a grandchild or a grandparent" (463c). That family feeling would be particularly powerful during warfare:

[The guardians] are highly likely to fight well against enemy forces, insofar as they are highly unlikely to abandon one another, since they regard one another as brother, father, son, and call one another by these names.... I am sure this would make our militia completely invincible. (471d)

Significantly, Plato lists a failure to distinguish between citizens and foreigners as one of the characteristics of a regime which is degenerating towards egalitarianism: "it starts to make no difference whether one is a citizen or a resident alien, or even a visitor from abroad: everyone is at the same level" (563a). Those who lack discernment and identity are no longer able to distinguish between those who share their blood, culture, upbringing, and civic responsibilities, and those who do not.

RACIAL/ETHNIC SOLIDARITY AMONG GREEKS

Plato had a very strong sense of Greek identity which was both cultural and racial (or ethnic). In a striking passage, Plato argues that war between Greek city-states should be considered limited internal "conflicts," whereas truly brutal "war" should be reserved for non-Greek outsiders:

Greeks are bonded to one another by internal ties of blood and kinship, but interact with non-Greeks as people who are foreign and live outside their domain.... When Greeks and non-Greeks fight, then, we'll describe this as warfare [πολεμεῖν, or making war], and claim that they are natural enemies and that the term "war" should refer to this type of hostility. But when Greeks get involved in this kind of thing with other Greeks, we'll claim that they are natural friends, and that in a situation like this Greece is diseased and in conflict, and we'll maintain that the term "conflict" [στασιάζειν, to be in conflict] should refer to this type of hostility. (470c-d)

Plato argues that Greeks who wage brutal war with one another should not be considered "patriotic," again using a family analogy: "if they were [patriotic], they would stop short of ravaging their nurse and their mother" (470d). Instead, Greeks should "reserve for non-Greeks the treatment Greeks currently give one another" (471b). Practically, Greeks should not enslave, humiliate, or ruin each other:

Socrates: Do you think it's right for communities of Greeks to enslave other Greeks? Shouldn't they do their best to prevent any other community from enslaving Greeks and make the norm to spare anyone of Greek stock, for fear of themselves being enslaved by non-Greeks?

Glaucon: It's absolutely crucial that they spare Greeks.

Socrates: Not only should they not own Greek slaves themselves, then, but they should also advise other Greeks to follow their example.

Glaucon: Yes. That should encourage them to concentrate on non-Greeks and leave one another alone.

Socrates: And we won't be taking arms and armor to our temples as trophies either, especially if they came from Greeks, if we're the slightest bit interested in being on good terms with other Greeks. We're more likely to be afraid of the possible pollution involved in robbing our kin of their weapons and taking them to a sacred site, except when the practice is divinely sanctioned.... What about devastating the land and burning the homes of Greeks? ... I think they'll avoid both practices and only steal the annual crop. (469b–470b)

The mere theft of crops was preferable to permanent damage as, "it smacks of aiming for reconciliation rather than perpetual warfare" (470e).

Furthermore, beyond the political boundaries of the city-state, Plato argues that Greeks could cultivate their common identity and feeling of kinship through shared religious practices: "Won't they feel warmth for their fellow Greeks? Won't they regard Greece as their own land and join all other Greeks in their common religious rites?" (470e).

To this day, Plato is revered as one of the founders of the Western philosophical tradition and one the greatest philosophers of all time. Thus, for we heretics, it is comforting to know that such a great figure should take so seriously notions of race and nation: genetic influences on behavior and thus the composition of the gene pool as a self-evident matter of public interest, patriotism as an extension of family feeling and an obvious good, a respect for the sacred that advances the interests of the entire group, and the importance of solidarity among kin peoples. The goal of politics was to prevent the bad, defined as a society or individual who was of bad "breed" and "uncultured," and to promote the good (559d-e).

Plato had a reputation as a man whose head was stuck in the clouds contemplating abstractions. Yet I am struck by the 'modernity' and practical implications of many of his arguments. He posited an ideal society ordered and cultivated through comprehensive education, good culture (including music, religious myths, and rituals), rigorous mental and physical exercises, and eugenics. Plato's social program is both refreshingly cognizant of basic human realities and decidedly holistic and systematic. Ethnocentric and hereditarian thought has the finest pedigree. We are in illustrious company.

THE *LAWS*: PLATO'S SACRED ETHNOSTATE

Plato's *Republic* is one of the world's most famous books. So long as it has had readers, people have wondered whether the ideal state presented in that work was meant as a serious political proposal; or was it only meant as an intellectually-stimulating utopia or even merely a symbolic analogy for the perfect soul? I for one am surprised by the confusion. More important in the *Republic*, or any of Plato's dialogues, than the specific provisions are the principles underpinning them. From this, we can be quite assured, for instance, that Plato was a fundamentally aristocratic thinker, seeing the recognition of inequality as the foundation of ethics, deeply concerned about ensuring right hierarchy, good culture, and good breeding.

Furthermore, we do have Plato's longest yet less famous final work, also on politics: the *Laws*, which describes his "second-best city," called Magnesia. There is our same Plato: the same uncompromising defense of altruism, the same paradoxical 'totalitarianism' in service of the community, the same fear and loathing of egalitarianism and 'pop culture,' the same meritocratic proto-feminism, the same quest for perfection. If Callipolis is a philosophical Sparta, Magnesia is a Spartanized Athens, taking the institutions of the moderate democracy founded by Solon and imbuing the society's culture with a basically Dorian, austere, communitarian, and demanding spirit. Much of what modern liberals find objectionable in the *Republic* can be found repeated, evidently meant seriously, in the *Laws*.

Actually, I believe the *Laws* merely explicitly spells out the implications in a particular concrete example of what one could reasonably infer from the *Republic*. At the eve of life, Plato apparently wished to cross all his Ts and dot all his Is. Indeed the work sometimes goes into rather tedious detail, perhaps inevitable for a legal treatise. I would stress again that much of Plato's authoritarianism was in fact not unique to him, but simply reflected the community-centered ethics and practice of citizenship of the ancient Greek *polis*. Glenn Morrow, the definitive historical interpreter of the *Laws*, writes that it has been "declared, with some exaggeration but with essential insight, that Plato's *Laws* is a collection and codification of the whole of Greek law."[205] This would explain why there is so much overlap between Plato's *Laws* and Aristotle's similarly-encyclopedic *Politics* (though the latter, as lecture notes, are far

---

[205] Glenn Morrow, *Plato's Cretan City: A Historical Interpretation of the* Laws (Princeton: Princeton University Press, 1993), p. 6.

easier for a modern to read). It also suggests that the *Laws* must be read not as a philosopher's pie-in-the-sky dreaming, but as synthesis of centuries of practical Greek political experience.

In the *Republic*, Plato is arguably radicalizing Socratic insights on self-discipline, the rule of expertise, and good breeding, and projecting them to the level of a polity. Similarly, in the *Laws*, Plato is systematizing and occasionally radicalizing many of the underlying assumptions of the practice of ancient Greek politics. Whereas the *Republic*'s radically utopian aristocratic and eugenic principles can be summarized briefly, in the *Laws* Plato goes into considerable detail on specific measures to be taken.

One can see why the *Laws* has resonated less with passing generations than the *Republic* has. The *Laws* meanders and suffers from some contradictions. Some blame the elderly Plato's failing mental abilities, others the fact that the work was unfinished at his death, to be edited from wax tablets by his disciple Philip of Otis.

All this said, the *Laws* remains stimulating and provocative. The dialogue portrays three men—a mysterious "Athenian Stranger" similar to Socrates, a Cretan named Clinias, and a Spartan named Megillos—on a pilgrimage to the shrine of Zeus' birthplace on Mount Ida, where the legendary Cretan king Minos had received his laws from the supreme god. As Sparta's austere customs were said to have originated in Crete and the Spartan lawgiver was supposed to have been inspired by Apollo, the *Laws* showcase a kind of return to the historical and divine origins of the prestigious Spartan constitution. The Athenian Stranger will then, as a thoughtful philosopher, help shape these laws through dialogue with his two interlocutors.

Plato, while retaining his pious moral earnestness, often jokes about his old age and has kept his ability to engage in the most stimulating paradoxes. Probably the most famous of these in the *Laws* is the long discussion in Book I on the merits of drinking-parties. Alcohol is a supreme gift enabling us to discern virtue in men: those who are able to maintain their self-discipline under its influence thereby show they have the kind of virtue necessary to sustain good statesmanship under similar 'intoxicating' pressures while in power. *In vino veritas!*

Old age and jokes aside, the *Laws* remains supremely ambitious: Plato is discussing the basic law of a new city which, synthesizing the best of the various Greek traditions, would prove timeless. This would establish an eternally virtuous version of Athens, preserving its ideal of citizenship, but without the egalitarian excesses. Plato was evidently inspired by the great discipline of the Spartan constitution and the immemorial religious traditions of ancient Egypt. By 'law' the Greeks typically do not have in mind the fluctuating and ever-growing mass of legislation that we understand by the term. Rather, we are discussing a largely unchanging basic law and a set of customs, like those of Lycurgus, prescribing a way of life and educating the citizens. Plato wishes for a new state, a new lawgiver, this time however inspired by philosophy and reason as well as the uncertain visions of a god, promoting virtue and not merely militarism. And if Lycurgus' law had by Plato's time lasted almost three centuries, the philosopher again aimed higher, taking as his model Egyptian customs which, like the famous pyramids, were said to have endured for millennia.

In all this, the reproduction of the citizenry and their kinship are fundamental. Plato waxes lyrical about the sacred duty citizens have to produce the best children possible in order to "participate in eternity." The city-state is conceived not merely as a collection of individuals, but as a timeless community including all past and future generations. Of great interest from an evolutionary perspective, the social order and ethics of Plato's *Laws* are founded on kinship, both familial and ethnic. We find in Plato's thought concentric circles of kinship and reciprocity: to the family, to the city, and ultimately to the Greek nation as a whole against the barbarians. Furthermore, Plato is emphatic on the duty of ensuring the biological and cultural quality of the citizenry, to be achieved notably: by an initial wholesale purge of bad elements, strict immigration policies, and the careful regulation and promotion of childbearing marriage.

In stressing the principle of kinship, Plato is embracing and systematizing wider Greek beliefs. Arnold Gomme writes: "The idea of kinship as the basis of membership in the state was fundamental throughout Greece, and in this respect the nationality of the mother was as important as that of the father."[206] Morrow says we can assume that Plato adheres to the Athenian notion of citizenship being limited to those with two native-born parents.[207] Given all this, just as Lycurgus is said to have founded Sparta as the first ethnostate, I believe it is not anachronistic to speak of Magnesia as Plato's sacred ethnostate.

What kind of city-state is Magnesia? Plato's second-best city is not as radical and elitist as Callipolis. The holy order of philosopher-kings gives way to the rule of the laws themselves. Plato is far closer to Aristotle's moderate and conventional notion of an ideal regime. In Magnesia, all native-born soldiers and veterans are citizens. Every male citizen has some property and each is expected to live happily with a moderate amount of wealth. Every citizen-soldier is expected to become a family father by begetting children. Most officials are elected by the Assembly of all citizens, the rich being given more voting power. Plato says this propertied democracy with oligarchic elements is meant to be a happy mean between Persian despotism and Athenian egalitarianism. On all this, Aristotle might approve.

Plato however is more prescriptive concerning the basic law. Magnesia's democratic Assembly is to be constrained and the citizenry educated towards virtue through Spartan-like disciplines stipulated by a largely immutable basic law. The philosopher is portraying a state in which all would live in harmony and piously, constantly training themselves and joining in communal activities: an aristocratic Athens, a philosophical Sparta, with folkways as eternal Egypt's.

Plato envisions numerous measures to prevent decadence and the degeneration of the law. Economic inequality and

---

[206] Arnold Gomme, *Essays in Greek History and Literature* (Oxford, 1937), 86-87. Quoted in Morrow, *Cretan City*, p. 117.
[207] *Ibid.*, p. 116.

poverty are checked by limits on capital accumulation and by maintenance of the number of households at 5,040. Plato favors virtuous self-sufficiency to corrupting intercourse with the outside world. Commerce is to be kept to a minimum (the city happily has no access to the sea), usury is to be banned, and the low trading professions are to be consigned to a class of non-citizen foreigners "whose corruption will not harm the state unduly" (919c).

In sharp contrast with Aristotle, Plato remains a meritocratic proto-feminist. He thinks it "stupid" that half the society, women, is kept in the private sphere and instead makes them potential citizens (albeit propertyless), eligible for office, grants them their own common meals, and enlists them in the armed forces if necessary. Even if women are on the whole less suited to war, politics, or abstract thinking, Plato cannot accept that so much potential remain untapped and even imagines female soldiers helping their menfolk by "gallantly resisting the destruction threatening their native land" (807b). Plato blames the lack of regulation and participation of women in Sparta for the rise of luxury in that state, saying the lawmaker should have covered both sexes: "A legislator should go the whole way and not stick at half-measures" (806c). Plato imagines women becoming citizens from the age of 40, once their duties as mothers have been largely completed.

Plato's obsession with an unchangeable and highly prescriptive basic law, intruding even into the smallest aspects of life and culture, can seem megalomaniacal and unrealistic. This reflects however not only his obsession with preventing decadence, but also the assumptions of his time and his philosophy. If law is inspired by the most enlightened, it would naturally override or channel men's various spontaneous and random movements, especially those of the less gifted. If nature and reason are eternal, and law is meant to reflect these, then the better the law is the more timeless it would be. This somewhat static vision makes particular sense in the context of the ancient world, when technological innovation was very slow, humanity's subsistence existence was in many respects basically unchanging, and one could indeed say there was "nothing new under the sun."

I will go into some detail on the regime and principles Plato describes in the *Laws*. I believe this is warranted on several grounds. Firstly, the *Laws* shows that Plato's aristocratic, communitarian, and eugenic principles as described in the *Republic*, which philosophy teachers tend to gloss over, were meant in earnest. Secondly, my readers are unlikely to wish to read the 500-odd pages of this difficult work, from which I have extracted the very substantial biopolitical themes.[208] Finally, even academics explaining the *Laws* have also tended to gloss some of its biopolitics. Charles Khan writes that in Morrow's 600-page explication of the *Laws*: "There is almost no mention in the present work of those passages in the slave law which, as Morrow put it, 'do not make pleasant reading!' Nor is there much said here about the preliminary population purges, nor the implications for home life of Plato's system of 'marriage inspectors.'"[209] Yet, the piety, rigor, and radical nature of Plato's biopolitical vision may yet have relevance for our times.

THE HOLISTIC RULE OF LAW AS THE REIGN OF A GOOD CULTURE

Plato's main innovation in the *Laws* is to have pioneered the notion of the "rule of law." He constrains the Magnesian regime within a complex system of laws and courts of appeal,

---

[208] A Penguin Classics translation by Trevor Saunders is available, as well as bootleg editions of a nineteenth-century translation by Benjamin Jowett. Both have useful introductory texts but seem to lack supporting endnotes.

[209] Charles Kahn, "Foreword," in Morrow, *Plato's Cretan City*, xxvi. I note that in 1940 Morrow wrote an article distancing Plato's philosophy from National Socialism and Communism, on the grounds that the *Laws* is founded upon the rule of law. That is fair point, but it must also be conceded that Plato and indeed Aristotle's communitarian politics are quite at odds with the modern liberals' hypertrophied individualism and egalitarianism. See also Guillaume Durocher, "Plato, Hitler, & Totalitarianism," *Counter-Currents*, March 23, 2017.

guaranteed by the so-called Guardians of the Laws, by which all officials were liable for prosecution for misdeeds. Plato asserts boldly: "any state without duly established courts simply ceases to be a state" (766d). Plato the 'totalitarian' is also the forerunner of the very notion of the rule of law and checks and balances, which would prove so influential for Montesquieu and the American Founding Fathers.

Another innovation: the laws are to have preambles, meant to persuade the citizens by rational argument of the necessity of a given action, before coercion if that fails. Thus the laws use two methods: "compulsion and persuasion (subject to the limitations imposed by the uneducated masses)" (722b). The law, devised by reason, is to be a "golden and holy" cord, pulling upon the souls of the citizens, towards virtue. Plato advocates a reformative penology aiming to improve criminals rather than harm them (854a). He expects the citizen to "exact the vengeance of his fatherland" against those who would subvert the laws (856b).

While aware of the disadvantages of an inflexible and too general law, Plato hopes nonetheless to escape the rule of men and establish the rule of reason embodied in law. The Greek word *nomos* means both 'custom' and 'law,' and indeed Plato's holistic notion of law often extends to a society's culture and traditions as a whole. He observes, as many have since, that the constitution and laws ultimately depend on "unwritten customs" and "ancestral law," which "are the bonds of the entire social framework, linking all written and established laws with those yet to be passed. They act in the same way as ancestral customs from time immemorial, by virtue of being soundly established and instinctively observed, shielding and protecting existing written law" (793b-c). For Plato, politics and lawmaking are not merely a matter of administration or management, but of education and customs. This is to say that, for Plato, *culture* is at the center of the statesman's work. Indeed, Plato considers culture to be so important that he makes the Minister of Education the city's most important official.

Plato's high ambition is again evident: his *Laws* is not

aiming for some perfect legal text, but is imagining a society whose traditions, customs, basic law, and regime are all working to make the citizens tend towards virtue. This notion of law and custom obviously rejects the modern notion of a 'private sphere' supposedly outside the domain of politics. Plato points out that "the state's general code of laws will never rest on a firm foundation as long as private life is badly regulated, and it's silly to expect otherwise" (790b). In this, Plato is not being uniquely authoritarian, but shares a view in common with Aristotle and Greek legislators in general.

The law will appeal to citizens' feelings of guilt and shame to prevent them from becoming criminals (647a). The citizens are above all to be pulled away from following their emotions and their bellies, and towards piety and reason. While athletes succeed in delaying gratification to win sporting events, Plato would like to see such disciplines used to overcome the craving for pleasure:

> [R]ight from the earliest years we're going to tell them stories and talk to them and sing them songs, so as to charm them, we trust, into believing that this victory is the noblest of all ... the conquest of pleasure. If they win this battle, they'll have a happy life — but so much the worst for them if they lose. (840c)

Plato argues for a prescriptive and constant basic law on the grounds that individuals do not have the ability to both discern what is good and to enforce that good on a day-to-day basis. The first challenge is effectively to overcome 'libertarian' solipsism:

> The reason is this: no man has sufficient natural gifts *both* to discern what benefits men in their social relationships *and* to be constantly ready and able to put this knowledge to the best practical use. The first difficulty is to realize that the proper object of true political skill is not the interest of private individuals but the common good. This is what knits a state together, whereas private interests make it disintegrate. If the public interest is well served, rather than the private, then the individual and the community alike are

benefited. (875a-b)

Plato argues by analogy, just as when doctors tend to person's limbs, or a craftsman builds something, so in a community: "the parts contribute to the good of the whole, not vice versa" (903d). Furthermore: "complete freedom from all authority is infinitely worse than submitting to a moderate degree of control" (698b).

The Magnesian regime then aims to discipline and educate its citizens towards unity and virtue. The means used are largely inspired by Spartan practices. Citizens are to be required to eat meals in common to build social cohesion. Youths are to dance in armor and compete in games using real weapons, despite the risks, as a preparation for war. The young are to be forbidden from criticizing the laws. Certain books and poets, deemed demoralizing by the authorities, are to be banned (634d-e). There is to be a ban on convertible currency and sharp limitations on foreign travel. All these measures can be ascribed to Sparta. Inspired by Egyptian practice, Plato furthermore says that authorized songs and dances are to all be religious ones, so that people's reverence for them make them unchanging and eternal across the centuries. The entire society is to regularly engage in ritualized dancing and song together, so as to turn their spontaneous, random gestures into harmonies.

All these measures are aimed at fostering social unity and virtue; and preventing luxury and decadence. Plato says Magnesia will have no city walls, quoting a poet: "a city's walls should be made of bronze and iron, not stone" (778d). Plato has scorn for those who dream of a lazy, consumerist lifestyle:

Must each of them get plumper and plumper every day of his life, like a fatted beast? No: we maintain that's *not* the right and proper thing to do. A man who lives like that won't be able to escape the fate he deserves; and the fate of an idle fattened beast that takes life easy is usually to be torn to pieces by some other animal—one of the skinny kind, who've been emaciated by a life of daring and endurance. (807a-b)

The citizens are to become as psychologically homogeneous and synchronous as possible: "the same state and the same citizens (who should all be the same sort of people, as far as possible) should enjoy the same pleasures in the same fashion: that is the secret of a happy and blessed life" (816d). Young men must learn to rule and be ruled in turn, individual action being eliminated, to notably ensure victory in war:

> [W]e must condition ourselves to an instinctive rejection of the very notion of doing anything, if possible, except by combined and united action as members of a group. No better and more powerful or efficient weapon exists for ensuring safety and final victory in war, and never will. This is what we must practice in peacetime, right from childhood — the exercise of authority over others and submission to them in turn. (942c)

Plato is emphatic: we must train ourselves so that each of our individual actions is not a random spasm, but serves the public good in some way.

PLATO, A PRACTICAL INEGALITARIAN

Plato's *Laws*, despite its democratic Assembly, does not represent a surrender to egalitarianism. The lawmaker, Plato says emphatically, must not follow the mob but be their teacher. The laws' strictures will both educate the people and constrain their will within certain bounds. Plato urges the statesman to be bold in going against public opinion where necessary:

> Of course, most people only ask their legislators to enact the kind of laws that the population in general will accept without objection. But just imagine asking your trainer or doctor to give you pleasure when he trains or cures your body! (684c)

Plato notably remarks that his suggestion that newlywed women not be confined to the home but have their own common meals — and thus also be educated and participate in the life of the city — would be particularly scorned by the average misogynistic Greek of his day. However, the philosopher and lawgiver must tell the truth: "the common man will find our policy this time more difficult to swallow than ever. However, we should never shrink from speaking the truth as we see it, Clinias" (779e).

More generally, while most public officials and generals are to be democratically elected by the Assembly, these appointments should ideally be based on merit. Plato lists seven generally accepted claims to rule: that of parents over children ("in general ... universally acknowledged," he observes), high birth over low, old over young, masters over slaves, strong over weak, wise over ignorant, and by lot (the famous, largely defunct practice of democratic election by choosing a random citizen, Plato staffs most offices through a mixture of voting and the lot). Of these, Plato claims the rule of the wise over the ignorant is by far the most legitimate. While the poet Pindar of Thebes had claimed that the rule of the strong over the weak was a "decree of nature," Plato writes that this is only true in the animal kingdom:

> [T]he most important claim will be the sixth, that the ignorant man should follow the leadership of the wise and obey his orders. In spite of you, my clever Pindar, what I'd called the "decree of nature" is in fact the rule of law that governs willing subjects, without being imposed by force; I'm certainly not prepared to say it's *un*natural. (690b)

If the best and wisest shall rule, the means to choosing them will be "equality of opportunity" (744b), not to pursue equality as an end in itself, but to give honor and power to citizens in precise proportion to their worth: "the citizens must be esteemed and given office, so far as possible, on exactly equal terms of 'proportional inequality'" (744c). For Plato, "practicable and appropriate duties should be specified for each individual," including women (785b). In Magnesia, one acquires the authority to rule the state by having served it well:

> No one will ever make a commendable master without having been a servant first; one should be proud not so much of ruling well but of serving well—and serving the

laws above all (because this is the way we serve the gods), and secondly, if we are young, those who are full of years and honor. It is vital that everyone should be convinced that this rule applies to us all. (762e)

The *Laws*, like the *Republic* and Aristotle's *Politics*, engages in lengthy denunciation of egalitarianism, worth reprinting here:

> You see, even if you proclaim that a master and his slave shall have equal status, friendship between them is inherently impossible. The same applies to the relations between an honest man and scoundrel. Indiscriminate equality for all amounts to *in*equality, and both fill a state with quarrels between its citizens. How correct the old saying is, that "equality leads to friendship"! It's right enough and rings true, but what *kind* of equality has this potential is a problem which produces ripe confusion. This is because we use the same term for two concepts of "equality," which in most respects are virtual opposites. The first sort of equality (of measures, weights, and numbers) is within the competence of any state and any legislator: that is, one can simply distribute equal awards by lot. But the most genuine equality, and the best, is not so obvious. It needs the wisdom and judgment of Zeus, and only in a limited number of ways does it help the human race; but when states or even individuals find it profitable, they find it very profitable indeed. The general method I mean is to grant much to the great and less to the less great, adjusting what you give to take account of the real nature of each— specifically, to confer high recognition on great virtue, but when you come to the poorly educated in this respect, to treat them as they deserve. We maintain, in fact, that statesmanship consists of essentially this—strict justice. This is what we should be aiming at now, Clinias: this is the kind of "equality" we should concentrate on as we bring our state into the world. The founder of any other state should also concentrate on this same goal when he frames his laws, and take no notice of a bunch of dictators, or single one, or even the power of the people. He must always make *justice* his

aim, and this is precisely as we've described it: it consists of granting the "equality" that unequals deserve to get. Yet on occasion a state as a whole (unless it is prepared to put up with a degree of friction in one part or another) will be obliged to apply these concepts in a rather rough and ready way, because complaisance and toleration, which always wreck complete precision, are the enemies of strict justice. You can now see why it was necessary to avoid the anger of the man in the street by giving him an equal chance in the lot (though even then we prayed to the gods of good luck to make the lot give the right decisions). So though force of circumstances compels us to employ both sorts of equality, we should employ the second, which demands good luck to prove successful, as little as possible. (756e-758a)

Thus, Plato's concession to democracy is halfhearted and pragmatic. Giving each a near-equal say in government is a way of giving him a stake in the regime and of building social solidarity, but given the inequality of men in wisdom and virtue, this is necessarily suboptimal.

Plato's views on 'pop culture' have also certainly not changed. He is emphatic: a society's culture and values must *not* be determined by the low and fickle tastes of a mob. At the risk of sounding coarse, this is also obviously suboptimal. Cultural aristocracy is paramount: the society's culture and values ought to be inspired by its most enlightened members. Consider Plato's denunciation of awarding prizes by popular majority:

For instance, the law now in force in Sicily and Italy, by truckling to the majority of the audience and deciding the winner by a show of hands, has had a disastrous effect on the authors themselves, who compose to gratify the depraved tastes of their judges; the result is that in effect *they* are taught by the audience. It has been equally disastrous for the quality of the pleasure felt by the spectators: they ought to come to experience more elevated pleasures from listening to the portrayal of characters invariably better than their own, but in fact just the opposite happens, and they have no one to thank but themselves. (659b-c)

I would add that politicians who seek to be crowd-pleasers inevitably worsen their own character in the same way. I can furthermore do no better than reproduce Plato's scathing account of the rise of "theatrocracy":

People of taste and education made it a rule to listen to the performance with silent attention right through to the end; children and their attendants and the general public could always be disciplined and controlled by a stick. Such was the rigor with which the mass of the people was prepared to be controlled in the theater, and to refrain from passing judgment by shouting. Later, as time went on, composers arose who started to set a fashion of breaking the rules and offending good taste. They did have a natural artistic talent, but they were ignorant of the correct and legitimate standards laid down by the Muse. Gripped by a frenzied and excessive lust for pleasure, they jumbled together laments and hymns, mixed paeans and dithyrambs, and even imitated pipe tunes on the lyre. The result was a total confusion of styles. Unintentionally, in their idiotic way, they misrepresented their art, claiming that in music there are no standards of right and wrong at all, but that the most "correct" criterion is the pleasure of a man who enjoyed the performance, whether he is a good man or not. On these principles they based their compositions, and they accompanied them with propaganda to the same effect. Consequently they gave the ordinary man not only a taste for breaking the laws of music but the arrogance to set himself up as a capable judge. The audiences, once silent, began to use their tongues; they claimed to know what was good and bad music and instead of a "musical meritocracy," a sort of vicious "theatrocracy" arose. But if this democracy had been limited to gentlemen and had applied only to music, no great harm would have been done; in the event, however, music proved to be the starting point of everyone's conviction that he was an authority on everything, and of a general disregard for the law. Complete license was not far behind. The conviction that they *knew* made them unafraid, and assurance engendered effrontery. You see, a reckless lack of respect for one's betters is effrontery of peculiar viciousness, which springs from a freedom from inhibitions that has gone much too far. (700c-701b)

The judgment may seem harsh and yet also justified whenever we consider the vulgarity and childishness of so much cultural production today. Plato does not believe anything should be done merely because it 'feels good,' but must actually serve the good in some way. Plato writes elsewhere on the threat to the younger generations posed by those selling them sensual pleasures and ever-changing superficial novelties: "we must also stop pleasure-mongers seducing them" (798e). The rise of modern pop culture shows that Plato's concerns were quite justified: public culture in a good society simply *cannot* be determined by what feels pleasurable to the lowest members in their lowest moments.

I would note that Plato, while extremely ambitious and prescriptive in his paper-polities, is not exactly a gratuitous 'totalitarian.' One should legislate as necessary, being more prescriptive insofar as the people need it: "When the majority of people conduct themselves with moderation in sexual matters, no such regulations [concerning child-bearing] should be mentioned or enacted; but if there is misbehavior, regulations should be made and enforced" (785a). The more naturally gifted and virtuous one's population, the less need there will be for coercive legislation to keep people on the straight and narrow.[210]

The *Laws* also clarifies the sometimes otherworldly ethics of the *Republic*. Plato believes selfishness is never justified, but conversely, he is realistic about the need for harshness to protect the common good. He says that tackling evil is impossible without "righteous indignation" (731c) and that "when you have to deal with complete and unmanageably

---

[210] Which perhaps explains the extreme severity of Sharia?

vicious corruption, you must let your anger off its leash. That is why we say that it must be the good man's duty to be high-spirited or gentle as circumstances require" (731d). Furthermore, Plato spells out the paradoxical counterpoint to his advocacy of unconditional altruism in the *Republic*, that the only thing to be done with the incurably antisocial is to put them down:

> We may use absolutely *any* means to make him [the citizen] hate injustice and embrace true justice—or at any rate not hate it. But suppose the lawgiver finds a man who's beyond cure—what legal penalty will he provide for this case? He will recognize that the best thing for all such people is to cease to live—best even for themselves. (862d-e)

And again:

> [The legislator will] do his best to banish ignorance and incontinence and cowardice and indeed every sort of injustice from the hearts of those criminals whose outlook can be cured. However—and this is a point that deserves constant repetition—when a man's soul is unalterably fixed in that condition by decree of fate, our erudite judges and their advisers will deserve the commendation of the whole state if they cure him by imposing the penalty of death. (958a)

Plato is however most different from Aristotle—at least what remains of him in the *Politics*—in the general spiritual tenor of the society. For Aristotle, religion is scarcely mentioned, being virtually an afterthought. Not so for the heaven-grasping Plato. He takes seriously the traditional Greek and Socratic view that piety is adherence to law, and vice versa. The city-state of Magnesia is openly inspired by a god, its officials occasionally appeal to the oracles, and indeed atheists face persecution. For Plato, as for most in the Socratic tradition, there is a kind of transcendental equation: nature = the divine = reason. Plato wants us to forever strive to be god-like: "we should run our public and private life, our homes and our cities, in obedience to what little spark of immortality lies in us, and dignify these edicts of reason with the name of 'law'" (714a).[211]

Plato simply cannot abide a life of randomness and frivolousness. He is, as ever, an enemy of slouching nihilists, relativists, and belly-chasers:

> I maintain that serious matters deserve serious attention, but trivialities do not; that all men of good will should put god at the center of their thoughts; that man, as we said before, has been created as a toy for god; and that this is the great point in his favor. So every man and every woman should play this part and order their whole life accordingly, engaging in the best possible pastimes — in a quite different frame of mind to their present one. (803c)

Plato elsewhere excoriates "all idle and thoughtless *bons vivants* ... just the kind of people the poet [Hesiod] said were 'like nothing so much as stingless drones'" (901a).

Plato wishes us to live by reason and walk with god, forever, to be as eternal as the stars. Particularly relevant to us in this respect, and quite rare for mystics, is Plato's emphasis on the duty of reproduction. He provides the following preamble to a law requiring citizens to have children:

> A man must marry between the ages of thirty and thirty-five, reflecting that there is a sense in which nature has not only somehow endowed the human race with a degree of immortality, but also planted in us all a longing to achieve it, which we express in every way we can. One expression of that longing is the desire for fame and the wish not to lie nameless in the grave. Thus mankind is by nature a companion of eternity, and is linked to it, and will be linked to it, forever. Mankind is immortal because it always leaves later generations behind to preserve its unity and identity for all time: it gets its share of immortality by means of procreation. It is never a holy thing to voluntarily deny oneself this prize, and he who neglected to take a wife and have children does precisely that. (721b-d)

---

[211] A pious sentiment which, I believe, also moved William Pierce.

I must say the phrase strongly resonates with me personally: each of us is "by nature a companion of eternity."

FILIAL PIETY: THE FOUNDATION OF SOCIAL ORDER

Kinship, both familial and ethnic, has a central role in the Magnesian regime. Plato cites Homer's Cyclopes as a metaphor for the family being prehistoric humanity's first society. In this family, the patriarch rightly rules on grounds of kinship:

> [T]he eldest member rules by virtue of having inherited power from his father or mother; the others follow his lead and make one flock like birds. The authority to which they bow is that of their patriarch: they are governed, in effect, by the most justifiable of all forms of kingship. (680e)[212]

Plato goes into lengthy detail on the honor children owe their parents as a sacred imperative and on "the worship of the gods and the services to be rendered to our ancestors" (723e). We frequently find such statements pairing blood and spirit: the highest moral imperatives are those to our kin and to the divine. Plato writes on the need for children to respect their parents:

> It is meet and right that a debtor should discharge his first and greatest obligation and pay the debt which comes before all others; he must consider that all he has and holds belongs to those who bore and bred him, and he is meant to use it in their service to the limit of his powers ... give to the old people what they desperately need in view of their age: repayment of all that anxious care and attention they lavished on him, the longstanding "loan" they made him as a child. Throughout his life the son must be very careful to

---

[212] Interestingly, this chronology was also followed by the Prussian king Frederick the Great, perhaps due to readings of Plato and Aristotle, writing in one political treatise arguing for fatherly monarchic rule: "It seems probable that family fathers were the first legislators." Guillaume Durocher, "Enlightened Patriarchy: Frederick the Great's Principles of Lawmaking," *Counter-Currents*, November 9-10, 2016.

watch his tongue in addressing his parents, because there is a very heavy penalty for careless and ill-considered language; Retribution, messenger of Justice, is the appointed overseer of these things. If his parents get angry, he must submit to them, and whether they satisfy their anger in speech or action, he must forgive them; after all, he must reflect, it's natural enough for a father to get very angry if he thinks he's being harmed by his own son. (717b-d)

Anyone whose parents live at home with them should venerate and care for them as "living shrines" (931e), care for whom is more valuable than prayer to gods, because they might join our own prayers.

Conversely, the killing of parents and relatives is the supreme crime, only possible to those with "such an ungovernable temper" that they cede to "an insane fury" (869a) in which one "has plundered the shrine that is his parent's body" (869b). There are "deliberate and wholly wicked murders of relatives ... murders that are absolutely the most detestable in the sight of Heaven" (872d). Fortunately: "Justice stands on guard to exact vengeance for the spilling of the blood of relatives" (872e).

A matricide, Plato says, will be reborn a woman in the next life and killed in the same way by their own children: "If a citizen is ever shown to be responsible for such a crime—to have perpetrated, that is, some great and unspeakable offense against the gods or his parents or the state, *the penalty* is death" (854e). Interestingly, Plato suggests such retribution is a "law of nature" (870d). Plato endorses the Athenian practice of disenfranchising those who mistreat their parents—such as by beating them or failing to support them in old age. Implicit is the assumption that society is held together by respect for the gods, the family, and the city-state.

Plato adheres to the traditional Greek view that happiness means a prosperous posterity. He assures that those who are pious towards their family will be rewarded with fertility: "If a man honors and respects his relatives, who all share the worship of the family gods and have the same blood in their veins, he can reasonably hope to have the gods of birth look with benevolence on the procreation of his own children" (729c). Conversely, wrongdoing hurts one's line: "we should put our trust in the traditional view of such conduct—that it injures our descendants" (913b-c).

The combination of pious and familial sentiment enables Plato to overcome the tension between private property and the public good. Plato no longer advocates the communism he described in the *Republic*, however, like Aristotle, he sees private property as something like a gift to individuals guaranteed by the state and meant to serve the public interest. The state will distribute land among the founding settlers and this property must be cherished as that of one's family and gods:

> [E]ach man who receives a portion of land should regard it as the common possession of the entire state. The land is his ancestral home and he must cherish it even more than children cherish their mother; furthermore, Earth is a goddess, and mistress of mortal men. (And the gods and spirits already established in the locality must be treated with the same respect.) (740a)

Kinship is also central to Plato's subordination of individual interests to those to the community. This is most explicit in the Athenian's discussion of inheritance, which should be regulated in accordance with the interests of the community (especially, to fight a common Greek problem and trend, the tendency for testaments to lead to concentration of property in few hands, the creation of a landless underclass):

> I, as legislator, rule that neither you nor this property of yours belongs to yourselves, but your whole clan, ancestors, and descendants alike; and your clan and its property in turn belong, even more absolutely, to the state ... I shall legislate with a view to nothing except the interest of your clan and the entire state, relegating (as is only right) that of the individual to second place. (923b)

The statesman legislates not merely for the current generation, let alone a mere aggregate of individuals, but *for one's entire people and lineage,* from one's ancestors to one's to descendants, in a single unbroken chain.

MARRIAGE & REPRODUCTION: THE FAMILY'S CONTRIBUTION TO THE COMMUNITY

Each family father holds his property as a sacred duty in the service of the community. This is part of the wider Greek claim, shared by both Plato and Aristotle, that the family is an institution created not for the mere convenience or pleasures of two consenting individuals, but to promote the community's well-being and perpetuity. Hence, the Athenian says:

> Well then, in heaven's name, what will be the first law our legislator will establish? Surely the first subject he will turn to in his regulations will be the very first step that leads to the birth of children in the state. (720e)

The begetting of children for Plato is not some frivolous affair, like whether or not one decides to adopt a hamster or a poodle. He says: "we should become partners in eternity by leaving a line of descendants to serve god forever in our stead" (774a). Like Aristotle, Plato considers children to belong to the community first, and hence education must be compulsory "for every man and boy" (804d).

The lawmaker is to create conditions in which mate selection can both take place and be done in an enlightened way:

> [W]hen people are going to live together as partners in marriage, it is vital that the fullest possible information should be available about the bride and her background and the family she'll marry into. One should regard the prevention of mistakes here as a matter of supreme importance—so important and serious, in fact, that even the young people's recreation must be arranged with this in mind. Boys and girls must dance together at an age when plausible occasions can be found for their doing so, in order that they may have a reasonable look at each other; and they should dance naked, provided sufficient modesty and

restraint are displayed by all concerned. (771e-772a)

Men are to marry between the ages of 30 and 35 and women between 16 and 20. Those who fail to do so will pay a yearly fine "of a sum to be specified; that ought to stop him thinking that life as a bachelor is all cakes and ale" (721d). For couples who refuse to have children, female officials are to "enter the homes of the young people and by a combination of admonition and threats try to make them give up their ignorant and sinful ways" (784c). Furthermore: "The Guardians of the Laws must chastise the disobedient as a philistine who has never been trained to appreciate the melodies of the Muses of marriage" (775b). Those found guilty will be officially disgraced, will not be given the normal honors accorded to the old, and will be banned from attending weddings and baby showers. Elderly unmarried and childless citizens will not have the right to shame disorderly young people, but can be beaten with impunity.[213]

Plato takes a pragmatic view of marriage as aimed above all towards the production and education of children. If a marriage fails to produce children, the citizen "must be obliged to remarry so as to beget sufficient children for his home and for the state" (930b-c). Furthermore: "The minimum acceptable number of children is to be fixed by law as one of each sex" (930c-d). After the child-bearing years, marriage for pure companionship and mutual assistance in old age would also be possible. Adultery is a particularly evil crime in the child-bearing years, but merely a source of shame once a woman is infertile (784e).

Plato is realistic on the supreme power of the sex drive. He sees humans as driven by the cravings for food, comfort, and sex. These impulses must be channeled towards constructive

---

[213] This provision shows the nature of a traditional society, in which people are sharply policed by elders. A Mauritanian Muslim friend of mine once told me that he was shocked when he first came to Europe seeing young people kissing and touching on the train. He thought to himself: "When is an old man going to come over to smack them?"

ends by the legislator:

> Give a man a correct education, and these instincts will lead
> him to virtue, but educate him badly and he'll end up at the
> other extreme.... . Our third and greatest need, the longing
> we feel most keenly, is the last to come upon us: it is the
> flame of the imperious lust to procreate, which kindles the
> fires of passion in mankind. These three unhealthy instincts
> must be canalized *away* from what men call supreme
> pleasure, and *towards* the supreme good. (782d-783a)

In this effort, the legislator uses "fear, law, and correct
argument," as well as appeals to the gods.

Plato is explicit that couples should consider having
children in a eugenic and communitarian light, aiming for
quality and the public good. He writes: "The bride and groom
should resolve to present the state with the best and finest
children they can produce" (783d-e). Man and wife should
have children in a cooperative spirit and "with a sense of
responsibility." It follows from these premises that citizens
should ideally marry to produce the best children, not for
selfish reasons such as physical beauty or wealth: "One general
rule should apply to marriage: we should seek to contract the
alliance that will benefit the state, not the one that we
personally find most alluring" (773b).

Plato recognizes that specific bans on marrying particular
individuals may be unrealistic and appear ridiculous,
nonetheless: "we must resort to our charms and try to persuade
everybody to think it more important to produce well-balanced
children than to marry his equal and never stop lusting for
wealth" (773e). Plato correctly points out that men and women
of similar personality types tend to be attracted to one another.
He worries this could be dysgenic, as their coupling would
produce children with an even more marked personality type.
As a response, he suggests the primitive eugenic measure of
pairing opposites to produce more balanced children. Plato
also suggests that marrying for wealth should be shamed but
not illegal. As all citizens will have some property and
economic means, he believes men and women will be less

likely to marry for wealth. Weddings should be relatively small and not expensive and showy.

Plato, like Aristotle, suggests that particular care should be taken to ensure infants are born healthy. Children should not be conceived in a state of drunkenness, for this will produce unbalanced children. The well-being and virtue of pregnant women should be particularly closely monitored:

> I'd even say, at the risk of sounding flippant, that all expectant mothers, during the year of their pregnancy, should be supervised more closely than other women, to ensure that they don't experience frequent and excessive pleasures, or pains either. An expectant mother should think it important to keep calm and cheerful and sweet-tempered throughout her pregnancy. (792e)

Plato even proposes that women should engage in prenatal activities to improve the coming infant, through what he calls the "athletics of the embryo": just as bird-keepers carry birds around to make them fit, so women should be invited to take a stroll to the temple each day (789e).

Writing in a prescientific age, the actual effectiveness of Plato's proposals in the *Laws* is highly uneven. Some, such as that expectant mothers should be both physically active and psychologically relaxed, are recommended by health professionals to this day. Plato's proposals in the *Republic* are more definitely eugenic and strikingly in line with modern genetic science. The wider principle however, that having or not having children has a fundamental impact on society and therefore both the lawmaker and couples should approach the issue according to the public interest, producing the best and healthiest children possible, is extremely sound.

Plato is quite impressed by the social taboo against parent-child incest. He believes this shows the power of public opinion to dictate behavior, given that children unanimously hear everyone condemn the practice from their youngest years. Megillos notes: "when no one ventures to challenge the law, public opinion works wonders" (838d). Plato returns to the notion that to enforce laws one should spread the belief that what is illegal is evil not only in the eyes of the state but of religion as well. There should be a taboo against homosexuality "in which the human race is deliberately murdered" and men should be kept "away from any female 'soil' in which we'd be sorry to see a seed develop" (839a). Plato argues this is "a *natural* law."

For Plato as with Aristotle, the production of the new generation in appropriate numbers and of the best possible quality is a civic duty: it is incumbent upon both individual citizens to found good families and statesmen to create propitious conditions for this. Bearing children being a sacred duty, Plato's community can live forever in piety: "The young couple should produce children and bring them up, handing on the torch of life from generation to generation, and always worshiping the gods in the manner prescribed by law" (776b).

POPULATION POLICIES: THE PURGING & EXCLUSION OF UNDESIRABLES

Following a Cretan decision, Magnesia is to have a founding population of Dorian Greeks drawn from various parts of both Crete and the Peloponnesian mainland. The settlers then will not have exactly the same customs or civic habits. The Athenian observes the pros and cons of this: the lack of homogeneity and identity will undermine common feeling and joint actions; however there will also be an advantage for the lawgiver, as it will be easier for him to replace their diverse traditions with new ones:

So it won't be all that easy for the Cretan states to found their colony. The emigrants, you see, haven't the unity of a swarm of bees: they are not a single people from a single territory settling down to form a colony with mutual goodwill between themselves and those they have left behind. Such migrations occur because the pressures of land-shortage or some similar misfortune: sometimes a given section of the community may be obliged to go off and settle elsewhere because it is harassed by civil war, and on one occasion a whole state took to its heels after being overcome by an attack it could not resist. In all these cases, to found a state and give it laws is, in some ways, comparatively easy, but in others it's rather difficult. When a single people speaks the same language and observes the same laws you get a certain feeling of community, because everyone shares the same religious rites and so forth; but they certainly won't find it easy to accept laws or political systems that differ from their own. Sometimes, when it's bad laws that have stimulated the revolt, and the rebels try in their new home to keep the same familiar habits that ruined them before, their reluctance to toe the line presents the founder and lawgiver with a difficult problem. On the other hand, a miscellaneous combination of all kinds of different people will perhaps be more ready to submit to a new code of laws — but to get them to "pull and puff as one" (as they say of a team of horses) is very difficult and takes a long time. (708b-d)

Morrow points out that, despite their apparent diversity, the settlers will be entirely of Dorian stock, which is to say populations with a similarly austere culture and experience living under similarly strict laws.[214] The rigorous Dorian ethos evidently appealed to Plato in contrast with his native Athens.

Plato is not in favor of being undiscerning concerning any city's founding stock. On the contrary, he argues for a vigorous "purge" of the population through exile or execution, of inferior and crime-prone stock, drawing direct comparisons with animal breeders. He particularly singles out any elements of the poorer classes engaging in egalitarian revolutionary activity as "a disease ... in the body politic."[215] In Magnesia, such a purge may be unnecessary if the settlers are very carefully screened for quality. Plato goes into considerable detail:

---

[214] Morrow, *Plato's Cretan City*, p. 11.

[215] Certainly, the reasoning here seems quite similar to that of early twentieth-century fascist movements, which sought to eliminate Marxist rabble-rousers and unite the body politic.

Anyone who takes charge of a herd of animals — a shepherd or cattle-man or breeder of horses or what have you — will never get down to looking after them without first performing the purge appropriate to his particular animal-community: that is, he will weed out the unhealthy and inferior stock and send it off to other herds, and keep only the thoroughbreds and the healthy animals to look after. He knows that otherwise he would have to waste endless effort on sickly and refractory beasts, degenerate by nature and ruined by incompetent breeding, and that unless he purges the existing stock these faults will spread in any herd to the animals that are still physically and temperamentally fit and unspoiled. This is not too serious in the case of the lower animals, and we need mention it only by way of illustration, but with human beings it is vitally important for the legislator to ascertain and explain the appropriate measures in each case, not only as regards a purge, but in general. To purge a whole state, for instance, several methods may be employed, some mild, some drastic; and if a legislator were a dictator too he'd be able to purge the state drastically, which is the best way. But if he has to establish a new society and new laws without dictatorial powers, and succeeds in administering no more than the mildest purge, he'll be well content even with this limited achievement. Like drastic medicines, the best purge is a painful business: it involves chastisement by a combination of "judgment" and "punishment," and takes the latter, ultimately, to the point of death or exile. That usually gets rid of the major criminals who are incurable and do the state enormous harm. When there is a shortage of food, and the underprivileged show themselves ready to follow their leaders in an attack on the property of the privileged, they are to be regarded as a disease that has developed in the body politic, and in the friendliest possible way they should be (as it will be tactfully put) "transferred to a colony." Somehow or other everyone who legislates must do this in good time; but our position at the moment is even more unusual. There's no need for us here and now to have to resort to a colony or arrange to make a selection of people by a purge. No: it's as though we have a number of streams from several sources, some from springs, some from mountain torrents, all flowing down to unite in one lake. We have to apply ourselves to seeing that the water, as it mingles, is as pure as possible, partly by draining some of it off, partly by diverting it into different channels. Even so, however you organize your society, it looks as if there will always be trouble and risk. True enough: but seeing that we are operating at the moment on a theoretical rather than a practical level, let's suppose we've recruited our citizens and their purity meets with our approval. After all, when we have screened the bad candidates over a suitable period and given them every chance to be converted, we can refuse their application to enter and become citizens of the state; but we should greet the good ones with all possible courtesy and kindness. (735b-736c)

From this we can surmise that Magnesia would reject any 'economic migration' which is not beneficial to the city-state of people coming from Crete or the mainland "on the grounds that the population in the individual cities has exceeded the number that be supported by the land" (707e). Furthermore, Plato demands that all beggars be expelled: "No one is to go begging in the state. Anyone who attempts to do so, and scrounged a living by never-ending importunities, must be expelled ... so that the land may rid itself completely of such a creature" (936c-d).

Like Aristotle later, Plato observes that a diverse population of subjects, lacking a common identity and solidarity, is easier to rule. Hence, he says of Magnesia's agricultural slave population: "if the slaves are to submit to the condition without giving trouble, they should not all come from the same country or speak the same tongue, as far as can be arranged" (777d).

Whatever one makes of the specific measures, the broader point is one shared by Aristotle: the composition of the population is a fundamental political issue on which the statesman is empowered to act by whatever means appropriate. In the case of Plato, possible measures vary from a discerning immigration policy to the expulsion of undesirable elements.

PLATONIC CONFEDERALISM
GREEK UNITY AGAINST BARBARIANS

The city-state was virtually the exclusive focus of Greek political science, at least in the literature which survives, perhaps surprisingly given the pervasiveness of multi-city leagues, including both military alliances and political confederations. Nonetheless, Plato does suggest, if somewhat allusively, in his various works a kind of lawful and ethnocentric confederalism for Greece. The Yugoslav scholar Slobodan Dušanić argues from numerous passages in Plato's works that the philosopher was deeply interested in the question of confederalism between city-states, that is to say of limited political unity on grounds of kinship and defense against external threats. Dušanić argues that Plato engaged with "that epoch's patriotic federalism," was moved by "his barbarophobia and laconophilia," and endorsed as "just wars" all "pan-Hellenic defensive actions against the attacks of foreign nations."[216]

Plato's Hellenic confederalism was grounded in a critique of Athenian imperialism following the trauma of defeat and collapse in the Peloponnesian War. The philosopher drew an analogy between the selfish, greedy, grasping, and self-destructive soul of the man lacking self-control, and the selfish, greedy, grasping, and ultimately self-destructive behavior of democratic and imperial Athens. The democracy was a rapacious, belly-chasing regime, so willing to crush fellow Greek in the pursuit of coin (recall that many Athenian citizens profited from imperial expansion through employment in the

---

[216] Slobodan Dušanić, "Plato's Projects for a Confederate Sicily and the Constitutional Patterns in the Third Book of the *Laws*," *Aevum* (2010, 1), pp. 61, 66, 67.

Athenian navy and imperial bureaucracy). As Malcolm
Schofield observes: "For Plato, Pericles was merely a late
episode in a story of self-indulgence and consequent
degeneration that he himself told in one mode or another again
and again."[217]

In contrast with the Athenian experience, Plato argued for
peace and gentleness among Greeks, under the consensual
leadership of the best city-states. From the ideal regimes
described in the myth of Atlantis and the *Laws*, and from his
practical political activity as described in the *Letters*, we can see
that Plato advocated for the creation of regional Hellenic
confederations of city-states, with varying degrees of
centralization, grounded in a shared identity, common laws,
and a joint struggle against barbarian threats.

THE DORIAN LEAGUE AS PROTECTOR OF GREECE

In the *Laws*, Plato analyzes politics as taking place within
ever-widening concentric circles of kinship and loyalty. After
the family, the collection of families, and the city-state have
been "founded in succession over a vast period of time," finally
"we discover this fourth state (or 'nation,' if you like)" (683a).
Beyond the city-state, Plato then considers the generally loose
and fractious leagues or confederations of Greek city-states as a
potentially even higher form of social organization.

Plato discusses the semi-legendary history of three city-
states founded by the descendants of Hercules prior to the
Persian Wars—Sparta, Argos, and Messene—which had
together formed the Dorian League, an association which
included a common army. The confederation was meant to
protect not just itself but the entire Greek nation:

> Well then, it's pretty obvious that they intended the
> arrangements they made to protect adequately not only the
> Peloponnese but the Greeks in general against any possible
> attack by non-Greeks—as for example occurred when those
> who then lived in the territory of Ilium trusted to the power

[217] Malcolm Schofield, *Plato: Political Philosophy* (Oxford: Oxford
University Press, 2006), p. 212.

of the Assyrian empire, which Ninos had founded, and provoked the war against Troy by their arrogance. You see, a good deal of the splendor of the Assyrian empire still remained, and the dread of its united organization was the counterpart in that age of our fear of the Great King of Persia today. Troy, which was part of the Assyrian empire, had been captured a second time [as recounted in the *Iliad*]. To meet such dangers the Dorian army formed a single unified body, although at that period it was distributed among the three states under the command of the kings (who were brothers, being sons of Hercules). (685b-d)

Plato laments however that the Dorian League was short-lived: "if they had done as they intended and had agreed a common policy, their power would have been irresistible, militarily speaking" (686b).

Both Argos and Messene degenerated, Plato says, while only Sparta maintained itself through the inspired laws of Lycurgus, which combined a mixed monarchic-oligarchic-democratic regime with extremely tough legislation aimed towards training the Spartiates for unity and warfare. Had Argos and Messene avoided luxury and decadence, and had the three cities been united, Plato suggests the Persian Wars would have been prevented:

> But if anyone ... had been able to control the various offices and produce a single authority out of the three [city-states], he would have saved all the splendid projects of that age from destruction, and neither the Persians nor anyone else would have sent a fleet to attack Greece, contemptuously supposing that we were people who counted for little. (692c)

Plato then portrays the Dorian League as a marvelous but wasted institution, which fell apart because of the bad laws of Argos and Messene. The failure to maintain the unity of these three states and to protect Greece against foreign aggression informs and frames the entire rest of the discussion in the *Laws*. The Greeks, Plato suggests, must learn from these mistakes. The Persian Wars had almost led to the annihilation of the Greek people through universal miscegenation:

If it hadn't been for the joint determination of the Athenians and the Spartans to resist the slavery that threatened them, we should have by now virtually a complete mixture of the races — Greek with Greek, Greek with barbarian, and barbarian with Greek. We can see a parallel in the nations whom the Persians lord it over today: they have been split up and then horribly jumbled together again into the scattered communities in which they now live. (693a)

This was no idle threat, Herodotus tells how the deportation and scattering *en masse* of entire tribes was a common way for the Persians to permanently eliminate national resistance. The first prerequisite for anything was to maintain the existence of one's people. Plato furthermore says that a sense of shame was what motivated the Athenians to resist even after their city was occupied. Without "Lady Modesty," the Athenians "would never have combined to defend themselves or protected temples, tombs, fatherland, and friends and relatives as well, in the way that they did. We would all have been split up and scattered over the face of the earth" (699c-d).

Plato gives some brief indications of how to maintain unity among the states of a confederation. The member states are ruled by different branches of the same royal family, have common laws, and maintain a confederal army. The kings and peoples of each city-state "exchanged oaths in accordance with mutually binding laws which they had to adopted to regulate the exercise of authority and obedience to it" (684a). The people swore loyalty to the king on the condition that he would not expand his power. Plato suggests an original model for ensuring the maintenance of confederal law across the League: "Whenever a given state broke the established laws, an alliance of the other two would always be there to take the field against it" (684b).

Plato's history, like much of Herodotus, must be considered mythological or customary. Nonetheless, there is no reason to think that his historical account was not meant in earnest, based on the traditions of his time. Plato clearly considered Dorian League as a model to followed, with its flaws corrected, for the unity and defense of Greece.

NATIONAL LEADERSHIP & CONFEDERALISM IN THE MYTH OF ATLANTIS

Another example of Plato's confederal thought is found in his famous myth of Atlantis, as expressed in the *Timaeus* and the unfinished *Critias*. The tale had supposedly been heard by the Athenian lawgiver Solon, who himself is said to have heard it from Egyptian priests. It tells of a great war which occurred 8,000 years before Plato's time, between the mysterious and powerful empire of Atlantis and Ur-Athens, to which the historical Athenians were distantly related. The point of the story is to show another version of Socrates' ideal state, Ur-Athens, in action, engaged in that most demanding of human activities: war.

In the myth, the Atlantids are semi-divine beings, descendants of Poseidon who have been shepherded by the gods themselves (*Critias*, 109b). However, they have since degenerated due to dysgenic breeding with mortals. The Atlantids had been virtuous, moderate, and frugal "as long as their divine nature survived … But when the divine portion in them began to grow faint as it was often blended with great quantities of mortality and as their human nature gradually gained ascendancy" (*Critias*, 121b-c). In so doing, these blessed creatures became worse than animals.

The myth then presents Plato's political ideals in two distinct forms: in pre-fallen Atlantis and virtuous Ur-Athens. The decadent Atlantids have greedily expanded across the world and threaten to conquer Greece and all Europe. The allegorical story again showcases Plato's obsession between a virtuous and frugal land-power (Ur-Athens) and a decadent and materialistic sea-power (Atlantis). As an ideal city, Ur-Athens was fit to lead the Greeks: "Preeminent among all others in the nobility of her spirit and in her use of all the arts of war, she first rose to the leadership of the Greek cause" (*Critias*, 25b-c). Furthermore, we are told that this mythical city had a perfectly stable population and led the Greek nation both militarily and culturally:

This was the manner of their life: they were the guardians of their own citizens and the leaders of the rest of the Greek world, which followed them willingly. And they kept their population stable as far as they could—both of men and women—for generation after generation, maintaining the population of those who had reached military age or were still of military age at close to twenty thousand at most ... they directed the life of their city and of Greece with justice. Their fame for the beauty of their bodies and for the variety and range of their mental and spiritual qualities spread through all of Asia and all of Europe. (*Critias*, 112d-e)

Plato writes: "the finest and best of all the races of humankind once lived in your [Athenian] region. This is the race from whom you yourself, your whole city, all that you and your countrymen have today, are sprung, thanks to the survival of a small portion of their stock" (*Critias*, 23b-c). Ur-Athens as a mythical model then showcases Plato's biopolitical and ethnocentric ideal.

Plato's federalism is however even more evident among the Atlantids. Atlantis is supposed to have been an enormous continent to the west, a federation of ten kingdoms, one of which was a leader-kingdom. Each king was sovereign concerning his domestic affairs, however "as for their common empire and federation, the kings were regulated by the laws of Poseidon" (*Critias*, 119c). The kings gathered every few years in the sanctuary of Poseidon and "deliberated on matters of common concern and held an assize to determine if anyone of them had broken the law, and they gave judgment" (*Critias*, 119d). Each king swore on "both himself and his descendants" to rule "in conformity with the laws of their father" (*Critias*, 120a). Like the Dorian League, the Atlantid federation was a military alliance within which there were to be no wars among themselves and whose common federal laws were enforced by a majority of member states:

> There were many other particular laws concerning the prerogatives of each of the kings, but the most important of these were those forbidding them to bear arms against one

another and commanding them to help one another should anyone in any of their cities make an attempt to overturn the divine family; that they should deliberate together, as had their ancestors before them, over their decisions concerning war and their other actions, but that they should cede leadership to the royal family of Atlantis; and, finally, that the king should have power to put none of his kinsmen to death, if he could not obtain the approval of the majority of the ten kings. (*Critias*, 120c-d)

The myth of Atlantis then showcases the same principles of Platonic federalism: biopolitics based on demographic and hereditarian realities, consensual national leadership, and federation based on shared blood, internal peace, and law.

PLATO'S SICILIAN PROJECT

There is evidence that Plato promoted solidarity among Greek city-states not just in his philosophical works, but also in his political activities advising statesmen. According to Plato's so-called *Letters*, especially the *Seventh* and *Eighth*,[218] the philosopher sailed to Syracuse three times in the hope of converting the ruling tyrants to philosophy. While Plato had gone so as not to be considered merely an impractical theorist, his attempts failed before the capriciousness of the Sicilian despots. Plato's ambitions and proposals for Sicily, however, are not without interest.

The Greeks of Sicily had been weakened, both by conflict between cities and within Syracuse, torn between tyrannical and democratic factions, and were increasingly threatened by

---

[218] Scholars are divided on the authenticity of the *Seventh Letter*, which is one of our only extensive sources for Plato's life and has traditionally been ascribed to the philosopher. In any case, if the letter is not by Plato, then all admit that it must have been written by a follower deeply steeped in Platonic literature and philosophy. Even if the *Seventh Letter* were to be inauthentic, we can then consider the document's ideals to be typical of the kind of politics Plato inspired in his followers.

the Carthaginians. In the *Letters*, written to the followers of Dion, a Sicilian politician whom Plato had tried to advise, Plato presents a clear project for the renewal of Hellenic Sicily and the expulsion of the Semitic barbarians. Syracuse, under a wise ruler, could unite Sicily under common laws, govern with restraint and consensus, and return to living in the frugal "Dorian fashion" (Sicily was notorious for luxurious living). Plato expresses a passionate Hellenic patriotism:

> [Given the Sicilian Greeks' infighting], eventually, if things take their natural course (which god forbid!), the whole of Sicily will have practically lost the Greek language and will have come under the empire and dominion of the Phoenicians or the Opici [an Italic people].

> This is a prospect which should incite every Hellene to search for a remedy with all his might. If anyone has an apter or a better plan than the one I am going to offer, let him bring it forth and he will rightly be called a loyal Hellene. (*Letter VIII*, 353e-354a)

Against this prospect, Plato argues for a politics of moderation and law in both domestic and foreign affairs. There is a clear conciliatory and pan-Hellenic message. After a civil war or revolution, he advises the victors "to select the most eminent Greeks they can discover ... to make laws, binding them upon oath to award no more to the victors than to the vanquished, but to consider only the equal and common good of the whole city" (*Letter VII*, 337b-c).

In foreign affairs, Plato criticizes the coercive hegemony of Syracuse over other Sicilian Greek cities as unjust and unsustainable. He compares imperialist plunder to confiscating wealth from the rich, condemning "the head of a great city ruling over many lesser ones, [who] unjustly assigns the wealth of the smaller ones to his own city" (*Letter VII*, 351b-c). Dionysius I, one of the great but brutal tyrants of Syracuse, had "united all of Sicily into a single city (for he knew that he could trust no one) [but] was scarcely able to survive, for he was poor in friends and loyal followers" (*Letter VII*, 332c). Against this, Plato advises foreign relations of moderation, unity, and trust among Greeks, and common laws. He contrasts Sicily with the early Athenian empire, which had liberated the Asiatic Greeks and, for a time, ruled them in a generous spirit.

Plato repeatedly describes a great project of uniting the Sicilian Greeks and liberating the island from the barbarians:

[I]f he [Dionysius II, the new tyrant of Syracuse] should resettle the deserted cities of Sicily, and bind them together with such laws and constitutions as would make them friendly to himself and to one another and a mutual help against the barbarians, he would have an empire not twice but actually many times as powerful as his father's had been; he would be ready to inflict upon the Carthaginians a far heavier defeat than they had suffered in the days of Gelon [the first tyrant of Syracuse], instead of paying tribute to these barbarians as he was doing at present under the agreement his father had made. (*Letter VII*, 332e-333a)

[If Dion had lived] he would have turned with ardor to the next task, that of resettling all Sicily and liberating her from the barbarians, driving out some of them and subjugating others ... (*Letter VII*, 336a)

[S]ummon others to help you in resettling all Sicily and equalizing her laws. Summon them not only from Sicily herself, but from the whole of the Peloponnese ... (*Letter VII*, 336d)

Finally, Plato even gives voice to his dead friend Dion, imagining what he would have said were he still alive:

I should have resettled the rest of Sicily and driven out the barbarians that now possess it, with the exception of those who made common cause with us in fighting for freedom against the tyranny, and I should have restored to their ancient and ancestral homes the former inhabitants of those Hellenic regions" (*Letter VIII*, 357a-b).

It is worth pausing on Plato's suggestion to "bind [the Greek cities] together with such laws and constitutions as would make them friendly to himself and to one another and a mutual help against the barbarians" and of "equalizing [their] laws." The term used, *isonomia*, is ambiguous in this context, but Dušanić suggests that Plato was arguing for giving each of these city-states the same basic constitution, thus promoting harmony between them even as each remained sovereign.[219] This interpretation is certainly in line with Plato's federal thought as expressed elsewhere. In any event, Plato's practical political projects, as for so many thinkers, came to naught. Nonetheless, the *Letters* show that Plato did not just speculate about Greek unity and survival, but actively and passionately worked towards this in his political life.

PLATO'S GROUP EVOLUTIONARY STRATEGY

Plato was evidently moved by a great sense of piety and a feeling that the universe was imbued with meaning. He happily quoted Thales on the wonder of existence: "everything is full of gods" (899b). Influenced by the disciples of Pythagoras, Plato argued for the study of astronomy and mathematics, in order to understand the elegant harmonies and eternal laws of the cosmos. He believed the reason in men was a small spark of that overarching divine harmony, and that we should seek to live in accordance with it. Plato laments that most Greeks of his day did not know the basics of geometry or astronomy: "I blushed not only for myself, but for Greeks in general" (819e).

Prefiguring an idea later taken up by the Stoics, Plato asserts there is a kind of a cosmic citizenship. Each of us is "a mere speck" with a duty to promote the well-being of the cosmos: "*you* exist for the sake of the universe" (903c). There is an idea of cosmic *eudaimonia* or flourishing, by the mystical equation of nature, reason, and the divine. This however did *not* imply a naïve rootless cosmopolitanism or undiscerning unreciprocated universal 'altruism.' Mankind should be elevated towards wisdom and virtue, which are indeed universal. But for Plato, virtuous solidarity was impossible

---

[219] Dušanić, "Plato's Projects," *Aevum* (2010, 1), p. 63.

and vicious frustration. There is clearly some truth to these, in the sense that both Christianity and Islam took on elements of Plato's thought. Perhaps Plato did not always follow his own advice when he wrote: "A first-class lawgiver's job is to have a sense of proportion" (691d). I would however also stress that neither Christianity nor Islam embraced some critical aspects of Plato's thought: the practice of citizenship, ethnocentric politics, and eugenics. His ideal man is a philosophical athlete, not a penitent monk.

While Plato's *Laws* aims to be timeless, in practice, there is a willingness to experiment in order to steadily improve one's laws. If a state has bad laws, Plato says the solution is the establishment of a new state through revolution, war, or emigration:

Rather than have the state tolerate the yoke of slavery and be ruled by unworthy hands, it may be absolutely necessary to allow it to be destroyed, or abandon it by going into exile. All that sort of hardship we simply have to endure rather than permit a change to the sort of political system which will make men worse. (770e)

In a corrupt old state unfortunately, politicians are often reduced to muddling through: "The only policy left them is to mouth pious hopes and make a little cautious progress over a long period by advancing a step at a time" (736d).

Plato does allow for some limited possibilities of reform. The Guardians of the Laws may draft proposals which—if approved by the Assembly, all major officials, and the oracles—will amend the basic law. This is a very high bar for reforms, meant to inspire awe in the law and not make it a frivolous, constantly-changed thing. Plato furthermore prescribes that the Magnesian regime would send out wise men to investigate other states and report any good customs or laws they have: "In the mass of mankind you'll invariably find a number—though only a small number—of geniuses with whom it is worth anything to associate," (951b) and these may live in poorly governed foreign states too.

In the *Laws'* final books, Plato introduces a mysterious

Nocturnal Council made up of the highest officials and promising young men, who would philosophize from dusk till dawn. The Nocturnal Council would apparently be empowered to reform the state, something which has puzzled interpreters ever since, being in apparent contradiction with the previous emphasis on the rule of law. Perhaps this is due to the unfinished nature of the *Laws*.

Ultimately, Plato seems to have been skeptical of the very notion of reform. There is something both tragic and realistic about this. In one sense, can a defective regime ever really heal itself? In such instances, there may be no alternative to a refounding through war or revolution. In any event, Plato is working within the historical practice of Greek city-states: the best regimes are established by semi-mythical lawmakers in hallowed and mysterious antiquity. The American Founding Fathers are revered in much the same way for having created a basic law meant to constrain tyrannical and democratic impulses, educating the citizenry towards a certain liberal ethos.

Morrow writes that the *Laws* were meant above all as a practical work, reflecting the fact that Plato and his Academy were often involved in the politics and legislation of new cities. The treatise was his final attempt, in old age, to save his people:

> It is not a Hellenic city in general that Plato draws for us, but an idealized Athens.... . It is the Athens of an earlier time, lifted from the past, but equipped with many of the inventions in law and politics that characterized the sophisticated century in which Plato wrote, that he makes into a model for the legislators of Athens and other Greek cities to follow.

> The Laws then is clearly a message prepared for Plato's own age and for his own people, a message delivered too late to have the effect that Plato doubtless hoped it would have.[220]

Plato clearly meant his *Laws* as an inspiration to generations to come. It exhorts the lawgivers of the future:

---

[220] Morrow, *Plato's Cretan City*, p. 592.

Colleagues and protectors of our laws, we shall—inevitably—leave a great many gaps in every section of our code. However, we shall certainly take care to outline a sort of sketch of the complete system with its main points, and it will be your job to take this sketch and fill in the details. You ought to hear what your aims should be when you do this. (770c)

In the *Laws*, the myth of Atlantis, and the *Seventh Letter*, Plato confirms his argument in the *Republic*: that kin states owe solidarity to one another. He goes further however, asserting that kin states must not only be gentle with one another, but should naturally be allied and perhaps have a degree of political unity against external aggression. The enlightened members of an alliance, furthermore, could have a duty to enforce such norms on decadent members. While admitting that fully-fledged political nationalism is a product of the modern era, born of the combination of our in-born tribal instincts and mass communication technologies, the fact is that many Greeks in the ancient world, Plato included, were already moved by a pan-Hellenic patriotism beyond their city-state.

Taken together, the Platonic corpus describes and proposes what I would go so far as to term a Group Evolutionary Strategy for the ancient Greeks: for Greek city-states to form a great tapestry of non-grasping, virtuous, and solidary city-states, reproducing and perfecting themselves biologically and culturally in perpetuity, at peace with one another and allied against barbarian threats, as members of lawful federations under the leadership of the best city-states. Such a Platonic confederacy would more resemble the relatively consensual Spartan-led Peloponnesian League than the tyrannical Athenian empire. Plato's advocacy of Greek unity may not have been as ineffectual as his Sicilian adventures either. Melissa Lane suggests that in later years, when the Greeks were debating whether to go to war with the Kingdom of Macedon: "Platonic imagery and vocabulary have been shown to be prevalent in the later speeches of the peace party, suggesting that Plato's thought was received and perhaps intended as a counsel against renewed war."[221]

Personally, I am impressed and touched above all by Plato's emphatic insistence that we must tell the truth as we see it, no matter how apparently unpalatable or unpopular or radical. He says that we should not "honor our own ego rather than the truth" and "every man must steer clear of extreme love of himself, and be loyal to his superior instead" (732a-b). I am also sensitive to Plato's piety. It is this piety which makes him a vehement enemy of nihilism and relativism. Plato cannot abide the general slouching into egalitarianism, individualism, and frivolousness. Plato offers us the psychological place where the enlightened may find the self-confidence and intensity to assert themselves, to personally live a life full of meaning, but also to find the strength to *dare* to lift up our own societies ethically and culturally. I sense this same piety in the thoughts and actions of the best of our people throughout the ages.

I am also struck at the enduring relevance of so many aspects of Greek politics and Plato's *Laws*. That we must live piously in accord with nature, reason, and the divine. For Plato, this means loving our family and nation as kin, ensuring cultural aristocracy and good breeding, and living life seriously, all according to a holistic rule of law. One must perpetuate one's line and serve one's community in light of truth. That is Plato's 'rooted cosmopolitanism.' With Plato, blood and spirit are in serene harmony, and I dare say we are indeed "partners in eternity."

---

[221] Melissa Lane, *Greek and Roman Political Ideas* (London: Penguin, 2014), p. 153.

BY WAY OF CONCLUSION...

This book has served as a literary survey of the Hellenic way of life in war and peace. We may conclude with a summary of ancient Greek biopolitics and some reflections on the decline of Hellenism in the past and the prospects for our own future.

The Greek citizen-soldier, raised on Homeric stories and civic life, established over a thousand city-states across the Mediterranean and maintained them for centuries. In evolutionary terms, Hellenism was eminently successful, a way of life of tremendous dynamism, growth and flourishing, culminating in some of the greatest intellectual, political, and artistic accomplishments of our species. The Greeks' achievements, it seems, were due to their own natural gifts, Homeric values, uniquely participatory and diverse systems of government, and their being the first people to unite the bulk of the Mediterranean into a linguistic and commercial network. Not until the age of Darwinism would Westerners again be so rigorously biopolitical.

Let us briefly recall the nature of Greek biopolitics. The Greeks believed that, despite their political divisions, they belonged to a common nation. As memorably recorded by Herodotus, they were "one race, speaking one language, with temples to the gods and religious rites in common, and with a common way of life" (Herodotus, 8.144). Patriotic pan-Hellenic rhetoric—on the supreme value of Greece and the glory of sacrificing oneself for her sake—is pervasive across centuries of Greek literature and political discourse.

The Greeks had a primitive and unsystematic racial theory. They believed that peoples gradually acquired characteristics due to their environment (e.g. Ethiopians became black because of the heat) and that these traits became hereditary. These observations certainly prefigure Darwin's later evolutionary theory.

The Europeans north of Greece were generally considered

barbaric and spirited, while Asians inhabiting Persia were considered cultured and submissive. Barbarians were often thought incapable of civic self-government. The Phoenicians were sometimes perceived as having certain Semitic stereotypes (mercantile, dishonest, greedy, mercenary) but could also be recognized as a fellow advanced people, comparably organized and capable in terms of trade, warfare, and politics.

The Greeks did not have a rigorous theory of racial differences in intelligence and it is often unclear to what extent they believed ethnic characteristics to be due to culture, geography and climate, or heredity. Racial variation in the ancient Mediterranean was typically clinal. Nonetheless, the Greeks were very struck by the physical differences of the few blacks they encountered, producing pottery contrasting Caucasian and Negroid features, in styles rather reminiscent of Western art of the nineteenth and early-twentieth centuries.

The Greeks had a primitive theory and practice of eugenics. Following the practice of animal breeding and simple observation, the Greeks understood that human physical and psychological traits were at least partly heritable. It was often said that men should choose the best women as wives so as to have the best children possible. Due to economic difficulties, infanticide through exposure was a cruel accepted practice, at the parents' discretion. In Sparta, the killing of deformed children was mandatory, an exercise in negative eugenics.

Greek and Roman political and social assumptions were grounded in the ancestral Indo-European religion. This was a patriarchal and exclusionary ancestor cult, which made a religious duty of having children in order to perpetuate the familial religion. The religion turned the family household into a sacred and inviolable sanctuary, under the authority of the father, obeyed by wife, children, and retainers, for the good of the family taken as a whole, including past and future generations.

This Indo-European familial religion and its assumptions were projected to the city-state as a whole, which was always a religious entity, every public act being accompanied by rituals.

By Way of Conclusion...

Hence, like the ancestral religion, the *polis'* ideal of citizenship was exclusionary (serving only citizens, typically defined by blood), communitarian (all could be regulated/expected to sacrifice for the whole, with a citizen-soldier ideal), and reproductive (marriage for the sake of children so as to perpetuate family and community, celibacy being often punishable). In seeking to regulate and improve the reproduction of the citizenry in the service of collective and eugenic goals, the Greeks were eminently biopolitical.

The city-state meant for the Greeks the actual people (they always called themselves "the Athenians," "the Spartans," etc.), their ancestors, and their gods. This patriotism was in political practice very much focused on the individual city, making its interests supreme, with little consideration for eventual imperial subjects, allies, or fellow Greeks in general.

These general observations are evident in the particular examples of Athens and Sparta. Democratic Athens had a racial notion of citizenship, Athenians supposedly being racially pure and "sprung from the Earth" (autochthonous), and under Pericles citizenship was limited to those with two full-blooded Athenian parents. Under the law of Lycurgus, Sparta famously made military training, marriage, the rearing of children, and fighting for the fatherland into a systematically-organized way of life—a clear example of a group evolutionary strategy. Sparta was an ethnostate composed of two separate, non-intermarrying peoples: Spartans and Helots, with strongly xenophobic attitudes preventing foreign influences on their way of life. Both Athens and Sparta claimed to be defending Greek freedom (whether against Persian rule or against the imperialism of fellow Greeks).

The Hellenic way of life combined a high degree of civilization with the aristocratic, competitive, and warrior ethos of the Indo-Europeans, developed over the course of millennia of struggle and expansion. This Aryan ethos is what so appealed to Nietzsche: a people not animated by pity or guilt, nor trying to achieve impossible or fictitious equality in an endlessly vain attempt to assuage feelings. Rather, Hellenic culture, driven by that aristocratic and competitive spirit, held up the ideal of being *the best*: the best athlete, the best warrior, the best poet, the best philosopher, or the most beautiful. This culture also held up the collective ideal of being the best as a whole society, for they understood that man as a species only flourishes as a community.

THE DECLINE OF HELLENISM

After the disasters of the Peloponnesian War, the Greeks were not redeemed by Plato's political schemes — indeed his works were preserved and treasured more for the spiritual-ethical revolution they contained than their politics. Renewal came not from philosophy but from a fresh dose of *barbarism* as the Macedonians conquered Hellas and enlisted the Greeks in their great imperial projects.

The *polis* was simply too small as more and more great empires consolidated around the Mediterranean. Empires are governed by their own universalist logic; which one would almost call cosmopolitan, but for the fact that empires are incompatible with civic life, reducing public affairs to court intrigue.

Xenophon in his *Cyropaedia*, a fictionalized telling of the rise of Cyrus the Great, imagined the founder of the Persian Empire adopting a policy of cosmopolitan meritocracy:

> And I would not have you fill [military offices] from our fellow-citizens alone, but, just as you choose your horses from the best stocks, wherever you find them, not limiting yourselves to the national breed, so you have all mankind before you, and you should choose those, and those only, who will increase your power and add to your honor. (*Cyropaedia*, 2.2.26)

Traditional Greek biopolitical notions of breed and loyalty are thus given an imperial twist throughout the *Cyropaedia*. Xenophon's work is suggestive of the ambitious Greek's dreams of empire.

These dreams were actualized, not by a Greek, but by Alexander the Great of Macedon. Alexander had his own biopolitics defined above all by imperial interests: his elderly veterans and wounded were settled in new cities across Asia; whole tribes were moved to cities to stabilize wild frontiers; and he ordered mass weddings of his officers with Persian noblewomen to fuse the Macedonian and Persian elites. These measures served no people in particular but were meant to solidify his vast empire spanning three continents. Upon Alexander's death by illness in the prime of youth, his empire collapsed into internecine warfare between his generals, who restyled themselves as rival kings.

Later, the original Greek lands would be conquered by the Romans, a people animated by a very similar martial spirit to that of the *polis*. The Romans were crucially different in one respect however: for while their conquests could be brutal and even exterminationist on occasion, they were also willing to gradually grant citizenship to their conquered subjects, thus giving them a stake in the empire.

Imperial conquest by outsiders did not mean the end of the Greeks. On the contrary, the Macedonian empire and Hellenistic monarchies established *koine* or common Greek as the lingua franca of the whole eastern Mediterranean, with Alexandria in Egypt emerging as an important Greek city for trade and scholarship. Under the Romans, Greek culture and language made up the whole eastern pole of the empire. The Greek-speaking world engaged in considerable trade, great artistic and architectural achievements, scientific and technological advances, as well as ethical innovations with the rise of Stoicism and Epicureanism. Indeed, even after the fall of the western Roman Empire, the Greek-speaking Byzantine Empire would endure for another thousand years. The full collapse of the Greeks would only occur with the Islamic conquests of the Arabs and the Turks.

The Macedonian and later empires may have unified and pacified the Greeks, but their loss of sovereignty coincided with a great loss of dynamism. Darwin himself had some thoughts on the decline of the Greeks, which required some explanation given their intellectual prowess. He speculated:

> The Greeks may have retrograded from a want of coherence between the many small states, from the small

size of their whole country, from the practice of slavery, or from extreme sensuality; for they did not succumb until "they were enervated and corrupt to the very core".[222]

The Greeks became more heterogeneous through the spread of their language and intermingling with other peoples. Many Greek-speakers who lived outside the mainland gradually lost their language and identity. In contrast with the patriotic *polis* and ethnocentric religions such as Judaism, the imperatives of empire are generally incompatible with the maintenance of national identity. The founder-nation tends to dissolve into a new human mass and the empire itself eventually collapses, either into its constituent nations or under assault from still-virile barbarians.

More generally, there was a shift away from biopolitical ethics to universalist and world-rejecting philosophies and religions. There is a palpable *fatigue* as Greco-Roman culture shifted from that of the founding aristocratic warriors to a culture more amenable to the suffering mass of the people.

From Socrates onward, ethics moves away from lordship, ambition, and worldly achievement towards ideals of conciliation, self-abnegation, and spiritual enlightenment. The Hellenistic philosophies of Cynicism, Skepticism, and Epicureanism are all marked by a rejection of the disciplines and constraints of the *polis*, seeking salvation instead in individual tranquility. Stoicism, in some ways the philosophy of the Roman Empire, emphasized both universal human brotherhood and familial and political duties.

These 'Axial' trends went further still with the popular religions Buddhism and Christianity, for indeed philosophy cannot touch the souls of the masses. The Buddha-Way flourished in the Greek kingdoms of northwest India and Gandhara, spread by Greek missionaries and glorified with magnificent sculptures in Hellenic style. Christianity spread first around the Greek-speaking eastern Mediterranean to the entire Roman Empire. Both religions were thoroughly world-rejecting and held up renunciation from the household as the

---

[222] Darwin, *Descent of Man*, p. 166-67.

highest way of life. The Hellenistic philosophies honored the detached sage and the Axial religions the mystical monk as their ideals.

In the fullness of time, the Roman Empire would decay and fall,[223] and the western Mediterranean would only be redeemed by another great dose of barbarism as the Germanic tribes founded the bulk of the great kingdoms of medieval Europe. Christianity's demanding morality fused with Germanic warrior values, most evocatively expressed in our gothic cathedrals, those uncanny stone and glass flourishings of Heaven and Earth

Much could be said of the biopolitics of the various religions of this world—Hinduism, Buddhism, Christianity, Islam … — and therefore their evolutionary consequences for the various nations of the human race, but this goes beyond the remit of this book.

TOWARDS BIOPOLIS

In the Greek political experience, we find much food for thought for us as their spiritual descendants in the twenty-first century. The practice of their diverse republics reminds us that there is no contradiction between a communitarian, aristocratic, and eugenic ethos and the uniquely Western practice of civic politics and the rule of law.

The successes and failures of the historic Greek leagues, and Plato's confederal proposals, continue to be of some interest to us today, given the persistence of a plurality of states and the emergence of novel confederations such as the European Union.

We live in a technologically advanced universal civilization of innovation and decay. We enjoy lives of comfort and

---

[223] For a recent view: David Engels, *Le Déclin: La crise de l'Union européenne et la chute de la République romaine—quelques analogies historiques* (Paris: Éditions du Toucan, 2016, 3rd ed.). Reviewed at Guillaume Durocher, "Decline and Empire in Ancient Rome and the Modern West: A Review of David Engels' *Le Déclin*," *The Occidental Observer*, July 12, 2018.

security, much of our experience defined by consumption of audiovisual media, cut off from the foundations of life. In this setting more than ever, we may renew ourselves by drinking from the ever-flowing fountain of Antiquity.

The Greek Classics remind us of both harsh truths we would prefer to ignore and of the mindset that enabled a remarkable people to flourish over two thousand years ago. Let the self-pleasing Modern lies — bastard children of misguided generosity and the most spiteful *amour-propre* — melt away. Let us find inspiration from these works, not as dead scribblings, but as exhortations to live better: as athletes and scholars, fathers and mothers, comrades and soldiers, statesmen and adventurers, and, yes, lovers of wisdom.

In an archeofuturist perspective, let our forebears be an inspiration in new times. In a world of spectacular social and technological change, not least with the emergence of human biotechnologies, we can only begin to imagine what shape may take the *biopoleis* of the future.

All life is marked by assay and experimentation with failures without number and occasional but enduring triumphs. This is no less true for the world's great spiritual and political systems. As John Adams observed:

> The systems of legislators are experiments made on human life and manners, society, and government. Zoroaster, Confucius, Mithras, Odin, Thor, Mahomet, Lycurgus, Solon, Romulus, and a thousand others, may be compared to philosophers making experiments on the elements. Unhappily, political experiments cannot be made in a laboratory, nor determined in a few hours.[224]

No system may last forever. The Greeks, adhering to a cyclical vision of history, were obsessed by how luxury, effeminacy, and decadence, the loss of ancestral traditions and manly virtue, doomed societies. But this doom may provide so much manure and sow the seeds of renewal, often in unexpected and novel forms.

---

[224] Adams, *Defense*, Preface.

By Way of Conclusion…

A world in tremendous flux and upheaval calls for new experiments and enterprises. Inspired by the Hellenic experience, we can imagine a renewal of the Western peoples in which futuristic technology and science will be combined with this archaic *vital* spirit, this communitarian ethos honoring excellence. Renewal cannot be decreed but must surge from the mysterious tumults of history. As ever, time will tell.

BIBLIOGRAPHY

PRIMARY SOURCES

Aeschylus, *Persians*, in Christopher Collard (trans.), *Persians and Other Plays* (Oxford: Oxford University Press, 2008).

Aristotle (trans. H. C. Lawson-Tancred), *The Art of Rhetoric* (London: Penguin, 1991).

——— (trans. David Ross, rev. Lesley Brown), *Nicomachean Ethics* (Oxford: Oxford University Press, 2009).

——— (trans. Anthony Kenny), *Poetics* (Oxford, Oxford University Press, 2013).

——— (trans. Ernest Barker, rev. R. F. Stalley), *Politics* (Oxford: Oxford University Press, 1995).

Arrian (ed. James Romm, trans. Pamela Mensch), *The Campaigns of Alexander* (New York: Anchor Books, 2010).

Diogenes the Cynic (trans. Robin Hard), *Sayings and Anecdotes* (Oxford: Oxford University Press, 2012.

Gethin, Rupert (trans.), *Sayings of the Buddha: A Selection of Suttas from the Pali Nikayas* (Oxford: Oxford World's Classics, 2008).

Herodotus (trans. Robin Waterfield), *The Histories* (Oxford: Oxford University Press, 1998).

Homer (trans. Robert Fagles), *Iliad* (London: Penguin, 1990).

——— (trans. Walter Shewring), *Odyssey* (Oxford: Oxford University Press, 1980).

Julian (trans. Emily Wilmer Cave Wright), *The Works of the Emperor Julian* (Loeb Classical Library, 1913), on wikisource.org.

Marcus Aurelius (trans. Robin Hard), *Meditations* (Oxford: Oxford University Press, 2011).

Old Oligarch, *Constitution of the Athenians*, in Xenophon (trans. E. C. Marchant), *Xenophon in Seven Volumes* (Cambridge, Massachusetts: Harvard University Press, 1984).

Plato (ed. John M. Cooper), *Complete Works* (Indianapolis,

Bibliography

Indiana: Hackett, 1997).

——— (trans. Robin Waterfield), *Republic* (Oxford: Oxford University Press, 1994).

Plutarch (trans. Richard Talbert), *On Sparta* (London: Penguin, 2005), incl. Xenophon, *Spartan Constitution*.

Polybius (trans. Robin Waterfield), *The Histories* (Oxford: Oxford World's Classics, 2010).

Sturluson, Snorri [trans. Jesse L. Byock], *The Prose Edda* (London: Penguin, 2005).

Thucydides (trans. Martin Hammond), *The Peloponnesian War* (Oxford: Oxford University Press, 2009).

Waterfield, Robin (ed. and trans.), *The First Philosophers: The Presocratics and Sophists* (Oxford: Oxford World's Classics, 2000).

Xenophon (trans. Rex Warner), *A History of My Times* [*Hellenica*] (London: Penguin, 1966).

——— (trans. Henry Graham Dakyns), *The Education of Cyrus*, (London: J. M. Dent & Sons, 1914).

——— (trans. Robin Waterfield), *The Expedition of Cyrus* [*Anabasis*] (Oxford: Oxford University Press, 2005).

SECONDARY SOURCES

Adams, John, *A Defense of the Constitutions of the United States* (1787), on wikisource.org.

Aurelio, Martin, "The Four Elements of National Identity in Herodotus," *Counter-Currents*, June 15, 2016.

Bronze Age Pervert, *Bronze Age Mindset: An Exhortation* (2018).

Cairns, Douglas, "The First Odysseus: *Iliad*, *Odyssey*, and the Ideology of Kingship," *Gaia: revue interdisciplinaire sur la Grèce Archaïque*, vol. 18, no. 1, 2015, pp. 51-66.

Cartledge, Paul, *Sparta and Lakonia: A Regional History, 1300 to 362 BC* (New York: Routledge, 2002)

——— *Ancient Greece: A History in Eleven Cities* (Oxford: Oxford University Press, 2009).

————— *Ancient Greek Political Thought in Practice: Key Themes in Ancient* History (Cambridge/New York: Cambridge University Press, 2009).

Clausewitz, Carl von (trans J. J. Graham and F. N. Maude), *On War*, (London: Wordsworth, 1997).

Devlin, F. Roger, "Greek & Barbarian," *Counter-Currents*, November 24, 2010.

Duchesne, Ricardo, *The Uniqueness of Western Civilization* (Leiden: Brill, 2011).

Dušanić, Slobodan, "Plato's Projects for a Confederate Sicily and the Constitutional Patterns in the Third Book of the *Laws*," *Aevum* (2010, 1), pp. 61-68.

Engels, David, *Le Déclin: La crise de l'Union européenne et la chute de la République romaine – quelques analogies historiques* (Paris: Éditions du Toucan, 2016, 3rd ed.).

Finley, M. I., "The Ancient Greeks and Their Nation: The Sociological Problem," *The British Journal of Sociology*, vol. 5, no. 3 (Sep. 1954), pp. 253-264.

Fustel de Coulanges, Numa, *La Cité antique* (Paris: Flammarion, 2009 [1864]).

Fragoulaki, Maria, *Kinship in Thucydides: Intercommunal Ties and Historical Narrative* (Oxford: Oxford University Press, 2013).

Galton, David, "Greek theories on eugenics," *Journal of Medical Ethics*, vol. 24, 1998, pp. 263-267.

Giesecke, Annette, "Mapping Utopia: Homer's Politics and the Birth of the Polis," *College Literature*, 34.2, Spring 2007, pp. 194-214.

Hamilton, Andrew, "Ethnic Cleansing in Ancient Attica & Lemnos," *Counter-Currents.com*, August 15, 2014.

Harrison, Thomas, *The Emptiness of Asia: Aeschylus' Persians and the History of the Fifth Century* (London: 2000).

Isaac, Benjamin, *The Invention of Racism in Classical Antiquity* (Princeton, New Jersey: Princeton University Press, 2006).

Johnson, Greg, "What's Wrong with Cosmopolitanism?," *Counter-Currents.com*, February 27, 2017.

Bibliography

Klosko, George, "The Nocturnal Council in Plato's *Laws*," *Political Studies*, vol. 36, 1988, pp. 74-88.

Lape, Susan, *Race and Citizen Identity in Classical Athenian Democracy* (Cambridge: Cambridge University Press, 2010).

Lane, Melissa, *Plato's Progeny: How Plato and Socrates Still Captivate the Modern Mind* (London: Bloomsbury, 2001).

———— *Greek and Roman Political Ideas* (London: Penguin, 2014).

Lomas, Kathryn, "The Polis in Italy: Ethnicity, Colonization, and Citizenship in the Western Mediterranean," in Roger Brock and Stephen Hodkinson, eds., *Alternatives to Athens: Varieties of Political Organization and Community in Ancient Greece* (Oxford: Oxford University Press, 2000).

Long, A. A., "The concept of the cosmopolitan in Greek & Roman thought," *Daedelus*, summer 2008, pp. 50-58.

MacDonald, Kevin, *A People That Shall Dwell Alone: Judaism as a Group Evolutionary Strategy, with Diaspora Peoples* (Lincoln, Nebraska: Writers Club, 2002 [1994]).

———— *The Culture of Critique: An Evolutionary Analysis of Jewish Involvement in Twentieth-Century Intellectual and Political movements* (Bloomington, IN: Authorhouse, 2002; originally published: Westport, CT: Praeger, 1998),

———— *Individualism and the Western Liberal Tradition: Evolutionary Origins, History, and Prospects for the Future* (Seattle: CreateSpace, 2019).

Mitchell, Lynette, *Panhellenism and the Barbarian in Archaic and Classical Greece* (Swansea, Wales: Classical Press of Wales, 2007).

Montesquieu, *De l'Esprit des lois* (Paris: Flammarion, 1979 [1748])

Morrow, Glenn R., *Plato's Cretan City: A Historical Interpretation of the* Laws (Princeton, New Jersey: Princeton University Press, 1993 [1960]).

Nietzsche, Friedrich, (trans. Carol Diethe), "The Greek State" (1871/2), in Keith Ansell-Pearson (ed.), *On the Genealogy of Morals* (Cambridge: Cambridge University Press, 2006).

Ojakangas, Mika, *On the Greek Origins of Biopolitics: A Reinterpretation of the History of Biopower* (London: Routledge, 2016).

Ollier, François, *Le Mirage spartiate* (Paris: E. de Boccard, 1933).

Pearson, Roger, "The Concept of Heredity in the History of Western Culture," *The Mankind Quarterly*, vol. 35, #3, Spring 1995, pp. 229-265.

Robert, Jennifer Tolbert, *Athens on Trial: The Antidemocratic Tradition in Western Thought* (Princeton: Princeton University Press, 1994).

Roper, Allen, *Ancient Eugenics: The Arnold Prize Essay for 1913* (Oxford: Oxford University Press, 1913).

Sale, William Merritt, *The Government of Troy* (Washington University, 1994).

Sanderson, Brenton, "A Review of *The Mighty Dead: Why Homer Matters* by Adam Nicolson," *The Occidental Observer*, May 15-24, 2016.

Schofield, Malcolm, *Plato: Political Philosophy* (Oxford: Oxford University Press, 2006).

Venner, Dominique, *Histoire et traditions des Européens: 30 000 d'identité* (Paris: Du Rocher, 2011).

——— "Homer: The European Bible," *Counter-Currents*, September 7-11, 2010.

Waterfield, Robin, *Why Socrates Died: Dispelling the Myths* (New York: W. W. Norton & Company, 2009).

Thompson, D'Arcy Wentworth, *On Aristotle as Biologist* (Oxford: Clarendon Press, 1913).

Made in United States
Orlando, FL
17 December 2024

55949105R00178